Sunset

PRUNING HANDBOOK

By the Editors of Sunset Books and Sunset Magazine

Lane Publishing Co., Menlo Park, California

Supervising Editor:
John K. McClements

Research & Text:
Philip Edinger

Design: **Joe di Chiarro**
Illustrations: **Jacqueline Osborn**
Photo Editor: **JoAnn Masaoka**

ACKNOWLEDGMENTS

Pruning principles are based on the knowledge of plant physiology—how a whole plant functions. But the art and practice of pruning rest on trial-and-error application of those principles. In preparing this manual of pruning, we have relied heavily on the personal experience of many horticulturists—experience acquired over a great stretch of time. We could not have written detailed and accurate pruning instructions for the hundreds of plants in this book without the benefit of the knowledge they gained and shared. For this sharing, we extend our greatest thanks to Robert Bartlett, Sr., Arboriculturist, Stamford, Connecticut; Robert Chittock, Landscape Architect, Seattle, Washington; Alan D. Cook, Senior Horticulturist at Dawes Arboretum, Newark, Ohio; Gene Joyner, Urban Horticulturist, West Palm Beach, Florida; Fred Lang, Landscape Architect, South Laguna, California; Dr. Ray R. Rothenberger, State Extension Horticulturist, Columbia, Missouri.

We thank everyone who allowed Sunset Books to photograph their plants for this book. We also give thanks to the following persons and organizations for helping Sunset Books find special plants to photograph: Anne Dickey, Cilker Orchards, Filoli, Jelich Ranch, White Flower Farm.

Photographers: **Derek Fell:** 58, 66, 79, 82. **Pamela Harper:** 55. **Jack McDowell:** 23, 26, 34, 71, 74, 87, 90, 95, 111. **Steve W. Marley:** 50, 63, 103, 106. **Ells Marugg:** 98. **Alan Mitchell:** 47. **Norman A. Plate:** 18. **Teri Sandison:** 39. **Darrow M. Watt:** 42. **Tom Wyatt:** 31.

Cover: Flowering cherry *(Prunus yedoensis* 'Akebono') needs only light pruning. Remove awkward or crossing branches while tree is in bloom, or cut branches for flower arrangements. Photograph by Jack McDowell. Design by Lynne B. Morrall.

Editor, Sunset Books: Elizabeth L. Hogan

Fifth printing January 1990

CONTENTS

INTRODUCTION: HOW PLANTS GROW

Some reasons for pruning:

To encourage fruit production

To repair storm damage

To thin dense growth

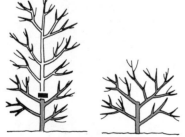

For special effect or renewal

At its best, pruning is an art solidly based on scientific principles. The principles of plant physiology—how a plant grows—dictate pruning practices. Art enters when you make a plant more attractive as you prune it.

This handbook consists of four chapters: pruning fundamentals, pruning tools, basic pruning techniques, and pruning encyclopedia that tells you how to prune specific plants. But before giving detailed instructions on pruning, we first need to ask, "Why prune at all?"

Prune to direct or control growth. Every time you make a pruning cut or pinch out the tip of a stem, you stop growth in one direction and encourage it in another.

Prune to encourage flower and fruit production. Woody plants normally bear flowers and produce fruit-encased seeds. By pruning in certain ways, you can direct flower and fruit-producing plants to produce better flowers or fruits—and sometimes more of them as well.

Prune to promote plant health. Some plants grow vigorous stems for just a few years, then stop producing strong new growth. To keep these plants young, frequently remove older stems so that a plant directs its energies toward new growth.

Leaves on the inside and lower parts of plants need light and air to stay healthy. You can improve the health and appearance of some plants by thinning out dense growth, allowing light and air to reach inner and lower leaves.

Prune to offset or repair damage. Strong winds, lightning, snow, and ice can all damage plants. Thin out growth on susceptible plants—those with brittle wood, for example—to lessen the chance of weather damage. If branches do break, you can prune them to remove broken parts.

Prune to achieve a special effect or an artificial form. Hedges are familiar examples of the result of this kind of pruning (see page 70). Other decorative pruning forms are espalier (page 50) and topiary (page 106).

Prune to alter, restore, or rejuvenate. These types of pruning help you make an established or neglected plant more attractive. One way you can alter an overgrown shrub, for example, is to remove lower limbs, transforming it into a multitrunked small tree. To restore a badly pruned plant, you can thin it, head it back, and remove any weak branches, enabling the plant to again display its natural beauty. To rejuvenate a healthy but overgrown plant, cut it back to a framework of main limbs or to the ground. New growth will form an essentially new plant.

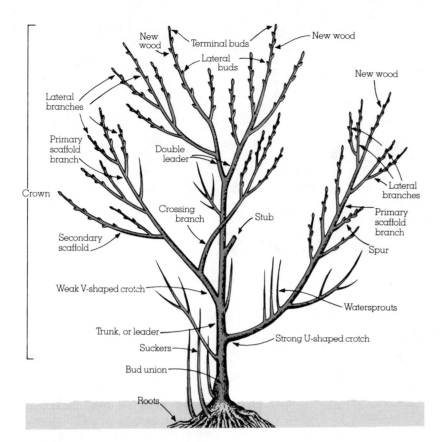

Labels (left to right, top to bottom): New wood, Terminal buds, New wood, Lateral buds, New wood, Lateral branches, Double leader, Lateral branches, Primary scaffold branch, Crown, Crossing branch, Stub, Primary scaffold branch, Secondary scaffold, Spur, Weak V-shaped crotch, Watersprouts, Trunk, or leader, Suckers, Strong U-shaped crotch, Bud union, Roots

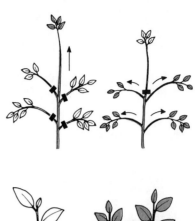

Pinch young stems to direct growth. Top: pinch side shoots and stem elongates; pinch tip and side shoots lengthen. Bottom: pinch stem tip and side shoots grow out.

Prune to compensate for transplanting. A healthy plant maintains a balance of nutrients between its roots and leafy top. When you dig up a plant for transplanting, you lose some roots, upsetting this balance. To help the plant compensate for the imbalance, you must prune its branches.

How a plant grows

In order to prune effectively, you should know something about how plants grow. With a little knowledge, you'll be able to predict the outcome of your pruning. The diagram on this page shows the plant parts that are important to a pruner. Become familiar with these terms; they appear throughout this book.

Function of stems. The stem (also called shoot, trunk, twig, branch, or limb) carries water and nutrients from the roots to the plant's growing points (buds, leaves, flowers). It also carries foods (sugars) that the leaves make to the roots. Because stems are conveying tubes, you can cut off a stem to divert the flow of nutrients to other buds and branches. By stopping growth in one direction, you encourage it in other directions, guiding the shape of the plant.

Importance of buds. Growth buds are undeveloped conveying tubes. As they grow, they divert water and nutrients from other parts of the plant. You can direct plant growth by removing selected buds. There are three types of growth buds.

The terminal bud grows at the end of a stem. It makes the plant grow in a line by elongating the stem. By removing a terminal bud, you divert energies to buds along the stem, encouraging a denser, bushier plant.

Lateral buds grow along the sides of a stem. As the plant grows, they may develop into lateral branches. By removing lateral buds, you channel energy into the terminal bud.

Latent buds lie dormant in a stem or beneath a plant's bark for many years. They grow only after pruning or injury removes growth above them.

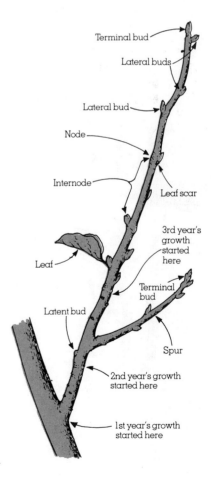

Labels: Terminal bud, Lateral buds, Lateral bud, Node, Internode, Leaf scar, 3rd year's growth started here, Leaf, Terminal bud, Latent bud, Spur, 2nd year's growth started here, 1st year's growth started here

PRUNING TOOLS

The number of tools available for pruning and the differences between them in quality and cost bewilder many home gardeners. To determine what tools are appropriate for you, consider your work habits and the kinds and number of plants you grow. A small garden usually calls for a few basic tools. A large garden with a great variety of plants will require a greater number of pruning tools, including some specialized ones.

What tools do you need?

The most basic tools are hand pruning shears and a pruning saw. Many gardeners can manage with just these two. If you have a large garden and a diverse or specialized group of plants, you might also want hedge shears, a pole saw and pruners, or a chain saw. When you consider pruning tools, don't forget the ones that every gardener already possesses: thumb and forefinger. A pinch in time can eliminate the need for pruning later.

Shopping for tools

When shopping for tools, look for good quality materials, construction, and design. A good pair of shears, though costly, can last a lifetime if you use them properly and give them reasonable care. Poor

quality tools, on the other hand, may not perform as well and will deteriorate faster; it's likely that you'll have to replace these.

Quality isn't the only important factor to consider when selecting pruning tools: be sure you obtain the right implements for each of your garden's needs. You'll make several different kinds of cuts when you prune. For best results—a sharp, clean cut with a minimum of bruising to the plant—don't depend on one tool to do them all. If you use the wrong tool, you may damage both the plant and the pruning tool. The information on these pages will help you choose the right tools.

Over the years, the basic designs and functions of pruning tools have changed very little. But manufacturers have introduced various styles and refinements. It's wise to shop before purchasing any particular tool. You need not only the right tool for the job, but also one that will feel comfortable as you use it. We can separate pruning equipment into three categories: cutting blades (the various shears and loppers), saw blades, and ladders and rasps.

SHEARS AND LOPPERS

A pair of pruning shears—the kind you work with one hand—is every gardener's basic pruning tool. Useful to patio gardeners and estate gardeners alike, shears vary in de-

One-hand hook and blade shears

One-hand anvil shears

sign but not in function. For particular types of pruning, specialized shears are available.

One-hand pruning shears

You'll find two basic designs. Anvil shears cut by the action of a straight blade against an anvil; hook and curved-blade shears cut as blade and hook pass one another (just as ordinary paper or nail scissors do). Some gardeners prefer one kind over another. Others think each kind performs equally well. Let quality and comfort (the feel of the shears in your hand) be the deciding factors when you choose between the two.

Refinements. Various manufacturers offer such refinements as blades with a nonstick coating, replaceable stainless steel blades, self-lubricating bearings, sap grooves (said to keep blades cleaner), different types of handles and grips, and one-hand-operable catches. Some shears have a ratchet that adjusts the cutting power of the blade—when you meet resistance, a slight release of pressure on the grip shifts it into another notch that gives you more leverage for the cut.

Specialized shears. Besides the two basic designs, you can find many other kinds of hand pruning shears, each designed for a specific purpose. Some, for example, are just for cutting flowers—and some of these will cut and hold on to the flower stem. Fruit shears are available for lemons, grapes, and other fruits whose stems don't break off readily. A Japanese-designed shear—originally intended for bonsai pruning—makes a concave cut that may heal more quickly and with less scarring than cuts made by either anvil or hook-and-blade types.

Two-hand pruning shears (loppers)

Two-hand shears have long handles (each gripped in a separate hand), giving you added leverage and therefore more cutting power than you get from one-hand shears. The long handles also extend your pruning range.

You have the same basic design choice with two-hand shears as with the one-hand types: hook-and-blade and anvil. With the hook-and-blade style, the hook helps hold the branch in place while the blade slices through it. Anvil-style loppers have a draw-in slicing action as the sharp blade cuts against the anvil.

Either type of lopper may have wooden handles or tubular steel handles covered with vinyl or rubber grips. Some have adjustable cutting action. Certain anvil loppers have an adjustable anvil, allowing you to sharpen the blade many times before you have to replace it. Both types come with handle lengths ranging from 15 to 35 inches.

Hedge shears

These two-handled, long-bladed shears are indispensable for maintaining formal hedges. They cut the same way as hook-and-blade hand shears but they consist of two blades of approximately equal size and shape. (The only alternative for hedge clipping is electric trimmers, described on page 9 under "Power Tools.")

Most hand-powered hedge shears have one serrated blade that prevents branches from sliding out from between blades as you cut. Many kinds also have a limb notch that lets you cut an occasional thick branch with these blades. Better shears have neoprene, rubber, or metal-spring shock absorbers between the handles just beneath the blades' pivot point to make shearing easier on the pruner's hands and arms.

The standard blade length is 8 inches. Handles come in several different materials. Metal ones usually have some sort of comfortable coating on the grips. Customarily, hedge shear handles are 10 to 12 inches long. Most manufacturers offer shears with extra-long handles of 20 to 22 inches, enabling the gardener to trim tall hedges while standing on the ground.

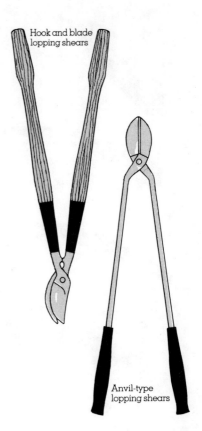

Hook and blade lopping shears

Anvil-type lopping shears

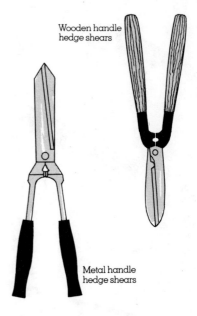

Wooden handle hedge shears

Metal handle hedge shears

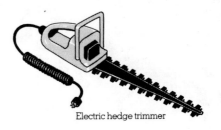

Electric hedge trimmer

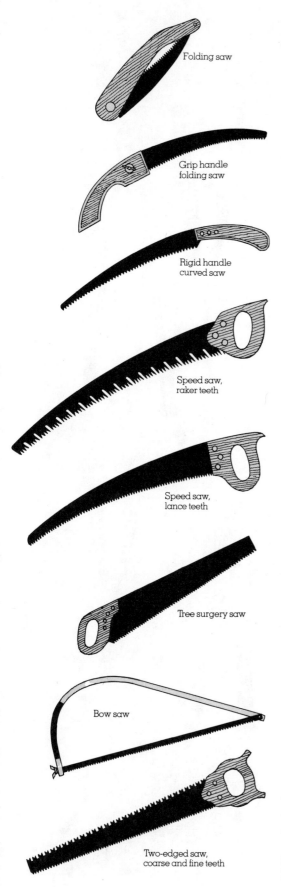

Folding saw

Grip handle folding saw

Rigid handle curved saw

Speed saw, raker teeth

Speed saw, lance teeth

Tree surgery saw

Bow saw

Two-edged saw, coarse and fine teeth

PRUNING SAWS

Whenever you must cut a woody stem that's more than an inch thick, you'll need a pruning saw. Using hand shears or loppers for thick branches strains both you and the tool. An overtaxed pair of shears or loppers will crush as it cuts, producing ragged or mashed edges. These heal more slowly than clean cuts and open the plant to disease.

Don't force a carpenter's saw to do garden duty. Only a pruning saw can cut a thick branch effectively. Pruning saws are designed to cut easily through green, wet wood. This is harder work for a carpenter's saw and quickly dulls it. Many pruning saws—all the curved blade ones—cut on the backward, or pull, stroke instead of on the push stroke as a carpenter's saw does. Because gravity helps you apply pressure, pull-stroke saws make cutting overhead branches much easier.

Evaluating a saw

When you evaluate a saw, first check the size of its teeth. Saws with large teeth (5 or 6 per inch) and large, heavy blades are suitable only for heavy, unconfined work. Saws with smaller teeth (up to 10 per inch) have smaller or slimmer blades that you use to tackle crowded limbs, smaller branches, dead wood, and hardwooded shrubs and trees.

After checking tooth size, look straight down the blade to see how the teeth are set. For the best cuts, choose a blade that shows a V of teeth alternately bent to the sides along the full length of the blade. Finally, remember comfort: lift the saw to gauge its weight and balance.

Pull-cut saws

You'll find many saws with this blade action, differing mainly in size and shape. They can be classified into the following types. (Pole saws are treated separately, on page 9.)

Folding saw. The most popular ones have blades ranging from 7 to 16 inches long. Small ones with fine teeth (8 or 10 per inch) are good for rose and basic shrub pruning. Larger ones (6 teeth per inch) will handle dormant-season tree pruning.

Folding saw with grip handle. This saw's handle is more comfortable for doing extensive work than the standard folding saw's hand grip.

Curved saw with rigid handle. Folding saws (above) may occasionally fold during use—with painful consequences. This saw won't fold, but it takes more storage space. Blades vary from 12 to 16 inches.

Speed saw with raker teeth. The fastest cutter of 3-inch and larger limbs, this saw is good for green wood because rakers (slots in place of every fifth tooth) pull sawdust out, keeping the blade from jamming.

Speed saw with lance teeth. This cuts deadwood better than the speed saw with raker teeth.

Push-cut saws

These have specific uses but are less versatile and less handy for the home gardener than pull-cut saws.

Tree surgery saw. This saw looks and works like a carpenter's saw, with teeth angled forward on a heavy 2-foot blade. It is useful on large limbs, but its unwieldy size is a handicap in close quarters.

Bow saw. Available in many sizes, from 15 inches up, this saw cuts on both push and pull strokes. It is hard to use among crowded branches, so its usefulness is limited.

Two-edged saw. One side of the blade has small teeth that cut on the push stroke, good for small limbs and deadwood. The other side has coarse teeth that cut on both strokes, and is particularly useful on larger branches and green wood. The saw has one drawback: it may be difficult to saw one branch without injuring, at the same time, another branch that's close to it.

Pole saw and pruner

These tools give you extra reach for cutting high branches. Most have blades that cut on the pull stroke.

Poles may be wood, aluminum, or fiberglass. Some telescope and lock into the desired length, others come with extensions and quick-connecting devices. Choose wood or fiberglass poles if there is any risk of contacting electric wires when you prune.

You can buy a pole saw and pruning hook in combination or purchase them separately with interchangeable pruning and saw attachments for the same pole. The most common type is a combination pruning saw and cord-operated or chain-operated cutting shears. The shears are inside a beaklike hook that you place over the branch you want to cut. You then pull a cord to draw the blade through the branch. Most pole pruning hooks will cut limbs up to an inch thick.

POWER TOOLS

Many gardeners have no need for the two common power tools. Others find them indispensable.

Power hedge trimmers. If you have a large hedge that you formally shear more than once a year, you'll appreciate how fast you can perform this task with a power trimmer. You have a choice of electric or gasoline-powered trimmers. Electric trimmers come either cordless or with a long cord. Many gardeners use both power and manual trimmers for hedges. You can use the power trimmer for the large, flat sides and top of a hedge; use manual trimmers for careful work on corners.

Chain saws. For home garden use, many models of lightweight chain saws are available for you to choose from. You'll seldom need one for routine garden pruning. To remove an occasional large limb, use a manual saw. Chain saws are most useful when you have a lot of heavy cutting to do. They're particularly

handy for clearing wooded property or for annually pruning a large home orchard. Exercise great caution in using a chain saw—it will cut indiscriminately. Study all directions and warnings in the instruction manual before you use the saw.

OTHER USEFUL TOOLS

The two tools described here are indispensable for larger pruning jobs.

Rasp. A surface-finishing tool that carpenters use to smooth rough edges of boards, a rasp finishes pruning cuts, especially large ones, leaving a smooth surface and edges. Hardware stores carry them.

Ladder. A good ladder can be an important aid to good pruning. Many bad cuts result when a pruner tries to reach too far from tiptoe. Well-constructed aluminum ladders will last a lifetime. Their chief advantage is also their main disadvantage: they're lightweight. You can carry them around easily, but they tip over easily, too, especially if you don't erect them on level ground, or if you overreach and lose your balance. Wooden ladders are more cumbersome and will deteriorate in time if exposed to weather, but they're steadier on their feet.

Be very careful when you use a stepladder outdoors. Set it firmly on a hard, flat surface. If you want a more stable freestanding ladder for high pruning work, rent or buy a three-legged orchardist's ladder.

MAINTAINING TOOLS

After using shears or a saw, wipe the blade clean. Use a solvent (kerosene, for example) to clean off any sticky sap residue. If residue is stubborn, or encrusted from previous neglect, remove it with steel wool. Wipe clean blades with an oily cloth before storing the tool.

When tools become dull, take them to a professional sharpener for best results.

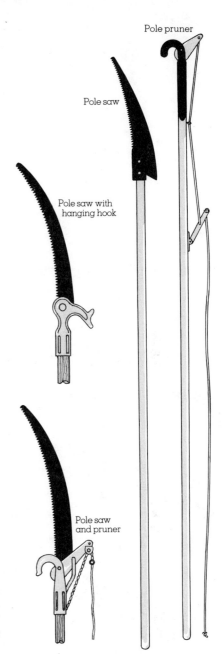

Pole pruner

Pole saw

Pole saw with hanging hook

Pole saw and pruner

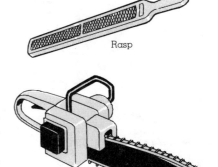

Rasp

Chain saw

BASIC PRUNING TECHNIQUES

Good pruning is removing plant parts *for a purpose beneficial to the plant*.

How much and how often you prune depends upon each plant and its individual needs. Some plants require heavy pruning each year. Others need only light pruning every few years. The Pruning Encyclopedia on pages 18–111 explains how to prune specific trees and shrubs. It tells you how much, how often, and when to prune them.

HOW TO START PRUNING

Most pruning novices ask, "How do I know which plant parts to remove and which to leave?" The answer lies in observing how plants in your garden grow. You also need to understand fundamentals of how all plants grow (see page 5), and how they respond to pruning.

The following procedure applies whether you're a pruning novice or an old hand. 1) Learn how to make correct cuts (see page 12). 2) Read instructions for the particular plant in the Pruning Encyclopedia, pages 18–111. 3) Study the plant from all sides to estimate how much and what kind of pruning it needs *before you make any cuts*. 4) Start by removing any obviously undesirable or damaged growth: dead, broken, or diseased branches; stems that

crowd or cross through the plant's center; wayward branches. Often, when you complete step 4, the plant will need no further pruning.

BASIC PRUNING METHODS

Pruning can range from pinching tips of new growth to cutting off large limbs. Most pruning involves four basic techniques: *pinching, thinning, heading back, shearing*.

Pinching

This is the most basic pruning technique. You use thumb and forefinger or clippers to remove stem tips of new growth. Pinching stops the stem from growing longer (see "How a plant grows," page 5) and stimulates side branches to grow along the stem. You'll treat a single-trunked tree, for example, as follows: 1) Pinch the tip of the leader (main trunk) to encourage side branches; 2) Pinch tips of side branches to encourage upward, not spreading, growth.

By pinching stem tips repeatedly, you promote the development of many branches; this in turn produces a bushy, compact plant.

Heading back

Pruning to shorten branches is called heading back or cutting back. You

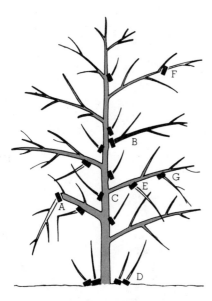

Subjects for pruning: (A) broken branches, (B) dead limbs, (C) watersprouts, (D) suckers, (E) crossing branches, (F) long, awkward limbs, (G) dangling branches.

can head back plants for several reasons: to make an oversize plant fit a limited space; to make a plant produce top quality flowers or fruits; and to remove branches that have been frozen by winter cold or damaged by a storm or accident.

Always head back branches to a growing point—a leaf, a dormant bud, or another branch. Prune to a point that will produce (or is producing) growth in a direction you want it to go. Don't leave branch stubs that will die back (see "How to Make Pruning Cuts," page 12).

Thinning (see below) should usually accompany heading back. Otherwise your plant will produce a dense mass of foliage and lots of twiggy stems. Light may not penetrate to the plant's interior, resulting in death for leaves and stems growing there. Because it cuts off potential flowering wood, too much heading back will also cut down or eliminate flowers and fruits.

Thinning

To thin, you remove whole stems at their points of origin. By thinning you reduce the bulk of a plant without obviously altering its size or form. Simply cut out superfluous side branches or remove whole large stems, cutting them to the ground.

Your goal in thinning is to re-move old, unproductive stems, to eliminate competing stems, and to open up a plant to let light and air reach its interior. This directs the plant's energies to healthy growth.

Thinning should normally accompany heading back (see above). Otherwise you'll have a plant with long, willowy branches that carry the weight of foliage and flowers at their ends. As a result, the plant tends to become floppy and its branches—under the stress of weather or their own weight—will break more easily.

Shearing

To shear a plant you simply clip its outer foliage (with manual or power trimmers) to create an even surface. Shearing differs from other kinds of pruning in two ways: only a formal hedge or a topiary plant routinely requires it (see pages 70 and 106), and it's a seeming exception to the guideline that tells you to make all cuts just above a growing point. Those plants best suited to roles as hedges or topiary will not be adversely affected by any amount of shearing; new growth will emerge close to any point where you prune.

Shearing has one drawback: a shrub or tree you've repeatedly sheared can't display any of its natural beauty.

Pinching

Thinning

Heading back

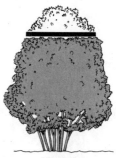

Shearing

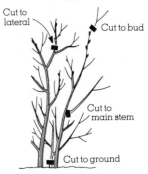

Cut to lateral
Cut to bud
Cut to main stem
Cut to ground

Where to make cuts

WHEN TO GET PROFESSIONAL HELP

Even the most experienced home gardeners shouldn't take on every pruning job themselves. Licensed, insured, professional tree care experts are best trained and equipped to handle the following tricky situations.

High chain-saw work. Standard advice to the weekend gardener is, "Never take a chain saw off the ground." Don't take a chain saw up a ladder or into a tree. Call for professional help instead.

Storm damage. Big trees with large broken limbs usually need someone who can climb the tree to remove the limbs and repair wounds.

Big tree rejuvenation. Restoring a large old tree to health by proper pruning requires a tree expert's knowledge, experience, and equipment.

Stabilizing a weak or damaged tree. Chaining or cabling can hold together a tree with weak or split crotches. Let a professional do this.

Power line problems. Any time you need to remove tree limbs or even small branches near electrical or telephone lines, get help. First, call the utility company. If they can't help, hire a professional yourself.

How to position pruning shears

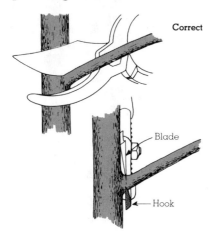

Correct

Blade

Hook

Right and wrong pruning cuts

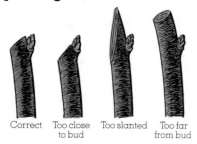

Correct   Too close to bud   Too slanted   Too far from bud

Removing large limbs

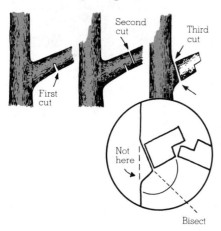

Second cut

Third cut

First cut

Not here

Bisect

HOW TO MAKE PRUNING CUTS

Make all pruning cuts just above (or beyond) some part of a stem that will continue to grow: to a leaf with a dormant bud at its base, to a dormant bud on a leafless stem, or to another branch. At these points of active growth, callus tissue will start to grow inward from cells at the edge of the cut; in time the wound will become closed over. In contrast, if you make a cut ½-inch or more beyond a growing point, the resulting stub will die back to the active growth; no callus cells will be able to close over the wound.

For successful pruning, you need sharp tools and know-how.

With shears. For the cleanest cut, be sure the blade side of shears is closest to the portion of the stem that will remain on the plant.

The illustration at left shows the best cut to make when you're heading back to the growth bud. The lowest point is opposite the bud and approximately even with it; the cut slants upward in the direction the bud is pointing.

With a saw. Use a pruning saw to remove any branch that is too large for hand shears or loppers. The illustration at left shows the correct angle for making the final cut to remove a branch. Make the cut on a slant that is roughly determined by bisecting the upper and lower angles the branch makes with the limb. This slant puts the cut at a point known as the "bark collar." In this region at the base of the branch (often easy to see because bark is slightly wrinkled), cell growth is especially active and the wound will cover over more quickly.

One danger in removing a branch is that the branch's weight will cause it to fall away just before you complete the cut, tearing a strip of bark from the limb beneath it. To prevent this, support the branch with one hand while you saw with the other. When a branch is too heavy for your free hand to support, use

three pruning cuts. First make a cut from underneath, about halfway through the branch; then cut off the branch several inches beyond the undercut. Finally, cut off the branch stub at the proper angle.

Removing diseased branches

Occasionally you may need to remove diseased branches to prevent the disease from spreading. Fireblight, which affects *Cotoneaster*, *Pear*, *Pyracantha*, and other members of the rose family, is a common disease you might encounter.

Some diseases can be spread if your shears touch diseased branches and you then use them to cut healthy stems elsewhere on the plant. To prevent this kind of transfer, make cuts at least 12 inches below obviously infected tissue and then disinfect your pruning shears (or saw) *after each cut.* Dip the blades in rubbing alcohol or a 5 percent solution of household bleach; then wipe them dry. Afterwards, be sure to wash all bleach off the blades to keep it from corroding the metal.

Getting rid of suckers

Two types of unwanted growth are called *suckers.* One kind, more properly called *watersprout,* is an extra-vigorous stem that grows straight up, parallel to the main trunk of a tree or bolt upright on a shrub with arching branches. True suckers appear on plants that have been grafted or budded onto the roots of other related plants. Suckers are stems from the rootstock rather than from the plant grafted onto it.

To remove watersprouts, cut them off flush wherever they arise. But, don't cut off suckers from understock; if you did, you'd leave a cluster of dormant buds at the sucker's base that would later grow into multiple suckers. Instead, pull off each sucker, including the stem's base with its dormant buds. If a sucker emerges from below the soil, dig soil away from it until you expose its base. Then grasp the sucker firmly and pull it off.

STARTING OFF YOUNG TREES

A tree's first few years are critical ones. Early training determines future growth. By giving a young plant careful pruning, you encourage it to develop into a healthy, beautiful, mature tree.

Pruning at planting time

At planting time it's necessary to prune trees to restore the balance of nutrients between top and roots that was upset when the tree was prepared for sale.

Trees are sold three ways: bare-root, balled and burlapped, and in containers. Each has its own pruning requirements.

Bare-root trees. Many deciduous trees are dug up with no soil around their roots, then sold during the winter dormant season. During digging, bare-root trees lose some roots, so you'll usually need to head back their tops to help compensate.

Some bare-root trees (whips) have no branches. If a whip is too

Pruning bare-root tree. At planting time, cut back leader and laterals on branched tree (left); cut back leader above bud on unbranched whip (right).

Three errors and their results

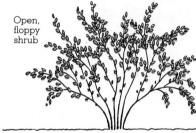

Twiggy, dense shrub

Repeated heading back with no thinning

Open, floppy shrub

Repeated thinning with no heading back

Stub will die back

Leaving stub when making cut

WHY DO YOU PRUNE WHEN YOU DO?

The Pruning Encyclopedia (pages 18–111) lists the best time of year to prune each plant included there. You may wonder why some times are better than others, and what might happen if you prune when it's not recommended. Here are answers to those questions and others.

● *When do you prune?* The best time to do any major pruning is when it will shock the plant least. Frequently this is while the plant is dormant.

● *When is a plant dormant?* There is no one time of year when all plants are dormant (not actively growing). Wherever winter temperatures are below freezing, plants are, by necessity, dormant in winter. Generally, deciduous shrubs and trees that are native to cool or cold-winter regions are dormant during their leafless period—from late autumn to early spring. Deciduous shrubs and trees from subtropical and tropical regions usually are most dormant during their leafless periods. But this stage may not be in winter.

Evergreen trees and shrubs generally are dormant during the coldest time of year. If they are native to mild or tropical regions, their dormancy *may* occur at other times.

● *What is the difference between winter and summer pruning?* Winter pruning removes weak and superfluous wood from an inactive plant. The goal is to maintain or increase a plant's vigor.

Summer pruning, on the other hand, reduces the amount of growth and also diminishes the plant's vigor somewhat. One caution: Where winters are severe, do any summer pruning early enough to allow new shoots a chance to harden before the first expected frosts.

● *Will you kill a plant by pruning it at the wrong time of year?* It's possible, but not inevitable, that pruning a plant at the wrong time will kill it. This depends on the kind of plant, your climate, the health of the plant, and how much you prune. Many plants will tolerate an occasional out-of-season pruning, especially if it's not severe.

In mild-winter regions, you can prune many plants, even heavily, at odd times with little harm. In cold-winter climates, the danger of freeze damage dictates that you avoid out-of-season pruning. You can damage plants by pruning them too late in summer for new growth to harden before autumn frosts.

Healthy plants are better able to endure any sort of pruning than are sickly ones. Light pruning, out of season, is less dangerous than heavy pruning. Some plants won't take heavy pruning at any time, because leafless wood won't send out new growth.

Well-placed tree limbs

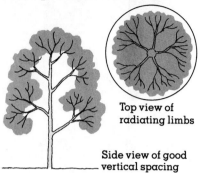

Top view of
radiating limbs

Side view of good
vertical spacing

How to develop single-trunk tree

1st spring

1st midsummer

1st winter

2nd summer

2nd winter

3rd summer

3rd winter

4th winter

short to form branches where you want them, do no pruning. If the whip is tall, head back the leader to a bud about a foot above where you want the lowest branches. If the tree has branches on the trunk, head back each branch to about two buds.

When you head back a bare-root tree, the top bud will grow upward to become a leader. Lower buds will become scaffold branches.

Balled and burlapped. Many conifers, most broadleaf evergreen trees, and some deciduous trees must have soil around their sensitive roots at all times. These trees are dug up from growing fields with a ball of earth around their roots. The soil ball is wrapped with burlap. These plants lose some roots during digging, but not as many as the bare-root plants, so at planting time they need only moderate pruning.

On broadleaf evergreen and deciduous trees, shorten branches that will be lower than you want the scaffold limbs. Thin out superfluous, twiggy stems. Don't prune coniferous evergreens at planting time.

Container-grown trees. Because they've spent their lives in containers, container-grown trees lose no roots. They seldom need pruning at planting time except possibly to remove wayward branches.

Training young trees

Don't rush to establish a young tree's final shape. Be sure not to cut off leafy shoots or branches along the trunk below the scaffold limbs. A young tree needs all its leaves to make food for growth. Also, trunk leaves and branches make the trunk grow thick more rapidly and protect young, thin-barked trunks from sunburn.

The training and pruning schedule that follows will guide you in establishing the framework of most trees.

First summer. Select the upright shoot you want to become the leader. Pinch or cut out any shoots that compete with the leader.

First winter. Head back any side branches on the trunk that have grown too long (but not permanent scaffold branches). Cut back these long branches to about a foot from the trunk, to two of their own side branches, or to two buds. Leave all other growth along the trunk.

Second summer. If the leader reaches 8 feet or more, pinch out the tip or head it back about 1½ feet above where you want scaffold branches to begin. The topmost bud will produce an upright shoot. Several buds 1 to 2 feet below it will grow and become the permanent limbs. Pinch or head back overly vigorous branches on the trunk.

Second winter. Select evenly distributed branches to form the tree's scaffold limbs. Thin out any twiggy and badly placed branches in the developing crown. Shorten side branches, if necessary, as described for first winter, but leave all other growth along the trunk.

Third summer. Let the crown scaffold branches develop. Head back any that make the tree lopsided. Pinch or head back vigorous branches along the trunk.

Third winter. Thin out any badly placed branches in the crown. Shorten long side branches.

Fourth winter. Cut off trunk branches below the scaffold limbs.

Thereafter, follow directions for specific trees in the Pruning Encyclopedia (pages 18–111).

TRAINING FRUIT AND NUT TREES

Commercial orchardists train and prune their trees to get crops with the greatest yield and quality. Below we present the three common commercial training systems.

If you want a primarily ornamental fruit tree, follow the preceding guidelines for training young trees. But to grow your fruit or nut tree as professionals do, use one of the following systems. For each fruit and nut tree the Pruning Encyclopedia list (pages 18–111), we name the preferred training system.

Open center system. After you plant a bare-root tree—usually a whip—head it back to a bud 24 to 36 inches above the ground. The 24 to 36-inch-tall shoot will become the trunk. Cut off any ill-placed side branches. Save any side branch located where you want your lowest scaffold limb; head it back to two buds.

First winter. Select three to four scaffold limbs. These should form a spiral around the trunk, each limb about 6 inches higher on the trunk than the next lower one. Select branches that grow out at a good angle (more than 45 degrees). Head back any long scaffold limbs to 2 to 3 feet from the trunk. Cut back very upright-growing limbs to outward-facing buds; cut back wide-spreading limbs to upward-pointing buds. Remove watersprouts, crossing limbs, poorly placed trunk limbs.

Second summer. Head back any scaffold limbs that become too long and droopy. To promote branching, pinch back to 2 to 3 feet long any limbs that weren't long enough for heading back the previous winter. Cut out any watersprouts.

Second winter. Select two strong laterals on each primary scaffold limb to become part of the main framework. Head back each main scaffold limb to the outermost lateral that you've selected. Head back chosen laterals to 2 to 3 feet if they are long enough. Otherwise pinch them back the following summer.

Thereafter. Follow routine training for the particular tree as detailed in the Pruning Encyclopedia, pages 18–111.

Modified central leader. To grow this kind of tree, you allow four to six scaffold limbs to develop on the trunk before stopping the central leader.

After planting, head back the whip to four or five buds. In the first growing season, select one shoot (usually the top) for the leader. Pinch back all other shoots so they stay leafy but don't grow.

First winter. Head back the leader to just above where you want the lowest scaffold branch. If the leader is still too short, let it grow

one more season. After this heading back, the top bud will grow upward as the leader, while a lower bud will form the first scaffold limb.

Second winter. Select more scaffold limbs, choosing ones that form a spiral pattern up the trunk, each limb about 6 inches higher than the next lower one. Choose branches that make good angles with the trunk (more than 45 degrees). Head back to 2 to 3 feet any long scaffold limbs.

Thereafter. Continue to select scaffold limbs until you have six. Then bend the leader over, making it the topmost branch. Continue to head back young scaffold limbs and secondary laterals to encourage a strong framework. Then follow directions given in the Pruning Encyclopedia, pages 18–111.

Central leader. This method of training produces a straight-trunked, pyramid-shaped tree.

At planting time, head back the whip to 24 to 32 inches, and cut back any side branches to two buds.

First summer. Make sure that the top shoot becomes the leader. Pinch back all other shoots.

First winter. If growth has been vigorous, you'll be able to select a first set of scaffold branches 2 to 3 feet from the ground. Choose 3 to 5 branches for this first set. These should spiral around the trunk, with about 4 inches vertical distance between succeeding branches. Cut off other side branches and vertical stems that compete with the leader. Head back the leader, but keep it as the highest part of the tree.

Second summer. Make sure that the top shoot of the pruned leader grows vertically again. Cut off any competing vertical shoots.

Second winter. Select another set of scaffold limbs 2 to 3 feet higher than the first set. If the tree didn't grow enough during the second year, do selecting the third winter.

Thereafter. Continue the process until you have three or four sets of scaffold limbs. In following years, remove watersprouts and crossing and unwanted branches. Keep lower limbs longer than upper ones.

Three training systems for trees

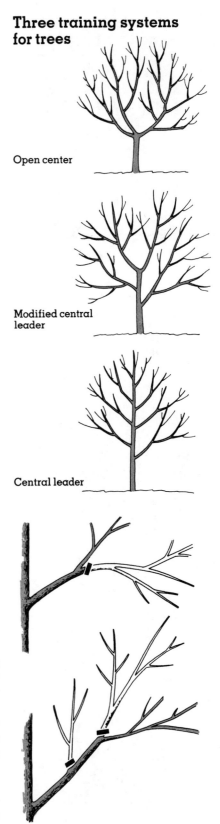

Open center

Modified central leader

Central leader

Prune to change direction of growth. (A) Cut spreading plant to upright limbs for increased height. (B) Cut off upright limbs to encourage spreading.

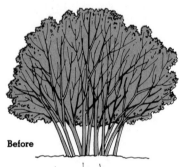

Convert multistemmed shrub into small tree by removing lower limbs, excess stems.

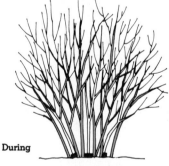

Before

During

After

Renovate overgrown shrub over a period of 3 years. Each winter, cut to ground one-third of oldest stems. Result is shorter, compact, leafy shrub.

SPECIAL KINDS OF PRUNING

The preceding pruning and training basics hold for all usual pruning operations. Below you'll find several ways to use basic methods to attain special goals.

Pruning for flowers

Not all flowering shrubs should be pruned at the same time of year. If you prune at the wrong time, you may reduce or stop flowering for that year. You can find the pruning time for each flowering shrub in the Pruning Encyclopedia, pages 18–111.

Most flowering shrubs bloom either in spring on laterals of stems formed the previous year, or in summer or autumn on strong new wood formed during spring of the same year. The sections that follow cover pruning methods for the two large general classes of flowering shrubs, as well as for perpetual-flowering ones, such as roses.

Spring-flowering shrubs. These shrubs, such as *Philadelphus* and *Syringa,* produce flowering laterals from stems formed the previous year. Prune them while plants are flowering or immediately after flowers fade. After bloom, these shrubs put out new growth that will bear the next year's flowers. Cut out weak and superfluous wood at this time to encourage strong new stems. If you wait until winter or early spring to prune, you'll cut away stems that are preparing to blossom.

Summer and autumn-flowering shrubs. These shrubs put out vigorous new growth in spring. In summer and autumn, flowers appear on the spring's growth. Typically you prune these plants in winter or early spring.

Perpetual-flowering shrubs. Modern roses—repeat-flowering hybrid trees, grandifloras, floribundas, polyanthas—represent the few shrubs that bloom on both old and new wood. To treat them as flowering shrubs rather than show-flower factories, prune year-old wood lightly in winter or early spring. Remove weak and badly placed stems. The remaining year-old stems will bear the first flower crop. Later flowers will come from last year's stems and vigorous new canes. For further information, see Rose on page 102.

An old shrub: Transformation vs. renovation

A shrub that has become old, woody, and ugly, and a shrub that's overgrown are challenges to the gardener. Should you discard and start anew, or should you try to restore the plant to attractiveness? Pruning offers an alternative to discarding.

Transformation. You can change an old, overgrown, straggly shrub into a good-looking small tree by careful pruning. If the plant has one sound, mostly upright stem, cut all other stems to the ground. Then cut off side branches on the remaining stem—now a trunk—up to the height where you want branches. If the plant has several good stems, you can leave them all and remove side branches on each one up to where you want branching. Either way, you get an instant small tree.

Renovation. Sometimes the way to handle a big, overgrown shrub is to cut it back drastically. Then, as it grows back, you can keep it under control. Many descriptions in the Pruning Encyclopedia mention whether or not a shrub will take severe cutting back. Some plants will regrow after being cut completely to the ground. But generally allow 4 years for renovation.

The first year, fertilize and water the plant well to make it as healthy as possible. During the next 3 years, cut back severely or completely one-third of the old stems each year. At the end of this time your shrub will be much smaller and will consist of branches no more than 3 years old. You can then thin out weak, badly placed, and crowding stems, leaving a good, young framework.

Pruning a freeze-damaged plant

Frost damage may be either obvious (blackened stems) or deceptive (healthy-looking but slow-to-sprout stems). If you know your plants have sustained freeze damage, take the following steps.

First, examine the stems for live growth buds. Withered, brown buds are dead. If you can't spot any live buds, choose a branch and scrape through the bark with your fingernail or a knife. If the cambium layer between the bark and heartwood is brown, the stem is dead.

On a plant that's partially alive, wait until growth starts and the danger of frost is past. Then cut away all dead and damaged wood. Cut back each damaged stem until the stem is totally green or green-and-white in cross section. Be patient. Some freeze-damaged plants need several months to start growing again. Even if all top growth is killed, some plants send up new stems from near or below the ground.

Freeze-damaged conifers drop their needles or scales. A plant that drops one-third or less should recover. Remove bare twigs later when it's clear which ones are dead.

A conifer that drops two-thirds or more needles may not live. Almost certainly the plant's symmetry will be altered if it does.

Pruning for decorative effects

Some kinds of pruning enhance a plant's natural form. Other pruning styles produce plants that differ radically from their natural shape. These are all decorative pruning.

Hedges. This common form of decorative pruning is fully discussed on page 70.

Espalier, cordon. These carefully manipulated plants are used for fruit production and garden ornament. Refer to page 50 for more information.

Topiary. Living sculptures can result from this whimsical plant shearing. Page 106 describes the practice in greater detail.

Pleaching. To pleach, you interlace the branches of trees planted in a row. The limbs grow together to form a high hedge on stilts.

Start by planting the trees in a row, spacing them 5 to 10 feet apart. Decide how high you want the foliage to begin, and keep the lowest branches of the trees above that height. Train the limbs of adjacent trees toward one another. As trees grow, remove branches that don't grow parallel (or nearly so) to the line of trees. Head back laterals on remaining branches so that branches will grow into one another and the trees will grow taller.

When branches reach those from adjacent trees, interweave them and tie them together. In time they may form natural grafts. When trees reach the desired height, cut out the leaders. Give further routine pruning as for hedges.

Hornbeam *(Carpinus)*, beech *(Fagus)*, sycamore or plane tree *(Platanus)*, linden *(Tilia)*, and even some maples *(Acer)* will adapt to pleaching.

Pollarding. A pollarded tree is one in which all new growth is cut back each year to the point from which it grew. The tree's crown remains about the same size year after year, but the branch stubs from which the stems grow become greatly enlarged and gnarled.

To pollard a tree, give it standard early training (see page 14) until it has formed several scaffold branches that are well placed and about wrist thick. Then cut back each limb to 2 to 5 feet long and head back the leader. The branch outline should be dome or mushroom shaped.

Each spring, the permanent limbs will send out slender, long branches that will bear the tree's leafy crown. Each winter you cut these shoots back to their bases.

Sycamore or plane trees *(Platanus)*, chestnut *(Castanea)*, Catalpa *(Catalpa)*, and horse-chestnut *(Aesculus)* all can be pollarded.

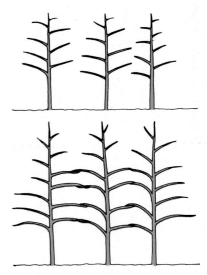

Pleaching. Plant young trees equally spaced in row. As trees grow, weave together branches that parallel the row. Limit height and spread in other directions.

Cut back branches

Cut back year-old stems completely

Large knobs form at branch ends

Pollarding. Cut back framework limbs of young established tree to stubs. Each winter afterward, cut back all new growth.

ENCYCLOPEDIA: A TO Z

In this 101-page pruning encyclopedia, you'll find instructions for pruning 422 popular trees, shrubs, and vines. Most plants are listed alphabetically by their botanical names. If you look up the pruning instructions for a plant by its common name ("Oak," for example), the common name entry will refer you to the plant's botanical name.

There are two exceptions to the botanical listing of names. One exception is that many common fruits and nuts are listed alphabetically by their common names rather than their botanical names: almond, cherry, fig, walnut, for instance. The other exception involves plants that are treated in special features, in which we give more detailed instructions for pruning some of the frequently used and frequently pruned plants. So if you look up a plant by its common name, you may find a cross-reference to the page that has the special feature.

For each regular entry, we list alongside the botanical name and common name, a brief description ("tree," "shrub," "vine," for example) and the best time of year to prune the plant.

Where illustrations accompany a set of pruning instructions, we've used a small black rectangle across a branch to represent a pruning cut.

Give crape myrtle thorough pruning each year after leaves drop, to stimulate growth of new branches that will bloom bountifully.

ABELIA. Evergreen, semievergreen, and deciduous shrubs. <u>Prune in autumn to early spring.</u>

Gracefully arching growth characterizes all abelia species. Summer blooms form on new spring growth. To promote flowering and maintain attractive plant form, remove oldest twiggy and unproductive stems to the ground; selectively head back any overlong stems to strong laterals. Pinch tips of new growth in spring to control height or spread and to make plants bushier.

You can shear plants into formal hedges, but this sacrifices flowers and beauty of plant. With selective heading back and pinching, you can use abelias for informal hedges.

In colder regions where stems freeze back but roots live over winter, cut back stems in autumn to about 4

Abelia. To keep graceful, arching form, cut ⅓ of old stems to ground.

inches and mulch the plant's crown. Plant will perform as a shrubby perennial, flowering in summer.

ABELIOPHYLLUM distichum. White forsythia. Deciduous shrub. <u>Prune in spring.</u>

White flowers of this forsythialike shrub bloom on wood produced in the previous year. Prune while in bloom (for cut flowers) or just afterward. Cut to the ground oldest stems that produced least amount of new growth in the last year. Vigorous new stems will arise to replace them.

ABIES. Fir. Coniferous evergreen trees. <u>Prune in spring, summer.</u>

The most important point is that you cannot restrict the size of a fir by pruning—if you try, you'll damage (and perhaps ruin) the natural shape. Plant a fir where it will have enough room for its ultimate size.

Pruning is rarely necessary except to remove damaged stems. Cut these back to the trunk or closest branch behind the damaged spot. Take care not to cut back to a bare, unbranched stem; no new growth will form. If the leader is broken, cut it off and tie a branch in the topmost whorl of branches into an upright position; it will become the new leader.

ABUTILON. Flowering maple, Chinese bellflower, Chinese lantern. Evergreen sprawling shrubs. <u>Prune in early spring.</u>

Rapid growth produces slender, flexible stems that form a floppy shrub.

(Continued on page 20)

Some are almost vinelike—easy to train as informal espalier. Pinch tip growth during spring, summer to promote bushiness; since plants bloom on new wood, moderate pinching will increase flower production.

Rejuvenate overgrown plants by cutting oldest stems to the ground; head back remaining stems to half their length. If frost has harmed plant, wait until new growth begins; then cut back all dead and damaged growth to vigorous new shoots.

ACACIA. Mostly evergreen shrubs and trees. <u>Prune during or after bloom; can be pruned at any time of year.</u>

Both tree and shrubby types can be grown as single or multitrunked trees (most shrubby species reach a height of more than 10 feet). To train any acacia as a single-trunked tree, allow the leader to grow upward, and shorten all side branches below the desired canopy height; remove shortened trunk branches when tree is self-supporting. To encourage shrubby growth, cut out leader and let side branches grow, or cut plant nearly to ground—while plants are young and trunks are less than 2 inches in diameter—and let several stems rise from the base.

Large trees need occasional thinning to allow light into the tree, and permit storm winds to pass through crown. Cut selected limbs back to main trunk or joints with other limbs. Cut off only limbs that are less than 3 inches thick, and make the cuts cleanly because acacias do not heal very well. Where trees grow fast, you may have to do a lot of thinning every 2 to 3 years to prevent storm damage. To keep trees clean-looking, frequently prune out dead branches and twigs.

ACALYPHA. Evergreen shrubs. <u>Prune whenever needed</u> (see below).

Both commonly grown species—chenille plant *(A. hispida)* and copperleaf *(A. wilkesiana,* formerly *A. tricolor)*—are vigorous, dense shrubs. Pinch back new growth and prune as much as needed to control size and bushiness at any time. Both species make colorful, informal hedges. For hedges, cut back stems and pinch tip growth; shearing destroys beauty of large leaves.

ACER. Maple. Deciduous (a few evergreen) trees and large shrubs. <u>Prune in summer, autumn, winter.</u>

There are three basic types of maples: trees—medium to large, usually with a single trunk and dense leaf canopy; character plants—large shrubs or smaller trees, grown for beautiful branch form or foliage pattern; and shrubs—dense and bulky, suitable for hedges.

Avoid pruning in spring just before and during time of active growth: most bleed sap profusely then.

Tree types. Trident maple *(A. buergerianum),* coliseum maple *(A. cappadocicum),* David's maple *(A. davidii),* paperbark maple *(A. griseum),* bigleaf maple *(A. macrophyllum),* Mt. Morrison maple *(A. morrisonense),* box elder *(A. negundo),* evergreen maple *(A. oblongum), A. paxi,* Norway maple *(A. platanoides),* sycamore maple *(A. pseudoplatanus),* red maple *(A. rubrum),* silver maple *(A. saccharinum),* sugar maple *(A. saccharum),* Shantung maple *(A. truncatum).*

To grow as single-trunked trees, train and stake them as described on page 14. Little pruning is needed; simply remove wood that is dead, broken, weak, or badly placed and interfering with other good limbs.

Character plants. *A. capillipes,* vine maple *(A. circinatum),* Amur maple *(A. ginnala),* fullmoon maple *(A. japonicum),* Japanese maple *(A. palmatum).* These occasionally grow as single-trunked specimens, but more often grow with multiple trunks or branch very low to the ground. Plants tend to determine their own shapes, can resemble large bonsai plants.

Prune only to accentuate the natural shape, removing any growth that obscures or detracts from a desirable irregularity. Thinning out entire limbs usually produces a better effect than heading back.

Shrub types. Hedge maple *(A. campestre),* Rocky Mountain maple *(A. glabrum),* Wasatch maple *(A. saccharum grandidentatum).* Hedge maple is a dense, compact, rounded plant that can be clipped as a high hedge or left as a bulky shrub. Rocky Mountain and Wasatch maples are multitrunked shrubby types that serve as garden accents (background shrubs or small trees). Prune by thinning out congested growth to reveal the beauty of the several trunks.

ACMENA smithii. Lilly-pilly tree. Evergreen shrub-tree. <u>Prune in early spring.</u>

Young plants may grow unevenly, taking on an irregular shape. If this is unattractive, shorten awkward limbs at good lateral branches or cut off limbs at main trunk.

ACROCOMIA.
See Palm.

ACTINIDIA. Deciduous vines. <u>Prune in winter, early spring,</u> before growth starts.

Kiwi *(A. chinensis)* is grown for fruit and for garden ornament; *A. kolomitka* is planted for its handsome variegated foliage. Both are rampant growers, good for covering walls, fences, trellises, patio overheads, and arbors. Prune ornamental plants annually to thin out entangling growth, leaving a well-spaced framework of main branches from which new growth will sprout.

For greatest fruit production, prune kiwi as you would cane prune grapes (see page 66). Initially, limit the plant to 1 or 2 strong, upright trunks and several main horizontal branches (cordons); these will be the vine's permanent framework. Fruit forms on shoots growing from wood formed the previous summer. Cut back these future fruit-producing shoots to 2 or 3 buds beyond the previous year's fruit stalks. Cut back to 3 buds the previous year's shoots that did not fruit. Remove weak, dam-

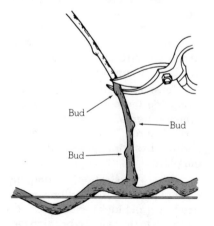

Actinidia. Prune kiwi annually to increase fruit production. Cut back last summer's growth to 2 or 3 buds.

aged, and entangling growth. On old vines, cut off a few of the oldest fruiting shoots each year. Newer fruiting wood will replace them.

ADAM'S NEEDLE.
See Yucca.

AESCULUS. Horsechestnut, buckeye. Deciduous trees or large shrubs. Prune in winter or early spring, just before growth starts.

Tree species need normal early training for a strong, single trunk (see page 14). With shrubby types you may need to remove excess branches arising from the ground. Otherwise, just cut off dead or damaged wood and any awkward-looking limbs.

AFRICAN BOXWOOD.
See Myrsine.

AFRICAN LINDEN.
See Sparmannia.

AFRICAN TULIP TREE.
See Spathodea.

AGATHIS robusta. Queensland kauri. Evergreen coniferous tree. Prune in late winter, early spring, before new growth starts.

This conifer naturally grows narrowly upright; open spaces between groups of branches give it a layered appearance. It requires little or no pruning. Occasionally a plant may develop a double leader; if so, remove the weaker of the two.

AGONIS. Evergreen trees. Prune in spring, after any danger of frost.

Adaptable growth lets you train them as trees (see page 14) or as informal espaliers (see page 50). If plant is frozen to the ground or cut back, several branches will arise; you then can train it as large shrub or multitrunked shrub-tree. Except for training, little or no pruning is needed.

AILANTHUS altissima (*A. glandulosa*). Tree-of-Heaven. Deciduous tree. Prune in winter.

This fast-growing, brittle-wooded tree is often condemned as a weed because of suckering and volunteer seeding, but is of great value as a shade tree where air pollution, heat, and drought are problems. Remove

broken or dead branches and periodically thin out branches to shape the tree and open up the canopy. Pull off root suckers as they appear, don't cut them back.

AKEBIA. Deciduous to evergreen vines. Prune in spring or summer.

Rampant and evergreen where winters are mild, these vines are deciduous and less vigorous in severe-winter regions. After spring bloom, thin out plant to remove weak and entangling branches. Prune, if needed, to direct growth onto a trellis.

For complete renewal, cut vine to the ground or cut stems back to 5 to 9 buds before growth begins. To limit growth and produce a more open vine, allow only 2 or 3 stems to grow from the ground.

ALBIZIA julibrissin. Silk tree (known as "Mimosa" in eastern United States). Deciduous tree. Prune in winter, early spring, or summer; in cold-winter areas, postpone pruning until after any danger of frost.

Silk tree naturally grows with several trunks or with single trunk and low branches. It needs careful tree training (see page 14) if you want a single-trunked tree. Growth is rapid to about 40 feet, but you can keep it to around 20 feet by heading back upward-growing branches.

For multitrunked clump, limit plant to number of stems you want; cut off excess stems at ground. As needed, thin out branches that are crossing or are crowded.

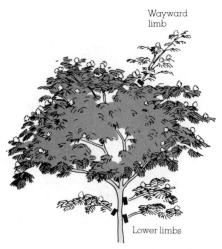

Wayward limb

Lower limbs

Albizia. On mature tree, cut off lower limbs, cut back wayward ones.

If frost or storm damages tree, cut back killed or broken branches to strong, healthy laterals or to the trunk.

Be careful not to leave stubs when you prune. They die back and become an entryway for diseases.

ALDER.
See Alnus.

ALDER BUCKTHORN.
See Rhamnus.

ALLAMANDA cathartica. Evergreen shrubby vine. Prune in late winter to late spring.

To use this plant as a vine, just remove excess, entangling growth and see that basic framework branches are tied to a support (vine is not clinging type). Pinch or head back poorly directed stems during growing season. To grow as a shrub, head back flexible, sprawly stems during growing season.

ALMOND. Deciduous tree. (For flowering almond, see page 54.) Prune in winter.

Newly planted trees need training for several years to form typical open center framework (see page 15). Once the basic framework is established, you prune primarily for wood renewal to ensure a steady crop.

Almonds bear along short fruiting spurs which produce for about 5 years; each winter, remove about a fifth of the oldest fruiting wood. At the same time, cut out dead wood and any crossing or crowded branches. A young almond tree grows vigorously and may put all its energy into vegetative growth at the expense of fruit-bearing spurs. If this happens, stop pruning for a season or two; this will slow excessive vegetative growth.

If you have an old tree to rejuvenate, cut out all twiggy branches and head back larger limbs to healthy lateral branches. Don't cut back large branches by more than a third.

ALNUS. Alder. Deciduous trees. Prune in winter or early spring.

Birch relatives that resemble birches in their clean (but not white) trunks and branching pattern. Some grow several trunks and are attractive planted as clumps. To grow as a single-trunked tree, select the strongest stem to train; remove all

(Continued on page 24)

APPLE

Apples are popular, long-lived fruit trees. With the right pruning they can become attractive ornamental plants as well.

Most apples form broadly upright trees. Typically you train the trees to either a central leader or to an open center system (directions for both follow). You can also train apples as espaliers and as cordons (see below). Dwarf and spur varieties need special pruning (see below).

Prune apples to achieve two goals: initially, on young trees, to encourage a strong framework of main limbs; later, on established trees, to assure fruit production.

The time to prune apple trees is in late winter or very early spring before new growth starts. On young and old trees, also remove all suckers that come from rootstocks. The best time to do this is during summer, when suckers are least likely to resprout. You can also purchase chemicals that will help to reduce suckering.

Young trees

A new apple tree you purchase will likely be either a 3 to 4-foot-tall whip (without branches) or a 4 to 6-foot-tall young tree with several branches. (Varieties grown on dwarfing rootstocks are an exception.) Prune young trees according to one of the following methods.

Central leader system. Training to a central leader produces a pyramid-shaped apple tree. This system is suitable for all apple varieties except the ones with naturally upright and slender growth (which are better trained to the open center system). Central leader training was most commonly used in the eastern regions of the United States. In the West, Midwest, and East, many orchardists now use the open center system. The central leader system is also shown on page 15.

If your newly planted tree has no branches, cut back the trunk to a height of about 32 inches. This will stimulate side branches to grow along the trunk. The topmost bud will become the central leader.

For a new tree that already has some side branches, cut back the trunk to 32 inches. Cut off any branches along the trunk between the ground and 24 inches. Cut back any remaining side branches to 2 to 4 inches, leaving no more than 2 buds on each branch stub.

During the next few years, follow the directions on page 15.

For a taller, more ornamental garden tree, train to the central leader system but let the lowest permanent framework branches start at 3 to 4 feet from the ground. Select scaffold limbs evenly spaced around the trunk, and 18 to 30 inches above the branches directly below them.

Open center system. Apples trained with an open center form a vase-shaped tree with no central leader—instead, several major limbs angle outward from the top portion of a short trunk. An open center tree is wider and shorter than a central leader tree. Use this system for upright-growing and extra-vigorous varieties so that trees will bear fruits at heights that are easy to pick from.

Cut back the newly planted tree to 24 to 32 inches, depending on how low you want the major limbs to form. Strong, well-spaced limbs that are 6 to 10 inches below the cut will become primary scaffold branches.

If the newly planted tree has some side branches, cut back the leader to 24 to 32 inches. Select well-placed side branches—ones that point out from the trunk in different directions in the 6 to 10-inch space

Young apple tree. Cut off weak and crowding limbs, leaving well-spaced ones for strong scaffold branches.

Dwarf apple tree. Annually remove weak, crossing branches. Cut back limbs to limit size when necessary.

Mature apple tree. Each year cut back too-vigorous branches and cut off weak, crowded, and dead limbs.

below the cut—to become scaffold branches. Cut back these well-placed branches to 2 to 4-inch stubs and cut off all other side branches. By the end of the first growing season the major scaffold limbs should be formed. See page 15 for full directions on the open center system.

Espaliers and cordons. You can grow apples as espaliers or as cordons. As ornamental plants they look best against a wall or fence, but you can also grow them in the open by training them on wires or lattice. Semidwarf and spur varieties (see below) are the best choices for espaliers and cordons because they grow slower and require less pruning than full-size varieties. Directions for espaliers and cordons are on page 50.

Dwarf and spur trees. Dwarf, semidwarf, and spur apples make smaller trees than ordinary 20 to 30-foot varieties. How much a tree is dwarfed depends on the rootstock to which an ordinary, regular-size variety is grafted. Dwarfs are about 6 feet tall and equally wide. Semidwarfs may reach three-fourths the size of a normal tree, depending on the rootstock.

Spur apples are mutations of familiar varieties. They grow only to about three-fourths normal size because their internodes are shorter. Overall they produce more fruiting wood (spurs) for the tree's size and less annual growth.

Usually you train these smaller apples to a central leader with some modifications. Cut back a newly planted dwarf tree to about 22 inches above the bud union. Cut back a spur tree to about 28 inches above the bud union. If the newly planted tree has side branches, cut them back to a length of 2 to 4 inches. Leave 2 buds per branch stub. Cut off any side branches closer than 18 inches to the ground. After that, train according to the directions for a central leader tree on page 15.

Prune apple mostly for size, shape.

Pruning mature trees

Apples produce flowers and fruit on long-lived (up to 20 years), stubby twigs called spurs. Each year a spur puts out blossoms, forms fruit, and grows just a bit longer to form a terminal bud that will repeat the performance in the next year.

Full-size trees. Annually remove broken branches, crossing limbs, weak stems, and any branches that grow toward the tree's center or grow vertically or downward. Thin out enough new growth to allow light to filter into the canopy when the tree has leafed out. Cut back to a sturdy side branch any too-long branches.

Dwarf and spur trees. Prune dwarf and spur trees annually about the same way as full-size trees. Since dwarf and spur trees grow less, you have less to prune.

When your dwarf or spur tree reaches a height you want to maintain, cut back the central leader by 2 or 3 feet (depending on the vigor of the tree) to a strong lateral. In later years, repeat this procedure whenever necessary.

Fireblight. In some areas fireblight disease affects apple trees. Some varieties are more susceptible than others. Fireblight requires pruning as soon as you notice it. If a twig or limb suddenly turns black and burned-looking, cut it off a foot below the affected part. Disinfect pruning tools after each cut to avoid spreading the disease.

others. Train the remaining stem as for young trees (see page 14). Mature alders need little pruning except to remove unwanted suckers at ground level, crossing branches, and dead wood.

ALOYSIA triphylla *(Lippia citriodora)*. Lemon verbena. Shrubby perennial. Prune in late winter.

Natural habit is leggy and open; grows to 6 feet or taller. Pinch growing branches frequently during spring and summer to control shape and increase bushiness. In dormant season remove old wood, spindly growth; if plant gets rangy, head back as much as you want.

AMELANCHIER. Shadblow, shadbush, service berry. Deciduous shrubs and small trees. Prune in late winter, early spring, before growth starts.

The most popular *Amelanchiers* are small trees, attractive with single or multiple trunks. For training single trunks, see page 14. Otherwise, you won't need to prune, except to occasionally remove crossing, crowded, and dead branches.

The most commonly planted shrubby species, *A. stolonifera*, sends up stems from the roots to form spreading clumps. Occasionally remove the oldest stems to ground level. You can limit the spread of clumps by digging out unwanted stems.

AMORPHA canescens. Lead plant, indigo bush. Deciduous shrub. Prune in late winter, early spring.

Summer flowers come on new wood formed in spring. Each year, before growth starts, remove the oldest, least vigorous stems.

AMPELOPSIS. Deciduous and semievergreen vines. Prune in early spring and summer.

Two vigorous, commonly grown kinds are the deciduous blueberry climber *A. brevipedunculata*, and the semievergreen peppervine *A. arborea*. Each year, thin and shorten selected stems to control form and spacing. Whenever necessary, cut back unwanted stems. Control underground spread of peppervine by digging out any unwanted suckers.

ANEMOPAEGMA chamberlaynii *(Bignonia chamberlaynii)*. Yellow trumpet vine. Evergreen vine. Prune in early spring and summer.

Summer flowers come on new spring growth. Head back any out-of-bounds growth in early spring, but remember that spring pruning sacrifices some summer flowers. After blossoms fade, thin out overcrowded and tangled stems, shorten exuberant lateral growth, and cut off all weak stems.

ANGEL'S TRUMPET.
See Brugmansia.

ANGOPHORA costata *(A. lanceolata)*. Gum myrtle. Evergreen tree. Prune in late winter, early spring.

This large, elegant eucalyptus relative needs routine tree training when young (see page 14), but little or no pruning in later years. You may need to thin out crossing branches in the developing crown; do this by cutting back branches to strong laterals or to the trunk.

ANISACANTHUS thurberi. Desert honeysuckle, chuparosa. Evergreen or deciduous shrub. Prune in winter.

True desert honeysuckle has 2-inch leaves and yellow orange flowers; a related plant *(Justicia leonardii)*, with red flowers and longer leaves, is sometimes sold as desert honeysuckle. Both plants benefit from the same pruning. Best foliage and flowers come on vigorous new growth. Cut plant to the ground before new growth starts, or prune back to framework of short branches.

ANISE TREE.
See Illicium.

ANNONA cherimola. Cherimoya. Briefly deciduous small tree or large shrub. Prune when out of leaf.

During first several years, trees need little pruning except to form good framework (see page 14); thereafter, remove crowding inner branches. Trees often branch low, so remove branches below the desired height as the tree matures. You can also train cherimoya as an informal espalier (see page 50).

APACHE PLUME.
See Fallugia.

APPLE.
See page 22.

APRICOT.
See page 26.

ARALIA. Deciduous large shrubs or small trees. Prune in late winter, spring, or summer.

Aralias grow as clumps of nearly vertical (and sometimes spiny) stems. Thin out stems as needed to create a more see-through effect. You can remove broken or dead stems at any time. Control spread of clumps by digging out suckers as they appear.

ARAUCARIA. Evergreen coniferous trees. Prune any time.

These distinctive trees from the Southern Hemisphere seldom need pruning except to remove damaged branches. If errant branch distorts tree's symmetry, head it back to a healthy pair of branches or to the trunk.

ARBORVITAE.
See Thuja, Platycladus.

ARBUTUS. Evergreen shrub-tree and tree. Prune in early spring, before growth starts.

Shrub-tree. Strawberry tree *(A. unedo)*. This type naturally grows as a multitrunked shrub, but you can train it as a single-trunked tree (see page 14). Without pruning, it makes a handsome dense screen. To restrict

Lower limbs

Arbutus. Remove lower branches to convert overgrown shrub to tree.

size and make plants more dense, cut back vigorous stems to clusters of branches from which they grew. On older unpruned plants, you can remove the lowest limbs and all twiggy growth to create a small multi-trunked tree.

Tree type. Madrone, madrona (*A. menziesii*). Tree grows erect and fairly symmetrical, but pruning or competition from other shrubs and trees will encourage irregular, picturesque shapes. Growth pattern comes from terminal buds surrounded by several secondary buds (see page 14). For a bushier plant, remove terminal buds on as many branches as you wish; the whorl of secondary buds will then grow into radiating clusters of branches.

ARCTOSTAPHYLOS. Manzanita. Evergreen shrubs. Prune in spring, after bloom.

The many species and named varieties of manzanita range in height from mat-forming ground covers to shrubs to small trees. Many shrubby and treelike manzanitas have beautiful irregular branching patterns and smooth, mahogany-colored limbs. They don't need much pruning, but you can pinch back stems to control their growth during summer.

To make manzanita more dense and uniformly compact, pinch tips of new growth to force branching. Cut back any lopsided stems to joints with other branches. Don't cut back into bare wood; the plant will not send out new growth from bare stubs.

Larger species, such as *A. manzanita*, naturally become treelike, usually with several trunks or with branches close to the ground. As plants grow, lower limbs die (in nature, they break off). Result is a canopy of leaves crowning a framework of handsome, angular limbs.

To give nature a hand, cut out all dead wood annually; remove any branches that you feel may obscure the beauty of the plant's largely self-determined form. You can remove large limbs and entire trunks without worry; cuts heal over well.

ARECASTRUM.
See Palm.

ARENGA.
See Palm.

ARISTOLOCHIA. Deciduous vines. Prune in winter.

Training during growing season is more important to these vines than pruning (you can cut out excess growth any time). If plant becomes too thick and tangled for selective thinning, you can cut back even to the ground during winter. With the California Dutchman's pipe (*A. californica*), you will lose a year's bloom; flowers come on year-old wood before plant leafs out.

ARONIA. Chokeberry. Deciduous shrubs. Prune in late winter, early spring.

The 2 tall-growing species, purple-fruited chokeberry (*A. prunifolia*) and red chokeberry (*A. arbutifolia*), are rather open, multistemmed shrubs that need only occasional thinning—cut oldest stems to the ground. You can restrict height and increase bushiness by heading back the upright stems.

Black chokeberry (*A. melanocarpa*) is much shorter, growing to about 3 feet. Thin out periodically and remove root suckers to prevent plant from spreading.

ARROWWOOD.
See Viburnum.

ARTEMISIA. Evergreen and deciduous shrubs and shrubby perennials. Prune in late winter, early spring.

Sagebrush (*A. tridentata*) is a true shrub. Thin out some crossing or crowded branches for beauty.

Shrubby perennials include deciduous southernwood, or old man (*A. abrotanum*); common wormwood (*A. absinthium*); and *A. arborescens*. To prune southernwood, thin out crowded stems annually; cut back remaining stems by half their length. If the other 2 kinds become floppy or too large, you may need to prune by cutting them back to half their size or lower; they will quickly fill out again. In mild-winter areas, you can cut plants to the ground or back to their woody base in late autumn. Plants will regrow in winter.

ASH.
See Fraxinus.

ASPEN.
See Populus.

ATLAS CEDAR.
See Cedrus.

ATRIPLEX. Saltbush. Evergreen and deciduous shrubs. Prune any time.

Grown as accent plants for their beautiful silvery gray foliage, these shrubs need little or no pruning. To grow them as hedges, give plants periodic trimming (see page 70)—how much and how often depend on whether you want formal or informal hedges.

AUCUBA japonica. Japanese aucuba. Evergreen shrub. Prune in early spring, summer.

Aucuba naturally grows dense and moderately tall—ultimately 10 to 15 feet high, if unchecked. Control size easily by cutting branches back to a joint with other branches, to a pair of buds, or just above a leaf. New growth will quickly fill in.

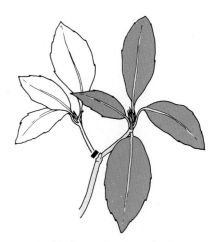

Aucuba. To shape plants, cut back wayward stems to branch joints.

AUSTRALIAN BLUEBELL CREEPER.
See Sollya.

AUSTRALIAN FLAME TREE.
See Brachychiton.

AUSTRALIAN FUCHSIA.
See Correa.

AUSTRALIAN PEA VINE.
See Dolichos.

AUSTRALIAN TEA TREE.
See Leptospermum.

AUSTRALIAN WILLOW.
See Geijera.

APRICOT

To keep it fruitful, prune apricot tree heavily.

Apricots are vigorous-growing deciduous trees that need heavy pruning for good fruit production. Train young trees as described on page 15. The open center system is best, but you can also train trees for a modified leader.

The time to prune is in winter, or *late winter before flowering starts.* Each year, routinely remove diseased, dead, or broken branches and any branches that cross through the tree's center or crowd major limbs.

Most fruit is borne on short spurs that form one year and begin bearing the next. Spurs bear well for about 3 years. To promote the growth of new fruiting spurs, remove older, unproductive branches with their played-out spurs; cut back to vigorous young branches bearing good fruiting spurs or to those new branches that will send out fruiting spurs as they grow (see diagrams at left and center, below).

To get bigger apricots, do this: after fruit has set, thin (pull off) the smallest apricots, leaving 2 to 4 inches between fruits.

Dwarf apricot trees—regular varieties grafted on dwarfing rootstocks—need similar pruning, but less of it.

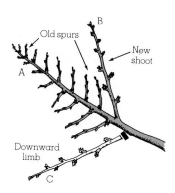

Apricot limbs. Fruiting spurs on (A) are 2 and 3 years old; (B) will grow spurs to replace them. Cut off limb (C).

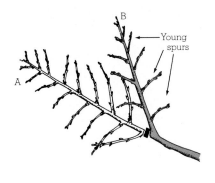

A year later. Old spurs on (A) won't bear much fruit. Cut back (A) to joint with younger limb (B).

Apricot tree. Cut back tall limbs, long side branches to control size. Remove old limbs as shown at left.

AUSTRALIAN WILLOW MYRTLE.
See Agonis.

AVOCADO (Persea americana). Evergreen tree. Prune after fruit harvest or after normal bearing season (this varies according to variety).

Give young trees routine training for the first several years (see page 14). After that, for plentiful fruit let tree take its natural form; this varies, according to variety, from upright to spreading, from symmetrical to irregular.

Mature trees usually need very little pruning; just remove weak, damaged, or dead branches. But where trees grow tall and are in danger of being uprooted by windstorms, prune tops back every few years to control size. Continual dieback of internal branches is normal; usually they simply fall off.

The bark of avocado trees sunburns easily. If you cut out live branches, be careful not to remove too much foliage, exposing previously shaded portions of trunk to full sunlight. Paint exposed trunks with whitewash to prevent sunscald.

AZALEA.
See Rhododendron, Azalea, page 98.

AZARA. Evergreen shrubs. Prune any time.

Azaras are large shrubs that can be trimmed up into shrub-trees or can be trained to grow as small trees (see page 14) or espaliers.

Two species, lanceleaf azara (A. lanceolata) and boxleaf azara (A. microphylla), produce long, arching branches. When plants are young, pinch or head back branches to offset legginess. Both kinds make fine espalier plants (see page 50). The densely branched, rounded A. dentata is useful for hedges or screens.

BACCHARIS pilularis. Coyote brush, dwarf chaparral broom. Evergreen shrub. Prune in late winter, early spring, before growth starts.

This shrub grows as a rather billowy ground cover. Remove any branches that look awkward, growing upright or rising too high above foliage. Each year, thin out some old wood and remove all dead branches to rejuvenate plant.

BALD CYPRESS.
See Taxodium.

BAMBOO. Giant grasses with woody stems. Prune any time.

This large group of related plants includes species of Arundinaria, Bambusa, Chimonobambusa, Phyllostachys, Pseudosasa, Sasa, Semiarundinaria, Shibataea, Sinarundinaria, Yushania, and many others less commonly sold.

Bamboos vary greatly in size, from foot-high ground cover and rock garden types to 60-foot-tall timber types. They can be used as clumps, high screens, even formal hedges.

All bamboos have woody stems that appear to be divided into sections by swollen nodes. Nodes on the upper stems produce buds that develop into branches. On larger bamboos, the branches divide into secondary leaf-bearing branches.

Bamboos spread by underground stems (rhizomes); like aboveground stems, they have nodes where growth buds appear. Based on their spreading habits, bamboos can be classified as clump-forming or running. Clumping bamboos grow rhizomes short distances underground before producing new stems; running bamboos can grow a rhizome many feet underground before sending up a new stem.

For all bamboos, cut out old and dead stems annually. To remove an entire stem, cut it flush with the ground or below ground level. Don't cut back young shoots until they have leafed out or they will often die to the ground.

Clumping bamboos. Specimen clumps need no special pruning. On taller clumping bamboos you can remove lower branches to create grassy shrub-trees; their bare stems make attractive silhouettes.

Shear the short, dense hedgetypes regularly. Cut back stems to desired height, shortening all new shoots that grow beyond that height.

Running bamboos. Controlling the spread of running bamboo is a serious challenge. Once established, these bamboos do not respect landscape or property boundaries.

To confine roots, make an impenetrable barrier 18 inches deep into the soil. Install a collar of galvanized sheet metal or pour concrete completely around an area where you wish to restrict roots; either should do the job. For closer confinement, use flue tiles, sections of well casing, or bottomless oil drums.

You can also corral wandering roots by digging a trench 1 foot wide and 18 inches deep completely around them. Disguise the trench by keeping it filled with dead leaves that continually shed from stems. Periodically check your leaf-filled trench to detect any rhizomes that threaten to cross the trench. Cut these back to the trench's inner edge.

On tall running bamboos, you can remove lower branches to create attractive, bare-stemmed shrub-trees.

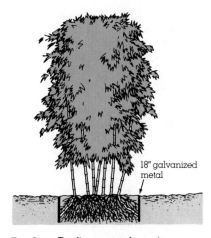

18″ galvanized metal

Bamboo. Confine roots of running bamboo to prevent spreading.

BANANA SHRUB.
See Michelia.

BARBADOS PRIDE.
See Caesalpinia.

BARBERRY.
See Berberis.

BASSWOOD.
See Tilia.

BAUHINIA. Evergreen to deciduous trees or sprawling shrubs. Prune most kinds in winter (see exception below). In tropical areas, prune spring through summer.

Common tree types include Hong Kong orchid tree (B. blakeana), B. forficata (also sold as B. corniculata or B. candicans), and purple orchid tree (B. variegata, usually sold as B. purpurea). Hong Kong orchid tree is more often single-trunked, the others multitrunked, but you can train all three to single trunks (see page 14).

After training, occasionally prune to remove excess or irregular growth, damaged or dead wood.

Shrubby red bauhinia (*B. punctata*, formerly *B. galpinii*), is naturally sprawling or vinelike; you can grow it as a flamboyant flowering espalier or as a sprawling 10- to 15-foot-wide mound. After flowering, thin and cut back heavily to maintain shape and encourage more bloom. Pinch back tips of new growth any time except in cold weather.

BAYBERRY.
See Myrica.

BEAUMONTIA grandiflora. Herald's trumpet, Easter lily vine. Evergreen vine. <u>Prune in late summer, autumn,</u> after flowering.

Prune only if needed to control form, height, or spread, or to get new wood. Flowers come on stems 2 years old and older, so don't remove too much growth or you'll sacrifice considerable bloom for a year. *Note:* In Florida, flowers appear on current growth. There, prune plants back more severely.

BEAUTYBERRY.
See Callicarpa.

BEAUTY BUSH.
See Kolkwitzia.

BEECH.
See Fagus.

BEEFWOOD.
See Casuarina.

BELOPERONE.
See Justicia.

BERBERIS. Barberry. Deciduous and evergreen shrubs. <u>Prune in winter, early spring.</u>

Various barberries are used as specimen shrubs and hedges; sizes range from 1½ to 10 feet tall. For specimen shrubs, thin out oldest wood and prune to shape after berries have gone. On vigorous growers, renew inner branches by selectively cutting back oldest branches to 4 to 6 inches from the ground. (This will prevent plants from becoming leggy and ratty.)

For formal hedges, give barberries the usual early training (see page 70). During the year, shear plants whenever needed to maintain shape of hedge. For informal hedges, cut back and pinch tips of stems at any time to control shape.

You can completely rejuvenate any neglected barberry by cutting it to the ground.

Note: discard all clippings. Thorns left on the ground can persist for years and painfully poke the fingers of unwary gardeners.

BETULA. Birch. Deciduous trees. <u>Prune in late summer, autumn, to mid-winter.</u> (Cuts will bleed the least sap if you prune trees at these times.)

Grow birches as individual feature trees, in grove plantings, or as clump plantings. Give single trees normal training (see page 14). Keep young trees staked so that the leader will grow upright.

Young birches often grow branches of equal size from the same point, forming weak V-shaped crotches; be sure you remove 1 of the 2 branches to develop a strong framework. On older trees, just remove weak, damaged, or dead wood.

You can train trees in grove plantings the same way as other young trees or let them develop naturally. In later years, you may thin out branches and remove any undesirable limbs.

To grow birches in clumps, plant several trees in 1 hole, tilting each trunk slightly outward. Or you can take a young tree that's grown in your garden for at least a year and cut it to the ground. When new stems sprout from the base, select the most vigorous and well placed to become the new trunks of the clump.

BIGNONIA. Trumpet vine.

Botanists have reclassified all but one of the trumpet vines once known as *Bignonia*, but the old names often stubbornly persist in the nursery trade. The following list of former *Bignonias* gives you their new reference names.

B. chamberlaynii. See Anemopaegma chamberlaynii.

B. cherere. See Distictis buccinatoria.

B. chinensis. See Campsis grandiflora.

B. jasminoides. See Pandorea jasminoides.

B. radicans. See Campsis radicans.

B. speciosa. See Clytostoma callistegioides.

B. tweediana. See Macfadyena unguis-cati.

B. venusta. See Pyrostegia venusta.

B. violacea. See Clytostoma callistegioides.

BIGNONIA capreolata. Cross vine, quarter vine, trumpet flower. Evergreen vine. <u>Prune in early spring.</u>

Vigorous vine can cover a large space, climbing by tendrils. Bright orange to red blossoms bloom on new wood from late spring to autumn. Before new growth starts, thin out crowded vines and remove all weak, broken, and dead stems. During the growing season, pinch or head back stems that grow out of bounds.

BIRCH.
See Betula.

BIRD OF PARADISE BUSH.
See Caesalpinia.

BITTERSWEET.
See Celastrus.

BLACKBERRY.
See page 30.

BLACK HAW.
See Viburnum.

BLACK OLIVE.
See Bucida.

BLACK WALNUT.
See Walnut.

BLUEBEARD.
See Caryopteris.

BLUEBELL CREEPER.
See Sollya.

BLUEBERRY. Deciduous shrubs (some are semievergreen). <u>Prune in winter, early spring,</u> before growth starts.

Blueberries are both food producers and handsome garden shrubs—low and spreading or upright. Your goal in pruning is to prevent plants from producing too much fruit, because overbearing decreases fruit size and slows plant growth.

For the first 2 years after planting, strip all flower buds off the plant during dormancy so that all plant energies contribute to growth. Remove drooping stems, crossing branches, and all dead, broken, and weak stems.

Once plants begin to bear, each year continue to remove crossing, dead, broken, and weak branches; cut off unproductive old branches and twiggy stems. To limit fruit production, cut back branches with many buds by one-third to two-thirds; cut back shoots that have fruited to 3 to 5 buds each.

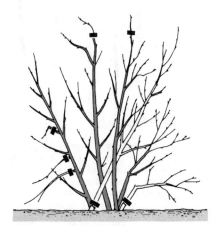

Blueberry. Cut off oldest, weak, dead, drooping, and broken stems. Head back stems that are too tall.

BLUEBERRY CLIMBER.
See Ampelopsis.

BLUE MARGUERITE.
See Felicia.

BOSTON IVY.
See Parthenocissus.

BOTTLEBRUSH.
See Callistemon, Melaleuca.

BOTTLE TREE.
See Brachychiton.

BOUGAINVILLEA. Evergreen shrubby vines. <u>Prune in spring, summer, early autumn.</u>

Vivid tropical bougainvilleas can be grown as vines on walls, arbors, and trellises; as ground covers; and as sprawling, mounded shrubs. They need to be pruned lightly, moderately, or heavily, depending on how much they grow.

Prune 2 to 3-year-old plants heavily after frost risk has passed, first removing any frost-damaged stems. If growth is crowded, thin out branches—cut off some entirely, cut back others, leaving short spurs where they join a main stem. Cut

back extremely long shoots to keep them in bounds. For wall-grown plants, pinch back long stems during the growing season to produce more flowering wood.

On plants grown for shrubs, cut back long, straggly shoots ("buggy whips") by one-third to one-half. If plants grow very slowly, cut them back to the ground the first or second year. For plants that will be used to cover the top of an arbor, limit the vine to 1 to 3 main trunks; top the trunks just above where you want branches.

Once plants have reached the size you want, prune them lightly or moderately to control shape and size—do this in summer and again in late summer or early autumn.

BOUVARDIA. Evergreen shrubs. <u>Prune in late winter, spring, and summer.</u>

The most popular *Bouvardia* species with a powerful fragrance, *B. longiflora* 'Albatross', is a floppy shrub with an intermittent flowering period. To prune, cut back stems that have flowered in order to stimulate new growth, and pinch out tips of new stems to encourage bushiness. Prune red-flowered species, *B. glaberrima* and *B. ternifolia*, in early spring, cutting back stems and removing dead or weak wood.

BOWER VINE.
See Pandorea.

BOX, BOXWOOD.
See Buxus.

BOX ELDER.
See Acer.

BRACHYCHITON *(Sterculia)*. Evergreen to partly or completely deciduous trees. <u>Prune any time.</u>

For the first several years, give newly planted trees recommended training outlined on page 14. After that, trees need little pruning except to remove broken, dead, cold-damaged, or weak limbs.

BRACHYSEMA lanceolatum. Scimitar shrub, Swan River pea shrub. Evergreen shrub. <u>Prune in early spring.</u>

These shrubs need no routine pruning. Occasionally thin out old straggly or twiggy stems.

BRASSAIA.
See Schefflera.

BRAZILIAN FLAME BUSH.
See Calliandra.

BRAZILIAN PLUME FLOWER.
See Justicia.

BREATH OF HEAVEN.
See Coleonema and Diosma.

BREYNIA disticha *(B. nivosa)*. Snow bush. Evergreen shrub. <u>Prune any time.</u>

Snow bush naturally grows as rather open shrub with zigzag branching pattern; most attractive in groups or as a hedge. For compact plants, pinch back new growth and cut back rangy stems.

BRIDAL WREATH.
See Spiraea.

BRISBANE BOX.
See Tristania.

BROOM.
See Cytisus, Genista, Spartium.

BRUGMANSIA *(Datura)*. Angel's trumpet. Evergreen shrubs. <u>Prune in early spring, after danger of frost.</u>

All are fast-growing, soft-wooded shrubs. Keep them shrubby by heading back to desired height and spread. You can also allow them to become shrub-trees with several trunks or with branches close to the ground. Annually remove all weak, dead, and crowded stems; cut back branchlets on main framework to 2 buds.

BRUNFELSIA pauciflora calycina *(B. calycina)*. Evergreen to semideciduous shrub. <u>Prune in spring or summer.</u>

Several varieties are sold: 'Eximia' is a shorter plant than the more common 'Floribunda', which can grow to 10 feet in part shade; 'Macrantha' is a more slender than rounded grower. Prune these varieties only to shape, removing straggling branches or wayward limbs. Plants tend to be more compact in sun, more open and rangy in part shade. With early training, they make attractive espaliers.

BRUSH CHERRY.
See Syzygium.

BLACKBERRY AND RASPBERRY

Blackberries and raspberries—deciduous, cane-forming plants—share an unusual growth pattern: roots are perennial, but canes are biennial. Canes emerge and grow the first year; with one exception (autumn-bearing raspberries), they flower and bear fruit the second year. Blackberries and raspberries are each subdivided into two groups, and each group needs special pruning and training. *Prune at time indicated in the instructions beneath the following illustrations.*

Blackberries

Blackberries are grouped into two growth patterns: trailing and upright. The many varieties include 'Boysen', 'Logan', 'Marion', 'Young', 'Ollalie', and dewberries (all trailing); and 'Darrow', 'Bailey', and 'Eldorado' (all upright).

Raspberries

Like their blackberry relatives, raspberries have two patterns of growth. Red and yellow raspberries produce long, straight canes. Purple and black raspberries have branching canes.

You can grow red and yellow raspberries as freestanding plants, but they're tidier and easier to manage if they're trained on trellises (as shown) or confined to hedgerows (pairs of parallel wires strung 3 and 5 feet above the ground along the outside of a row that's 12 to 24 inches wide). Pruning is almost the same for both situations.

Purple and black raspberries are clump-forming plants with arching canes. Grow them as freestanding shrubs or, to save space, train them to a 2½-foot-tall trellis.

Red & yellow raspberry

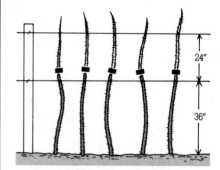

Autumn-bearing ("everbearing") raspberries bear fruit twice on each cane—in autumn of first year, then in summer of second year. Grow in rows (illustrated) or hedgerows. First year, let canes grow up; tie them to trellis. In autumn, fruit will appear on top third of each cane. After harvest, cut off fruit-bearing part of each cane.

Trailing blackberry

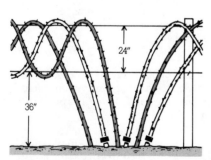

Trailing blackberries bear fruit on 2-year-old canes. In first year, let canes grow with no pruning. When growth starts in second year, tie canes to trellis; either cut off canes just above top wire, or weave long canes from wire to wire. Remove any weak, diseased, or dead canes. After canes on trellis bear fruit, cut them to the ground. Meanwhile new canes will grow from ground during spring, summer. Tie them to trellis in following year, when they will bear fruit.

Upright blackberry

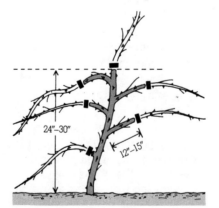

During first year, when new canes reach 2 to 2½ feet tall, pinch off tips to force branching. In second year, when new growth starts on year-old canes, shorten side branches to 12 to 15 inches and cut out dead and diseased canes. After the branched, year-old canes bear fruit, cut them to the ground. Meanwhile, new canes will be growing from the ground. To promote branches that will bear next year's crop, pinch off tips at 2 to 2½-foot height.

Red & yellow raspberry

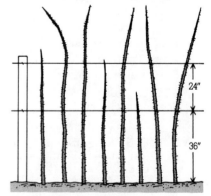

Summer-bearing red and yellow raspberries bear fruit just once, on 2-year-old canes. During first year that canes grow, tie them to a trellis when they get tall enough (or confine canes in a hedgerow). To keep rows neat, dig or pull up any canes that grow more than 12 inches from trellis (or outside hedgerow). Wait to do any other pruning until the following late winter or early spring, before growth starts.

—autumn-bearing

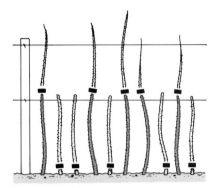

During second year, after year-old canes have borne summer crop on lower parts, cut those canes to the ground. As new canes emerge during summer, tie them to trellis; these will produce small crop in autumn. After new canes have produced autumn fruits, cut off top third of each. Then they are ready to give next summer's crop.

Blackberries and raspberries (left and right) need yearly pruning.

—summer-bearing

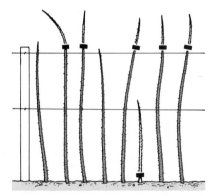

During second year, in late winter or early spring (before growth starts), cut out any weak, diseased and dead canes. Thin remaining canes to 6 to 8 inches apart along trellis (or in hedge-row). Cut back these year-old canes to 5 to 5½ feet (or 4 feet in hedgerow). After canes bear fruit, cut them to the ground. During summer, more new canes will grow. Tie them to trellis as shown at left. Following year, thin and cut back new canes as described above.

Purple & black raspberry

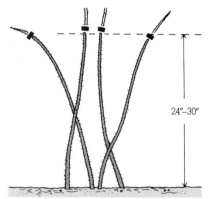

24"–30"

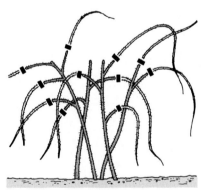

Purple and black raspberries are clump-forming plants with arching canes. Grow them either freestanding or on a 2½-foot trellis (not shown). During first summer, pinch off tips of new canes to promote growth of side branches that will bear fruit the second summer. Pinch off tips of *freestanding black raspberries* at 2 feet, *freestanding purple raspberries* at 2½ feet. Pinch off cane tips of *trellised black raspberries* at 2½ feet, *trellised purple raspberries* at 3 feet.

During second spring, before growth starts, remove all weak canes less than ½ inch thick. (If all canes are thinner, leave just the two strongest from each plant.) Shorten side branches of black raspberries to 8 to 10 inches; shorten side branches of purple raspberries to 12 to 14 inches. Side branches will carry fruit. After crop is picked, cut fruit-bearing canes to the ground. During growing season as new canes emerge, pinch them back as described at left.

BUCIDA buceras. Black olive, geometry tree. Evergreen tree. <u>Prune any time.</u>

Because of its slow growth and dense foliage, black olive needs little or no pruning. In time it will become a small tree; you can remove lower limbs to emphasize a treelike form. For use as a windbreak, occasionally cut back branches on the leeward side to maintain a uniform appearance.

BUCKEYE.
See Aesculus.

BUCKTHORN.
See Rhamnus.

BUCKWHEAT.
See Eriogonum.

BUDDLEIA. Butterfly bush. Deciduous shrub to small tree; deciduous to semievergreen shrub. <u>Pruning time differs for each.</u>

Fountain butterfly bush (*B. alternifolia*) bears spring flowers on growth made the previous year. Prune in late spring to summer, after flowering. Cut back oldest, least productive wood to the ground or within 2 buds of the ground; strong new stems will emerge. Thin out twiggy and crossing stems.

You can grow fountain butterfly bush as a tree, single or multitrunked, by removing unwanted growth from the ground and along trunk or trunks. After flowering, periodically cut out or cut back old, unproductive branches in crown.

Common butterfly bush (*B. davidii*) flowers in summer on new spring

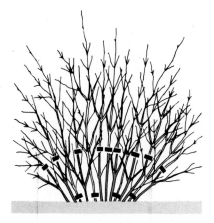

Buddleia davidii. Cut down weakest stems, cut back strong stems by ⅔.

growth. In coldest regions where stems freeze to the ground, many gardeners cut stems back 4 to 6 inches from the ground in late autumn to early spring; extremely vigorous new growth will renew the plant for the season.

For a less drastic approach, remove all but strongest stems and cut them back to one-third their length; new growth will emerge from cutback stems and from the ground. During the next pruning season, remove the stems previously cut back. Thin out youngest growth to the most vigorous stems, cutting them back to one-third their length. Repeat this procedure each year.

BUNYA-BUNYA.
See Araucaria.

BUSH ANEMONE.
See Carpenteria.

BUSH POPPY.
See Dendromecon.

BUTIA.
See Palm.

BUTTERFLY BUSH.
See Buddleia.

BUXUS. Boxwood, box. Evergreen shrubs, small trees. <u>Prune in early spring through autumn.</u>

Boxwood—including English boxwood (*B. sempervirens* and its varieties), Japanese boxwood (*B. microphylla japonica* and its varieties), and Korean boxwood (*B. microphylla koreana*)—is a classic hedge and topiary plant. Depending on the variety, sizes range from foot-high shrublets to bulky shrubs that can be treated as small trees.

You can formally shear boxwood hedges or prune them with a billowy informality that requires only a bit of clipping now and then (see page 70). If you wish to try boxwood topiary, refer to page 106.

Plants can take any amount of cutting. If a hedge becomes too tall, cut it nearly to the ground or back to a compact framework of branches; do this in spring, just as active growth is beginning. In colder areas where it grows, frost may damage tender new shoots of English boxwood. Do the final shearing or clipping at least a month before the expected first frost in autumn, giving new growth time to mature before winter.

CAESALPINIA (formerly *Poinciana*). Evergreen and deciduous shrubs, small trees. <u>Prune in early spring.</u>

Bird of paradise bush (*C. gilliesii*) grows as a large shrub or small tree, deciduous in cold winters. Prune only to remove dead or broken wood, crossing or crowded branches; remove lower limbs if you want a treelike shape. If plant grows too large, cut it back to about 2 feet tall and let it regrow as a shrub.

Dwarf poinciana (*C. pulcherrima*) is a bulky, dense shrub that needs no routine pruning unless it is frost damaged. In coldest areas where it grows, it may freeze to the ground in winter but will regrow vigorously in spring; remove all dead wood before new growth gets underway. To restrict plant's size, you can cut it to the ground early every spring and still have your crop of flowers in late spring and summer.

CALICO BUSH.
See Kalmia.

CALIFORNIA BAY.
See Umbellularia.

CALIFORNIA HOLLY.
See Heteromeles.

CALIFORNIA LAUREL.
See Umbellularia.

CALLIANDRA. Evergreen shrubs. <u>Prune after flowering.</u>

Pink powder puff (*C. haematocephala*, sometimes sold as *C. inaequilatera*) grows as a shrub or an espalier. Remove dead and crossing branches by cutting back to good laterals; this will reveal and maintain attractive branching pattern. On established plants, selectively cut oldest stems to the ground to promote renewal growth. For an espalier, frequently cut back to main framework.

Trinidad or Brazilian flame bush (*C. tweedii*, often sold as *C. guildingii*), needs the same sort of pruning to emphasize its interesting branch pattern. You can encourage branching and blossoms by pinching out tips of new growth. You can formally espalier this plant or train it to a wall or fence.

Two southwestern desert natives, *C. californica* and *C. eriophylla*, are short, rather loose shrubs. Prune to remove dead, damaged, or weak wood; cut back lightly to control spread.

CALLICARPA. Beautyberry. Deciduous shrubs. <u>Prune in late winter.</u>

Conspicuous clusters of purple berries in autumn are the main feature of this shrub. Flowers (therefore berries), come on new wood. In coldest areas where they'll grow, plants freeze to the ground and come up totally new in spring. In warmer regions, gardeners often cut plants to the ground even though stems are alive, just to encourage vigorous new stems. If you don't cut plants to the ground, cut back heavily and thin out all weak stems. Remove stems more than a year old by cutting back to new growth or to the ground.

CALLISTEMON. Bottlebrush. Evergreen shrubs or trees. <u>Prune in spring or summer.</u>

Most of the *Callistemons* in nurseries are medium-size to large shrubs. Some are naturally dense and compact; others are sparse and open. You can train the large shrubs as single-trunked trees (see page 14) or as multitrunked small trees. Denser, more compact species make good hedges, screens, and windbreaks; most kinds can be trained as informal espaliers.

For routine pruning, remove dead and weak branches. To promote denser foliage and control shape, cut back selected branches to laterals. Don't cut into bare wood beyond leaves: stems may fail to send out new growth. To keep hedges and screens uniform, don't shear growth; instead, cut back branches to laterals.

Large shrubs or trees. Lemon bottlebrush (*C. citrinus*, often sold as *C. lanceolatus*), stiff bottlebrush (*C. rigidus*), white bottlebrush (*C. salignus*), weeping bottlebrush (*C. viminalis*).

Shrubs. *C. citrinus* 'Compacta' and 'Jeffersii', *C. cupressifolius*, *C. pachyphyllus viridis*, *C. phoenicius*, *C.* 'Rosea', *C. viminalis* 'Captain Cook', narrow-leafed bottlebrush (*C. linearis*).

CALLUNA vulgaris. Scotch heather. Evergreen shrub. <u>Prune in late summer, autumn, and spring.</u>

Cut or shear off faded blooms, usually in late summer and autumn, removing any dead wood. If you wish more compact, bushy plants, shear or clip off about half the previous year's growth in early spring.

CALOCEDRUS decurrens (*Libocedrus decurrens*). Incense cedar. Evergreen coniferous tree. <u>Prune in early spring.</u>

A tall, symmetrical timber tree, incense cedar really needs no pruning, but you can remove lower limbs if they are in your way or if you want to emphasize beauty of trunk. You also can grow it as a tall hedge, screen, or windbreak. For these purposes, set your plants about 6 feet apart. Whenever needed to maintain uniformity, clip or shear cedars, topping plants at desired height. Grown this way, plants should retain foliage to the ground.

CALOTHAMNUS. Net bush. Evergreen shrubs. <u>Prune after flowering.</u>

Net bush naturally grows spreading, straggly; older plants show more wood than foliage. After flowering, cut branches back heavily, if necessary, to control size and shape, and to develop a smaller, denser plant.

CALYCANTHUS. Deciduous shrubs. <u>Prune in early spring.</u>

The eastern native Carolina allspice or sweet shrub (*C. floridus*) and the west coast native spice bush (*C. occidentalis*) are both clump-forming shrubs with slightly arching stems.

For both, annually remove oldest stems that have produced only twiggy wood; then thin out crowded and crossing branches. Plants are more attractive if you don't cut back the remaining growth. You can train the western native into a small multi-trunked tree by selecting several vigorous young stems for the trunks and removing all others.

CAMELLIA.
See page 34.

CAMPHOR TREE.
See Cinnamomum.

CAMPSIS. Trumpet creeper, trumpet vine. Deciduous vines or large, mounding shrubs. <u>Prune in early spring.</u>

Trumpet creepers are rampant growers—without thinning, they may become top-heavy and pull away from supporting surface. After one or more permanent trunks develop, shorten some branches each year to 2 or 3 buds; thin out others. Remove all dead and weak wood. Pinch back often during the growing season to keep plant bushy and covered with leaves at the base.

To train as a big shrub or bulky hedge, simply cut back long branches in spring and repeat whenever needed. If an old plant is hopelessly tangled, cut it to the ground and strong new growth will emerge; select a few strong stems for a new plant.

CANDLEBERRY.
See Myrica.

CANDLE BUSH.
See Cassia.

CANTUA buxifolia. Magic flower, sacred flower of the Incas. Evergreen shrub. <u>Prune after flowering.</u>

Growth is open, sprawling, rather vinelike—making this plant virtually impossible to shape into a compact shrub. Branches arch out from weight of flowers. Best used as informal espalier on a trellis or trained up a post. Thin or cut back branches only to direct shape.

CAPE HONEYSUCKLE.
See Tecomaria.

CAPE PLUMBAGO.
See Plumbago.

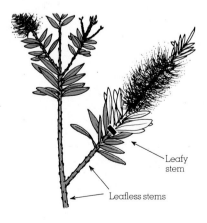

Callistemon. Makes cuts in leafy parts of stems, not in bare wood.

Leafy stem

Leafless stems

CAMELLIA

Prune camellias a little or a lot.

You can grow outstanding camellias as medium-size to large shrubs, but these broad-leafed evergreens come in a surprising range of shapes and sizes. Depending on the types, you can grow them as ground covers, hedges, screens, specimen shrubs, or small trees with one or several trunks.

Camellias don't need routine pruning to stay healthy and attractive, but you might want to do a bit of shaping from time to time for special purposes. *The best time for pruning is at the end of the flowering period when plants are dormant.* However, you can do minor snipping or even remove branches any time of year.

When young, some camellias grow more wide than tall; you may want to cut back horizontal branches to divert growth upward. Some camellias have sparse foliage (notably, kinds of C. *reticulata*), so you may want to pinch and cut back tips of stems to increase bushiness. It's best to do this when plants are young; it's more difficult to increase bushiness as plants grow older.

Some older plants are so full of leaves and small branches that they bear few flowers, or poor quality ones. Thinning out weak growth will increase both quantity and quality of flowers and improve the form of the plant. Finally, you may have a mammoth old specimen that is more impressive than beautiful. It might be a candidate for rejuvenation (see below).

Where to prune

The illustrations at left show how camellias grow and the results of thoughtful pruning, as opposed to indiscriminate pruning. An unbranched shoot will send out several branches if you cut it back to the obvious growth scar that marks the end of one year's growth and the beginning of another. But if you cut the stem in the middle of a year's

Camellia stem. To get branching, cut back to base of most recent growth.

After pruning, many new stems grow from buds below cut tip.

growth, only one branch will arise from the bud immediately below the cut. Removing the growth bud at a branch tip will stimulate several buds on the stem to grow.

Some camellias—notably *C. reticulata*—will not respond well to heavy pruning. To make these plants bushy, you must pinch the tips of new growth. Don't cut them back into bare wood of previous growth—buds seldom sprout to form side branches from bare wood.

Training

A few of the sasanquas (*C. sasanqua*) grow low and spreading—almost vinelike. To train them as ground covers, just cut off any stems that start to grow upward from the horizontal stems. If a vertical branch is growing where you need a gap filled in, tie the upright stem down to a horizontal position.

The sasanquas, many japonicas (*C. japonica*), and some hybrids are excellent plants for informal espaliers (see page 50).

When you decide to use camellias as hedges or screens, choose varieties with dense, compact growth. To trim hedges, cut back the irregular branches to growth scars (see "Where to prune," above) or to side branches within the plant.

You can train the large, open-growing reticulatas and vigorous japonicas as trees. For a tree, select a plant with a straight trunk and undamaged leader. As the plant grows in your garden, keep lower branches headed back so major growth is directed upward. When plant reaches the height you prefer for permanent branches, allow these branches to grow (pinch or prune only to promote bushiness or to remove irregular growth on these side branches). Eventually, when the trunk is thick and tree canopy has taken shape, remove the lower limbs that you earlier cut back to stubs.

Rejuvenation

A mammoth old camellia in the proper place is a beautiful plant. But if it is blotting out a window or looming too large as a somber mass in the garden, you can turn it into a tree or cut it back to a smaller shrub.

Tree conversion is the simpler and more immediately rewarding choice. It's also better for the plant and produces a more attractive result. Just remove limbs and branches from the plant's lower framework, aiming for good placement of remaining trunks and framework limbs. Cut off crossing or rubbing limbs from the framework and thin out the canopy, eliminating weak and twiggy wood.

Reducing the size of a large plant can be done in one or two steps (a year apart). *Warning:* Don't prune reticulatas this way; they may not sprout from the remaining branches.

As a single step, you can cut back a vigorous, well-established plant to a completely bare skeleton (much like a pruned rose bush). The remaining plant will send out new shoots profusely, especially if you fertilize the plant monthly during the growing season. From among these shoots, choose those aiming in the directions you want; pinch or rub out all others.

For a two-stage operation, remove all branches from the main trunk except for the top one-third; new growth will sprout from the cuts and form short branches. During the following dormant season, cut the plant down to the height you prefer and thin out any crowded branches on the remaining plant.

Canker disease

In some areas of the country, new stems occasionally will die back suddenly. This dieback is caused by a fungus. If dead twigs aren't removed, they'll form a canker that will spread the disease. Cut off each dead stem tip below the dead area in healthy wood. Disinfect the cutting tool after each cut.

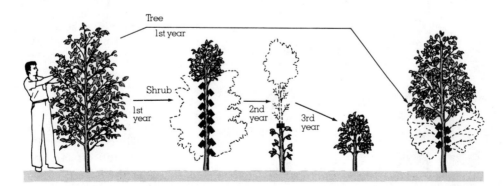

Two choices. For big camellia, prune either into shrub or tree. For shrub, in first year cut off side branches and keep leafy tuft. In second year, cut back top. For tree, cut off lower branches.

CARAGANA arborescens. Siberian pea shrub. Deciduous shrub or small tree. <u>Prune in early spring.</u>

Naturally inclined to grow as a shrubby small tree, Siberian pea shrub needs little attention—just remove dead, broken, crowded, and weak limbs. If you want a single-trunked tree, see page 14. You can plant shrubs closely as a windbreak or use them as a clipped hedge, shearing back as needed during the growing season. Remove spent flowers to stop seed formation and prevent bothersome volunteer seedlings.

CARICA. Papaya. Evergreen tree and shrub-tree. <u>Prune in early spring.</u>

Two papayas are grown: *C. papaya* for edible fruit, and mountain papaya *(C. pubescens* or *C. candamarcensis)*, as a foliage plant.

Fruiting papaya grows as a single-trunked tree to about 20 feet, topped by large, fanlike leaves. It bears fruit high under the leafy crown. Plants don't need pruning. Old leaves fall off by themselves. Plants are short-lived, bearing for perhaps 3 to 8 years.

Mountain papaya resembles a shorter, multitrunked version of the fruiting trees. Little pruning is needed; occasionally thin out oldest stems.

CARISSA grandiflora. Natal plum. Evergreen shrub. <u>Prune in spring.</u>

The basic kind is a vigorous, spiny, upright, and rounded shrub that occasionally sends out erratic shoots. Some named varieties have

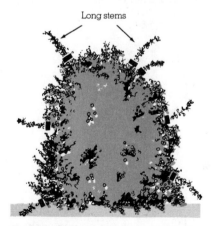

Long stems

Carissa. Cut back long branches flush with the outline.

different growth patterns—stiffly upright, short and compact, or mounding-spreading and are used as shrubs, hedges, and ground covers.

In early spring, remove weak, twiggy, and dead wood. Throughout the growing season, remove any lopsided strong new growth. For hedges, cut back stems to fit desired shape, but don't shear foliage.

CAROB.
See Ceratonia.

CAROLINA ALLSPICE.
See Calycanthus.

CAROLINA JESSAMINE.
See Gelsimium.

CAROLINA LAUREL CHERRY.
See Prunus.

CARPENTERIA californica. Bush anemone. Evergreen shrub. <u>Prune after flowering.</u>

Plant's growth is fairly compact and regular, so you have little need to prune. For occasional shaping or heading back to control size, cut branches back to pairs of opposite leaves or opposite branches.

CARPINUS. Hornbeam. Deciduous trees. <u>Prune in late winter, early spring,</u> before growth starts.

Young trees may need guidance as outlined on page 14. On older trees you usually need to remove only crossing, broken, or dead limbs. European hornbeam *(C. betulus)* makes a good hedge or screen—from a few feet tall to 12 or 15 feet. Shorten branches selectively to maintain an even surface.

CARROT WOOD.
See Cupaniopsis.

CARYA illinoensis *(Carya pecan).* Pecan. Deciduous tree. <u>Prune any time.</u>

Give young trees the early guidance outlined on page 14. Thereafter, you need to remove only dead, broken, and lopsided limbs.

CARYOPTERIS. Bluebeard. Deciduous shrubs. <u>Prune in late winter, early spring.</u>

In coldest areas where they grow, plants will freeze to the ground in winter. In spring, cut off dead wood; new growth will replace it. In milder climates, cut back heavily, leaving framework stems. During summer blooming season, lightly cut back branches after flowering—another crop of blossoms may come along.

CARYOTA.
See Palm.

CASCARA SAGRADA.
See Rhamnus.

CASIMIROA edulis. White sapote. Evergreen tree. <u>Prune in spring.</u>

Given only normal training for young trees (see page 14), sapote may grow 30 to 50 feet high and nearly as wide, but selective thinning and heading back can limit both height and spread. For fruit production and easy picking, keep tree low.

Unless you remove lower limbs, trees retain branches and foliage to the ground. Control height by cutting back leader to induce side branching. You can train sapote to umbrella shape if you continue to pinch out or head back vertical growth and encourage lateral spread. With diligence, you can even train it on an arbor.

Thinning in spring may reduce fruit crop in late summer-autumn bearing season, but mature trees can produce more than one household can use.

CASSIA. Senna. Evergreen, partly evergreen, or deciduous shrubs, trees. <u>Prune after flowering.</u>

Some cassias need only light pruning to shape the plant or to remove developing seed pods, which can grow several inches long. Others are rank growers; they need hard pruning to keep them from becoming floppy, unattractive monsters.

Tree types. Give *C. multijuga* and crown of gold tree *(C. excelsa,* also sold as *C. carnaval)* heavy pruning; thin out and head back to strong laterals. Prune gold medallion tree *(C. leptophylla)* only to shape, to contain spread, or to raise foliage canopy.

Shrub types. Give the following shrubs heavy pruning to control size and to produce strong, new, flower-bearing wood: *C. bicapsularis, C. didymobotrya* (also sold as *C. nairobensis),* candle bush *(C. alata),* flowery senna (C. corymbosa), golden wonder senna (C. splendida), and wooly senna (C. tomentosa). Note that C. bicapsularis can be trained to fences, walls, and houses as an informal espalier. C. didymobotrya is usually grown as a 5 to 6-foot-high, 10 to 15-foot-wide mounding shrub or ground cover.

Give these only light pruning: C. sturtii, C. surattensis (also sold as C. glauca), and feathery cassia (C. artemisioides).

CASTANEA. Chestnut. Deciduous trees. Prune in winter, early spring, before growth starts.

Give young trees the guidance outlined on page 14 to establish strong trunk and framework. In later years, remove crossing, dead, and broken branches; head back occasional limbs that detract from overall symmetry.

CASUARINA. Beefwood, she-oak. Evergreen trees. Prune any time.

Though not related to pines, these trees have a pinelike appearance. Give young trees basic training (see page 14). Later, remove lower branches if you wish. Thin out any weak or crowded branches in the tree's crown whenever needed. If plants are used in windbreaks, head them back to the desired height occasionally.

CATALINA CHERRY.
See Prunus.
CATALINA IRONWOOD.
See Lyonothamnus.

CATALPA. Deciduous trees. Prune in late winter, early spring.

Young plants need regular training as outlined on page 14; give special attention to developing a strong leader. When leader is established, shorten lower side branches up to the height you have chosen for the lowest limbs on the mature tree. Later, when trunk is self-supporting, remove the stubbed-back lower branches. With mature trees, prune out dead and broken limbs and cut short or remove any that look radically out of balance.

Umbrella catalpa, C. bignonioides 'Nana' (often sold as C. bungei), is a selected compact form grafted high on a regular catalpa trunk. Each winter, severely cut it back and thin out crowding stems. (After pruning, it looks like a bare stick with switches on the end.)

CAT'S CLAW.
See Macfadyena.

CEANOTHUS. Wild lilac. Evergreen shrubs, small trees, ground covers; also deciduous shrubs. Pruning times vary (see below).

In general, it's best to avoid heavy annual pruning which can lead to fungus attack and some kinds of dieback. Instead, control growth by frequently pinching or cutting tips of stems during growing season. For specific instructions, see the following.

Evergreen shrubs, trees. Different kinds range in size and shape from low and spreading, compact and bushy, upright and angular, to round-headed small trees. Flowers come on new growth produced by year-old wood, so prune after blooms have faded.

These plants do not take kindly to being restricted in size; with few exceptions, if you repeatedly cut back plants to fit a space, they look unattractive. Instead, direct growth by pinching new tip growth to increase bushiness, heading back young stems to control plant shape, or removing limbs entirely to enhance plant's structure or give it a new shape.

You can train the more rangy, angular growers as espaliers. Those that grow to tree size (C. 'Ray Hartman', for example) look best with multiple trunks or with branches very close to the ground. Young trees grow as ever-enlarging shrubs for a few years, eventually becoming big enough for you to remove lower branches from the main trunk or trunks. Avoid cutting off stems more than 1 inch in diameter; they don't heal well.

Deciduous shrubs. These plants flower in late spring or summer on new spring growth. Prune in late winter or early spring before growth starts, thinning out oldest unproductive stems. Cut back main stems to 1½ to 2 feet, and shorten lateral limbs to 2 to 6 buds.

Evergreen ground covers. Many kinds are shrubby, but wide-spreading, ranging from ground-hugging to about 3 feet tall. Pinch or cut off tips of new growth or cut back young stems to control spread and promote dense foliage. Cut out any stems that grow unattractively upright.

CEDAR.
See Cedrus.

CEDAR OF LEBANON.
See Cedrus.

CEDRUS. Cedar. Evergreen coniferous trees. Prune in spring.

Four true cedars—Atlas cedar (C. atlantica), Cyprus cedar (C. brevifolia), deodar cedar (C. deodara), and cedar of Lebanon (C. libani)—are very large trees that need little pruning; usually you just remove dead and broken branches. Two may require some special care.

Young Atlas cedars may look awkward, but give them time to grow and they often become quite pleasing. If necessary, pinch back tips of branches that seem too long and heavy. On older trees, remove branches that crowd the structure of the tree.

Deodar cedar looks best with lots of room to grow. To control spread and shape of young tree, cut back new growth of side branches halfway in late spring. By topping it yearly, you can make tree grow low. This plant will even stand shearing.

New growth

Cedrus. To shape tree, cut back new shoots halfway or completely.

CELASTRUS. Bittersweet. Deciduous vines. Prune in winter, early spring, before growth starts.

Bittersweets are vigorous, twining climbers. Unchecked, they can strangle shrubs and small trees, so routinely remove branches that are invading other desirable plants.

Each winter cut out all weak growth and fruiting branches; cut back the last year's growth by about one-third. If vines become too dense, thin out oldest and crowded stems. During growing season, control vines by pinching or removing overaggressive new growth. Rejuvenate old plants by cutting them to the ground.

CELTIS. Hackberry. Deciduous trees. Prune any time.

Young trees need only routine guidance in their early years (see page 14). After tree is self-supporting and has developed a permanent framework, just remove dead and broken branches. At times, thin out crowding or rubbing branches.

CEPHALOTAXUS. Plum yew. Coniferous evergreen shrubs and trees. Prune any time.

These slow-growing plants resemble true yew (Taxus), are compact and need little pruning. Use them as individual specimen plants or together for hedges or screens. Cut back new growth only to maintain plant shape or hedge form. Remove dead twigs now and then.

CERATONIA siliqua. Carob, St. John's bread. Evergreen tree or large shrub. Prune in winter.

By nature this is a tree-size shrub with branches to ground level; often, it has several trunks. To grow it as a tree, give it the training outlined on page 14. You can train the crown as high as you want; thin and shape tree each year until tree size and form are established. After that, you may only need to thin out crowded branches from time to time.

This large shrub can also be used as a hedge, screen, espalier, or windbreak. You can train it to be tall or compact; it will stand heavy pruning and reshaping.

CERCIDIPHYLLUM japonicum. Katsura tree. Deciduous tree. Prune in late autumn to early spring.

Katsura is naturally inclined to grow upright with several trunks that form a multistemmed clump; to train as a single-trunked tree, follow directions on page 14. To prune, now

(Continued on page 40)

CITRUS

Citrus are broad-leafed evergreen plants that include orange, lemon, grapefruit, mandarin orange (tangerine), lime, tangelo, kumquat, and various hybrids. Most standard citrus trees grow 20 to 30 feet high and nearly as wide. The most popular sorts are also available in some areas as 4 to 10-foot-tall dwarfs.

Prune citrus any time in frost-free regions; where frosts occur in winter, prune them from spring through early autumn.

Commercial growers grow their citrus as giant shrubs, with branches to the ground (fruit production is heaviest on the lowest branches). Some citrus growers prune only to remove twiggy stems, weak branches, and overvigorous growth on young citrus that would create a lopsided plant. Other citrus growers prune trees to keep them 8 to 10 feet tall for easier picking. Either method will work for the home gardener as well. In addition, you can grow citrus as single-trunked trees or as espaliers.

Basic training. Starting with a regular-size (not dwarf) 1-year-old tree from the nursery, cut back the central leader to a height of about 3 feet, and cut back side branches slightly. Allow the tree a year to get established; then start training for a strong framework of upright branches (weight of foliage and fruit will eventually bend branches down). Look for three to four vigorous, well-spaced laterals to form the framework; leave them alone and head back all others.

Leave lower branches on the tree to help strengthen the trunk, and because leaves will protect the trunk from sunburn. As tree gains size and strength in the next few years, you may remove these lower branches if you want a clean trunk, but in hot-sun regions, be sure to protect newly exposed trunk from intense sunlight. Coat trunk with white protective paint (often called "tree white"), or wrap with a commercial paper trunk band. You can even use common water-base house paint.

During these formative years, do whatever pruning seems necessary to shape the tree. Some vigorous plants will send out branches unevenly—beyond the mass of the tree. Cut these long shoots back to good side branches, or to buds that promise good side branches that will grow in better directions, or all the way back to their points of origin. Pinch back tips of new shoots that grow out too far.

Lemons usually have more undisciplined growth than most other citrus, calling for more attention to basic shaping. A vigorous young lemon tree usually produces some strong upright shoots each year; they emerge close to the base of the trunk and run vertically up the tree's center. If they grow from the base below the graft union, they are undesirable suckers. Snap them off.

If the vertical shoot grows from above the graft union and if the tree has gaps in its branch structure, you can turn one of these vertical shoots into a new scaffold branch. To make this conversion, grasp the shoot about a foot above the point where it joins the trunk, and slowly bend it in a large arc toward the ground. Ordinarily the shoot will stay in that position after you release it; if it springs back, weight it down into position. Soon, new side shoots will grow out along the top of the arc and begin to fill in the gap.

Lemons, too, often grow long, pendulous branches carrying foliage and fruits at the very ends. You can cut back these long branches severely to encourage fruiting growth closer to the tree's center.

On any mature citrus tree, prune yearly by heading back and pinching to maintain good shape, as mentioned above, and by removing dead and broken wood. Whenever you make large openings in the foliage canopy that expose the trunk or major limbs to hot sunlight, apply a protective coating to limbs and trunk, as described before.

Rejuvenation. As citrus trees mature, they often lose vigor, accumulate dead or scale-infested wood, and produce fewer new fruit-bearing stems. This is the time for some heavy pruning.

First, remove all dead wood and twiggy, unproductive stems to let more light through the branches and force some new growth all over the tree. Accompanied by fertilizing, this may be enough for satisfactory renewal. A second choice is to cut back side branches 1 to 3 feet. This encourages plenty of new growth.

If the tree has grown too tall to suit you, remove top limbs, two or three each year for several years, if necessary.

For a complete rejuvenation of an old plant, you can prune drastically. If you have a healthy, vigorous tree, you can expect a strong showing of new growth. The most severe method is to cut back all major limbs to 12-inch stubs. Do this in early spring, but only after all danger of frost is past. You can accomplish the same result more gradually by cutting back a third of the limbs in spring, a third in summer, and the final third in autumn.

A few weeks after each of these prunings, closely spaced new shoots will appear along the stubs, mostly near the ends. Remove up to half of these, leaving new shoots evenly spaced along the stems.

As these new shoots grow, do some additional thinning, leaving strong shoots that will form a symmetrical set of new branches. When the new branches are about a foot long, pinch out the tips to encourage further branching. With this renewal pruning, don't expect a fruit crop for 2 to 3 years.

Most citrus trees need only occasional shaping.

Dwarf trees. You can apply the same pruning principles to dwarf citrus, but on a smaller scale. Usually you grow dwarf citrus as shrubs, so give attention to forming a good branch framework; watch for, and head back, any lopsided growth.

Espaliers. Lemons, oranges, mandarin oranges, and limes make handsome espaliers against a warm wall or fence. You can train them formally, or let them branch naturally and prune back any side branches that stick out too far. For general information on espaliers, see page 50.

New shoots will sprout here

Lemon. Cut back long stems to force branching, keep plant compact.

and then you'll have to thin out crossing and rubbing branches; on mature trees, you usually remove only dead, broken, or weak wood.

CERCIDIUM. Palo verde (for Mexican palo verde, see *Parkinsonia*). Deciduous trees. Prune any time.

You need to prune these trees only to enhance their form—remove crossing or wayward limbs, or branches that are too low. Beware of sharp spines on the branches.

CERCIS. Redbud. Deciduous shrubs or trees. Prune in early spring, before growth starts.

Most grow as medium to tall shrubs; some can be trained as small trees (see page 14). To prune redbuds grown as shrubs, thin out crowded branches; remove dead, twiggy, and broken stems. Some shrubs—western redbud *(C. occidentalis)*, for example—send up strong new stems from the ground. Periodically remove oldest stems that aren't producing healthy growth.

With training, eastern redbud *(C. canadensis)* and Judas tree *(C. siliquastrum)* will grow as small trees (see page 14). Eastern redbud tends to develop horizontally tiered branches as it matures. You can accentuate this tendency by thinning out some limbs to reveal the layered pattern. Pruned this way, trees look interesting even in winter.

CERCOCARPUS. Mountain mahogany. Evergreen or deciduous tall shrubs or small trees. Prune in early spring.

Depending on the kind, mountain mahoganies grow as shrubs, hedges, screens, or small trees. For shrubs, prune to reveal branch patterns; thin out crowded and crossing limbs. To grow as a hedge or screen, selectively cut plants back—don't shear them. To train as trees, see page 14. When pruning trees, you need to cut out dead, broken, weak, and crowding branches now and then.

CESTRUM. Evergreen shrubs. Prune in spring and summer.

Cestrums are vigorous, rangy plants. Prune them in spring to remove frost-damaged wood. Prune again heavily after flowering or fruit-

ing to control the size of plants.

Grown for powerful fragrance are *C. nocturnum*, a vigorous 10-foot shrub, and *C. parqui*, about 10 feet tall and more lax in growth. Pinch tips of new growth regularly to produce fuller, more compact plants; thin out older, twiggy growth when necessary.

Showy flowers and fruits are features of *C. aurantiacum* and *C. elegans (C. purpureum)*. Both are lax, rangy plants, best used as espaliers or shrubby vines.

CHAENOMELES (some formerly called *Cydonia*). Flowering quince. Deciduous shrubs. Prune in winter or spring.

Many named varieties are sold; some grow rather tall and upright, others are low and spreading. All have attractive branching patterns, usually with many small branches and twigs (each plant becomes dense and thicketlike).

You can take advantage of this characteristic and grow them as informal hedges, or you can use them as individual flowering accent plants. Another use is to espalier flowering quince against a wall, fence, or trellis to make an attractive spring show.

One of the best times to prune is when flowers are opening; cut stems and take them indoors for bouquets. (It's also easier to see what to remove when plants are bare.) At all times, your major pruning work is thinning—remove old and weak wood, crossing and tangled branches. Head back any stems that are too long.

Renew old, neglected bushes in winter by cutting out one-third of old-

Chaenomeles. To renew old shrub, cut out one-third of old, weak stems.

est wood each year for 3 years. The result will be a vigorous "new" plant.

CHAMAECYPARIS. False cypress. Evergreen coniferous shrubs, trees. Prune in spring or late summer.

Different kinds range from timber trees to rock garden shrublets. Trees and large shrubs usually grow symmetrically and need no guidance. Small shrubs and shrublets are grown for their natural form—often irregular or picturesque. Larger ones make screens, hedges.

To maintain shape and keep height even, pinch out or cut back branch tips of new growth. You also can shear plants into formal hedges. Don't cut stems back into old leafless wood where new shoots will not sprout. Some varieties will take topiary training (see page 106), usually of the "Ming tree" sort, in which a cluster of foliage sits at the end of each selected branch.

CHAMAEDOREA.
See Palm.

CHAMAEROPS.
See Palm.

CHAMELAUCIUM uncinatum (sometimes sold as *C. ciliatum*). Geraldton wax flower. Evergreen shrub. Prune during or after flowering.

Loose, airy, rather sprawling shrub grows 8 feet high and wide; if you stake it, shrub becomes a small tree. To get stems for long-lasting indoor arrangements, prune plants when blooming. To make plant denser and control spread, prune after flowering by heading back to well-placed side branches. Do not cut back to bare, leafless wood.

CHASTE TREE.
See Vitex.

CHENILLE PLANT.
See Acalypha.

CHERIMOYA.
See Annona.

CHERRY. Deciduous fruit trees. (For flowering cherry, see page 54.) Prune in winter; late winter in severe-winter areas.

Three types of cherry trees are available to home gardeners: sweet cherries, sour cherries, and hybrids of the two, called "Duke" cherries. All 3 types bear fruit on long-lived spurs, so you don't have to prune trees specifically for fruit production. But because the three have different growth habits, there are differences in the way you train young trees and, later in the way you prune mature trees.

Sweet cherries. Growing to 35 feet with upright limbs, these large trees often spread as wide as they are high. Usually you train sweet cherry trees to the open center system. (In some areas, such as the Midwest, the modified leader system is preferred.) General directions for this training are on page 15, with additional information under Apple on page 22.

At the end of the first growing season, select 3 or 4 branches for the tree's primary framework. To develop a well-balanced vase shape, choose branches that are spaced 6 to 9 inches apart vertically on the trunk, and that point in different directions. (Don't select any branches with narrow crotches.) Cut back these primary branches, leaving stubs 24 to 30 inches long; they will form secondary branches in the next growing season. Remove all other branches from the trunk.

During the next winter, cut back the newly formed secondary branches, leaving stubs 24 to 30 inches long with only 2 well-placed secondary branches on each primary branch. This forms the basic framework of the tree.

After the tree begins to bear fruit, annually remove weak growth—especially twigs and branches that crowd the tree's center. Most trees won't need much pruning, especially in cold-winter regions. To shape the maturing tree, encourage outward-growing branches to balance the tree's natural tendency to grow upright. If you prune any branches, cut back to buds or side branches that face outward.

Thin branches enough to let sunlight filter through the foliage canopy. Don't remove so many branches that you leave gaping holes in the leaf cover—branches and trunks can be sunburned in hot-summer regions.

Sour cherries. Trees are shorter than sweet cherry trees, spreading rather than upright, and irregular in shape. The central leader system (see page 15) suits these cherries best.

Cut back any too-long branches to good laterals; cut out drooping branches. As the tree matures and begins bearing, prune out weak, crossing branches and any excess growth in the tree's center to let light filter into tree's canopy.

Duke cherries. These hybrids fall between sweet and sour cherries in size and shape. Train and prune as for sour cherries.

Cherry. Remove crossing branches; otherwise, prune very little.

CHESTNUT.
See Castanea.

CHILEAN JASMINE.
See Mandevilla.

CHILOPSIS linearis. Desert willow. Deciduous large shrub or small tree. <u>Prune in winter.</u>

Open and irregular in its growth pattern, plant develops shaggy bark and twisting stems as it ages. Grow desert willow as a character shrub or as a single or multitrunked tree. Prune to accentuate picturesque shape—cut out dead, weak, and crossing branches, and thin out crowded twigs, leaving sinewy framework of strong limbs.

CHIMONANTHUS praecox (*C. fragrans, Meratia praecox*). Wintersweet. Deciduous shrub. <u>Prune in winter or spring.</u>

Fragrant, winter to spring-flowering shrub is tall and open-growing, sending up many stems from ground. Prune during bloom or right afterward to promote growth of new wood that will bear next year's flowers.

To keep plant low, cut stems back

to buds that promise to develop into strong side branches; thin out branches that are dead, weak, and crowding. (Without heading back, plant will grow 10 feet tall.) To train as a multitrunked tree, cut weakest stems to the ground and remove twiggy growth from remaining trunks. Select 3 to 5 strong canes for permanent framework. Cut out all new stems that arise from the ground. Occasionally during the years, remove an old frame cane and replace it with a good new cane that has sprouted.

CHINABERRY.
See Melia.

CHINA FIR.
See Cunninghamia.

CHINESE ANGELICA.
See Aralia.

CHINESE BELLFLOWER.
See Abutilon.

CHINESE BOX ORANGE.
See Severinia.

CHINESE FLAME TREE.
See Koelreuteria.

CHINESE GOOSEBERRY.
See Actinidia.

CHINESE LANTERN.
See Abutilon.

CHINESE PISTACHE.
See Pistacia.

CHINESE SCHOLAR TREE.
See Sophora.

CHINESE TALLOW TREE.
See Sapium.

CHINESE WITCH HAZEL.
See Hamamelis.

CHIONANTHUS. Fringe tree. Deciduous trees. <u>Prune after flowering.</u>

Bearing lacy clusters of flowers in late spring or summer, these slow-growing plants can eventually become 20 to 30-foot-tall trees.

To grow as single-trunked trees, follow directions on page 14. For multitrunked trees (often the better choice for cold-winter climates), let several stems develop from the ground. Periodically remove dead and weak stems and congested branches.

To grow as a shrub, cut back branches to strong laterals, limiting height and spread. Occasionally cut oldest stems to the ground to encourage strong renewal growth.

CLEMATIS

Direct vine's growth by selective pruning.

Clematis includes deciduous and evergreen vines and a few deciduous shrubs. Pruning depends on when a clematis blooms, how vigorous it is, and how you train it.

Early training

Early training is the same for all deciduous vining clematis. At planting time, cut back the stem or stems of a dormant clematis to 2 or 3 pairs of buds, or to 6 to 12 inches from the ground, whichever is lower.

Following the first year's growth, prune heavily during winter or early spring. Cut back the first year's growth to 2 or 3 pairs of buds. As the vine begins to grow again during the second spring, start to train it. (For evergreen vines, don't prune, but start training after planting.)

Clematis vines climb by twining their leaf stalks around anything that gives support: stretched string, wire mesh, other plants' branches, their own stems. With support, you can train vines almost anywhere.

Vines: Three groups

Clematis can be categorized as spring-flowering, summer-flowering, and twice-flowering vines.

Spring-flowering. These plants produce flowers on stems that grew during the previous year. Wait until flowering is finished, then cut back stems that have bloomed.

How much you cut back will depend on the vine's vigor and how you are using it. You want the plant to produce strong new growth that will bear flowers the next year, but you don't want tangled stems.

For extra-vigorous species, such as evergreen *C. armandii* and deciduous *C. montana*, you will need to cut back stems that have flowered and to thin any excess stems. During the growing season, you may need to do more thinning and pinch-

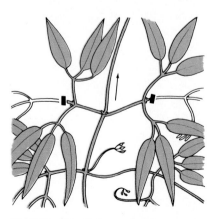

Clematis vine. To force growth upward, cut back side branches to lowest pairs of leaves of last year's growth.

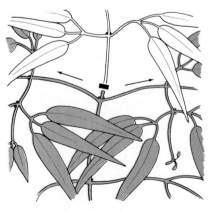

Encourage vine to grow horizontally by cutting off vertical stem just above joint at height you want.

ing to keep the vine in bounds and to prevent it from tangling. Cut back excess new growth on *C. armandii* to 2 or 3 nodes so it doesn't shade out the rest of the vine.

Less vigorous growers need less pruning. Thin out weak stems and remove extra entangling stems. Cut back stems that have flowered to about half their length.

Summer-flowering. These clematis bloom only on new growth produced in the spring. You will need to thin and cut back stems before growth begins. Do pruning either in late autumn after plant has become dormant, or in early spring as buds swell. Cut back the last season's growth to about 12 inches. Each year the vine will grow larger, denser.

Twice-flowering. Many of the popular large-flowered clematis hybrids are in this group. The first bloom comes on stems produced the previous year. Summer or autumn flowers form on stems that grow after the spring blooming.

In late autumn or early spring (before buds swell), prune lightly to thin and untangle stems. To ensure a good spring display, leave as much of the last season's new growth as possible. After spring flowers fade, prune more heavily so that plenty of healthy new stems will develop for summer blossoms. Follow the pruning guidelines for the summer-flowering clematis at this time.

Shrubby clematis

The two most common genuinely shrubby clematis species are *C. heracleifolia davidiana (C. davidiana)* and *C. integrifolia.* Each blooms during summer, but their pruning times are different. Prune *C. heracleifolia davidiana* in early spring before buds swell. Wait until after flowering to prune *C. integrifolia.* For each kind, cut back newest stems to about 2 pairs of buds.

CHOISYA ternata. Mexican orange. Evergreen shrub. Prune in spring, summer.

Fast-growing plant forms a rounded bush with dense foliage. Leaves cluster in fans, mostly at the ends of branches, hiding leafless interior.

During growing season, pinch back branch tips or cut back branches to control size and shape. Thin out older branches in the plant's center to force leafy new interior growth.

CHOKEBERRY.
See Aronia.

CHORISIA. Floss silk tree. Evergreen to briefly deciduous tree. Prune in spring.

These fast-growing trees usually need little pruning or training. At times, you may have to cut back a wayward limb or remove dead or broken branches.

CHORIZEMA. Flame pea. Evergreen shrubs. Prune after flowering.

Naturally sprawling plants with slender, graceful stems, flame peas are useful as tall ground covers or spilling down a slope. Pinch tips of new growth during growing season; this encourages plants to branch and become compact. After flowering, cut back to limit size and spread.

CHRISTMAS BERRY.
See Heteromeles.
CHRYSOLARIX.
See Pseudolarix.
CHUPAROSA.
See Justicia.

CINNAMOMUM. Camphor tree. Evergreen trees. Prune in spring or as needed.

Young trees need early training as shown on page 14; thereafter, you only need to remove dead and broken branches. Sometimes root rot (verticillium wilt) infects trees, causing sudden wilting of leaves and death of branches, usually on just part of the plant. Whenever this occurs, cut out the affected limbs.

CINQUEFOIL.
See Potentilla.

CISSUS. Evergreen vines. Prune at any time.

Vines require little attention. Whenever needed, prune to thin out tangled growth (sometimes you can just untangle stems and spread them out), and to remove dead, weak, and broken stems. Cut back to restrict size and to direct development of vine.

CISTUS. Rockrose. Evergreen shrubs. Prune after flowering.

Some gardeners don't prune rockroses at all, letting plants grow naturally in tumbled masses. However, on plants left totally alone, deadwood accumulates and good new growth diminishes.

To keep young plants low, pinch tips of new growth several times during growing season or lightly shear entire plant after flowering. As plants get bigger, each year remove a few older stems that aren't producing strong new growth; cut out all dead wood. You can cut stems back to side branches or to leaves, but don't cut back into bare wood.

CITRUS.
See page 38.

CLADRASTIS lutea. Yellow wood. Deciduous tree. Prune in summer after leaves are fully developed.

Give young trees the routine training outlined on page 14. Be particularly careful to remove the weaker of any two upright limbs that form a narrow V-shaped crotch. Sometimes limbs of young plants grow long, creating spread at the expense of height. To encourage growth of the leader, cut back these limbs to side branches. Established trees need only occasional attention: remove dead or broken branches and eliminate crossing or crowding limbs.

CLEMATIS.
See page 42.

CLERODENDRUM. Glorybower. Evergreen and deciduous shrubs. Pruning time varies (see below).

The largest of these is the deciduous Harlequin glorybower (*C. trichotomum*). It naturally grows as a many-stemmed shrub that becomes bare at the base. By cutting back the tallest stems, you can keep it shrubby and more dense. Cut some others to within a foot of the ground to stimulate new leafy growth low on the plant. Do this in winter or early spring, before plant leafs out.

Alternatively, you can grow Harlequin glorybower as a multi-trunked tree—remove excess stems, leaving only trunks you want, and remove any new growth that arises from the ground. To grow it as a single-trunked tree, start with a young plant, removing all but the strongest stem from the base. Train the tree according to directions on page 14.

Cashmere bouquet (C. bungei or C. foetidum) and C. fragrans pleniflorum are evergreen shrubs that spread by underground stems to form thickets. Both are rank growers. To keep plants compact, cut them back severely in early spring and pinch stem tips during the growing season. To control spread, cut out or dig up unwanted stems.

Unrestrained, the evergreen shrubby vine bleeding heart glorybower (C. thomsoniae or C. balfouri) will grow to 6 feet as an open shrub. By putting up a trellis for stems to twine upon, you can grow it as a vine. Clean up plants and prune lightly after summer bloom. For shrubs, thin out crowded stems. For vines, thin out entangling and unwanted stems, cut back long ones.

CLETHRA. Deciduous shrubs and evergreen tree. <u>Prune in early spring</u>.

Shrubby, deciduous summersweet or sweet pepperbush (C. alnifolia) grows strongly upright from 5 to 10 feet tall with many slender stems that slowly form broad clumps. Grow it as an unclipped screen or hedge, or as specimen shrub. Cut back any too-tall stems. Periodically remove oldest stems.

Evergreen lily-of-the-valley tree (C. arborea) is a neat, dense, upright small tree. Give it training outlined on page 14 for young trees. Needs little pruning once established—just remove dead, broken, frost-damaged branches and any crossing or rubbing limbs.

CLEYERA japonica (Eurya ochnacea). Evergreen shrub. <u>Prune in early spring</u>.

This camellia relative grows into a gracefully spreading, arching shrub with little need for pruning. Head back branches that are over-long or floppy, or that depart from the desired shape of the shrub. You can also train it as an espalier or informal wall plant, or trim it as a hedge.

CLIANTHUS puniceus. Parrot-beak, red kowhai. Evergreen shrublike vine. <u>Prune after flowering</u>.

Graceful shrub with drooping leaves and hanging flowers; grows at moderate pace to 12 feet. Cut out dead wood; thin out and cut back older stems and weak branches. This will encourage strong new growth for the next year's bloom. To train it as an attractive informal espalier, see page 50.

CLYTOSTOMA callistegioides (Bignonia violacea, B. speciosa). Violet trumpet vine. Evergreen vine. <u>Prune in late winter, spring, summer</u>.

Strong growing, vine climbs by tendrils, clinging to other nearby plants and its own stems. If necessary, in winter you can untangle stems, cut away from other plants, thin out and head back as much as you want to control size and direction of growth. After plant flowers in spring and summer, remove any unwanted long, new runners.

COCCOLOBA uvifera. Sea grape. Evergreen shrubs or tree. <u>Prune in spring to midautumn</u>.

You can grow sea grape as a shrub or tree, or you can even plant it as a windbreak in some areas. For a shrub or as a windbreak plant, let branches stay on stems all the way to the ground (control height by periodically cutting back upward growth). To train sea grape as a single-trunked tree, follow directions on page 14. After tree is established, prune only to remove dead, broken, weak, or crossing limbs.

COCCULUS laurifolius. Evergreen shrub or small tree. <u>Prune any time</u>.

This glossy-leafed, multi-stemmed shrub with arching, spreading branches can grow 25 feet high and just as wide. Use it as a big bulky shrub, a multitrunked shrub-tree, or a beautiful umbrella-shaped single-trunked tree (see page 14). You can also train it as an informal espalier (see page 50). To control

growth and shape, selectively remove whole branches from stems, or cut them back to strong side branches.

Cocculus. To shape plant, cut back stem to joint with larger limb.

CODIAEUM variegatum. Croton. Evergreen shrub. <u>Prune in spring to midautumn</u>.

Crotons have eyecatching foliage—almost countless varieties with different leaf shapes, colors, and degrees of variegation. They are grown as specimen shrubs or hedges in tropical areas. Prune for denser foliage that shows the least amount of branch. Pinch tips of new growth to encourage branching.

On old overgrown plants, cut back heavily to stimulate compact new growth and new stems from the base. Do this in two stages. First, cut back one-third to two-thirds of the old stems. Then, cut back and thin out the remaining stems once new growth is underway. At any time, head back wayward stems to side branches or to a pair of leaves.

COFFEEBERRY.
See Rhamnus.

COLEONEMA and DIOSMA. Breath of heaven. Evergreen shrubs. <u>Prune in spring</u>.

Graceful and airy, breath of heaven has slender branches and small, narrow leaves. To keep young plants compact, shear them after flowering. Emphasize their delicacy by thinning out weaker interior stems. You can try to renew neglected old plants by thinning out straggly growth and weak stems, then cutting back to half the original size, but plants don't always recover from this heavy pruning.

COLVILLEA racemosa. Deciduous tree. <u>Prune any time.</u>

Young plants need routine training as they grow (see page 14); beyond that, these trees need little or no pruning. They naturally grow a dense crown with many crossing branches. Remove only dead or broken limbs, cutting these back to laterals or to other major limbs.

CONVOLVULUS cneorum. Bush morning glory. Evergreen shrub. <u>Prune in late winter.</u>

Rapid-growing shrub stays compact in full sun, becomes looser and more open in shade. When plant gets leggy, cut back severely and thin out weak stems. To avoid need for heavy pruning, cut back and thin lightly late each winter. When growth starts, pinch tips of stems to increase bushiness.

COPPER LEAF. See Acalypha.

COPROSMA. Evergreen shrubs. <u>Prune any time.</u>

The ground cover, *C. kirkii*, is a 2 to 3-foot-tall wide-spreading plant. Shear back plant in spring or summer to keep it dense.

The large, polished-leaf shrubs are mirror plant (*C. repens* or *C. baueri*) and *C. 'Coppershine'*. A rapid grower, mirror plant becomes straggly and irregular if neglected. Cut back wayward branches twice a year to make plant neat and bushy. Or take advantage of irregularities and train it as an informal espalier (see page 14). *C. 'Coppershine'* is more compact. Pinch or cut back only to maintain desired shape.

CORAL BERRY. See Symphoricarpos.

CORAL TREE. See Erythrina.

CORDYLINE. Evergreen shrubby and treelike perennials. <u>Prune in spring to midautumn, if necessary.</u>

Except for shrubby *C. terminalis*, the treelike species of these yucca relatives bear palmlike puffs of sword-shaped leaves at branch ends. They seldom need pruning.

Tallest is *C. australis*, growing to 30 feet. Plants usually branch out high, but you can sometimes cut back a young plant to force low branching. Alternatively, plant several in a clump, cutting one to the ground each year until all develop multiple trunks.

Shorter *C. stricta* grows to 15 feet, branching low or from ground level. Keep lower by cutting tall stems to the ground. Blue dracaena, *C. indivisa*, is unbranching. Plant several of different heights for mass effect.

Shrubby Hawaiian ti plant (*C. terminalis*) forms clumps of leafy stems that grow to 10 feet in tropical regions. Control height and promote bushiness by cutting back stems to any desired height.

CORNUS. Dogwood. Deciduous and evergreen shrubs and trees. <u>Pruning time varies.</u>

Among the dogwoods are clump or thicket-forming shrubs, treelike shrubs, and full-fledged trees. Each group has particular pruning guidelines. Prune shrubs in late winter or early spring. Prune shrub-trees and trees after flowering. (Note: In severe-winter areas of the eastern United States, prune shrub-trees and trees in late autumn or early winter to prevent bleeding sap.)

Shrub types. These include bloodtwig dogwood (*C. sanguinea*), redtwig or red-osier dogwood (*C. stolonifera*, or *C. sericea*), Tatarian dogwood (*C. alba*), and their varieties. In cold-winter areas their blood-red twigs are brilliant against snow.

Since the most colorful stems are year-old growth, prune to encourage production of new wood each year. (Some gardeners even cut plants to the ground annually; this produces clumps of vertical stems with few branches.) For a more moderate approach, thin out stems that are 2 years old and cut back the year-old stems. New growth will sprout from the ground and from cut-back stems, producing a bushier plant than those cut to the ground.

Both *C. alba* and *C. stolonifera* (*C. sericea*) spread by underground stems. The latter may form roots if a stem tip touches the ground; you can control spread by digging out shoots that come up beyond desired area.

Shrub-trees. All of these kinds—cornelian cherry (*C. mas*), evergreen dogwood (*C. capitata*), pagoda dogwood (*C. alternifolia*), and *C. kousa*—will grow as tall as small trees, retaining branches and foliage to the ground. You can remove lower limbs to convert shrubs into trees (usually with several trunks); or you can train a young plant into tree form (see page 14).

Note that cornelian cherry usually looks best unpruned. Also, select either an upright or vase-shaped young *Cornus kousa*, depending on how you want the mature plant to look.

For pruning, remove dead and broken limbs. To emphasize the usually horizontal branching pattern, you can thin unwanted branches.

Tree types. These dogwoods are the most widely planted for flowers: medium-size flowering or eastern dogwood (*C. florida*), the much larger giant dogwood (*C. controversa*) and Pacific or western dogwood (*C. nuttallii*). Usually you grow them as single-trunked trees, but you can choose young plants with several trunks. Eastern dogwood has a tiered branching pattern and usually has dense lower branches that, on older trees, touch the ground.

Prune these trees as little as possible. Remove dead and broken limbs and branches that detract from desired shape. Also cut out galls and diseased limbs. *Caution:* Cuts heal slowly on shrub-tree and tree kinds—large wounds are open to infection. If possible, limit pruning to small branches and always cut back to a side branch or main limb.

Cornus. Prune shrubby dogwoods heavily. Cut off 2-year-old stems, head back year-old ones.

COROKIA cotoneaster. Evergreen shrub. <u>Prune whenever needed.</u>

The beauty of this shrub is its intricate, angular branching pattern. Foliage is small and sparse, allowing a clear view of branches. The plant seldom needs pruning. Occasionally, a stem from near the base of the plant will grow completely upright. Cut this out at its point of origin to preserve the shrub's picturesque branching quality. It's a good plant to use as a quick bonsai or in a container.

CORREA. Australian fuchsia. Evergreen shrubs. <u>Prune after flowering.</u>

Growth habits vary: *C. alba* is arching; *C. backhousiana* (*C. magnifica*) is upright and sprawling; *C. harrisii* is fairly short and compact; *C. pulchella* is short and wide-spreading, good for shrubby ground cover. Pinch back all kinds during growing season to promote compactness. After bloom, control height or spread by cutting stems back to laterals. Don't prune back to bare wood—these stems may not put out new growth.

CORYLOPSIS. Winter hazel. Deciduous shrubs. <u>Prune in late winter, early spring,</u> right after flowering.

These shrubs need little pruning. Plants grow slowly with attractive, delicate, open branching pattern. Occasionally you may have to remove dead or broken branches, limbs that detract from the overall pattern, or a weak stem at the ground.

CORYLUS. Filbert, hazelnut. Deciduous shrubs or small trees. <u>Prune in late winter.</u>

Most filberts grow as multi-stemmed shrubs. Some varieties of European filbert (*C. avellana*) and the major nut-producer, *C. maxima* and its varieties, may be trained as small single-trunked trees (see page 14). Filberts send out many suckers. Shrubby contorted filbert (*C. avellana* 'Contorta') sends out many suckers from below the rootstock graft. During training, remove all suckers that sprout from the ground, the trunk, or the rootstock.

Filberts grown as shrubs need little pruning. Cut some crowded stems to the ground and cut out all dead or broken branches. To prevent filberts from dying, cut off limbs with disease cankers as soon as cankers appear. Make cuts in healthy wood below cankers. Disinfect pruning tool after each cut.

CORYNOCARPUS laevigata. New Zealand laurel. Evergreen shrub or small tree. <u>Prune whenever needed.</u>

Slow growth and dense, handsome foliage make this a good candidate for informal hedge, screen, or background planting. For these uses, only prune back branches that are growing too wide or tall (in time this plant grows 20 to 40 feet high). To train as a tree, see page 14.

COSTA RICAN HOLLY. See Olmediella.

COTINUS coggygria (*Rhus cotinus*). Smoke tree. Deciduous shrub or tree. <u>Prune in late winter or early spring,</u> before growth starts.

You can grow smoke tree as a small tree (see page 14 for training guidelines) or as a low-branching or multitrunked large shrub. Little pruning is needed. Cut out dead or broken limbs and remove crowding and awkward branches.

COTONEASTER. Evergreen, semievergreen, and deciduous shrubs. <u>Prune in winter, early spring.</u>

The many cotoneaster species range from wide-spreading ground cover plants to upright small shrubs to shrubs and shrub-trees with graceful, fountainlike forms. Where they have room to develop naturally, these plants need little pruning. If you need to prune, prune deciduous types in winter and early spring, evergreen types in spring before growth starts.

For ground covers, periodically remove dead branches and any that grow awkwardly upright.

You can cut back upright-growing species to limit height and spread without harming the basic form. Cut oldest stems to the ground whenever they stop producing strong new growth. You can also grow the upright kinds as formal hedges.

For fountainlike shrubs and shrub-trees, occasionally cut old stems to the ground to allow new

(Continued on page 48)

CONIFERS

Conifers are the plants that gardeners in cold-winter regions call "evergreens" and that Westerners call "needle-leafed evergreens." The word conifer itself means "cone-bearing."

Some conifers have branches that radiate out from the trunk in whorls, and others have branches that grow along the trunk randomly. Pruning guidelines are different for these two groups.

Whorl-branching conifers

Conifers that branch in whorls include *Abies, Agathis, Araucaria, Cedrus, Cryptomeria, Cunninghamia, Larix, Picea, Pinus, Pseudolarix, Pseudotsuga, Sciadopitys.*

Prune whorl-branching conifers by cutting back selectively. Do not shear. New growth comes from buds at the tips of branches, from buds along the growing tips, and from buds at the bases of new growth. To stimulate branching, partially cut back or remove new growth just after it is fully formed. Generally you cannot force branching by cutting back into an old stem, *unless* you can see latent buds at the base of a previous season's growth.

To head back a wayward branch, cut back to a side branch or to obvious latent buds. Don't cut back to an area that's totally bare of foliage because you won't get regrowth below the cut.

Many whorl-branching conifers are trees with ramrod-straight central leaders. To keep trees growing upright, make sure that the central leader is not damaged. If it is, grow a replacement leader by staking one of the branches from the whorl immediately below into an upright position. It will become the new leader. If two leaders start to develop, remove the growing tip of the weaker one.

Random-branching conifers

Conifers that branch randomly include *Calocedrus (Libocedrus)*, *Cephalotaxus, Chamaecyparis, Cupressocyparis, Cupressus, Juniperus, Metasequoia, Platycladus, Podocarpus, Sequoia, Sequoiadendron, Taxodium, Taxus, Thuja, Tsuga.*

This group comprises trees, shrubs, and ground covers. New growth comes from buds at the tips of branches and erupts randomly along stems. Prune by shearing or by cutting back branches selectively.

It is risky to cut back most random-branching conifers to leafless stems and to expect regrowth—*Taxus* is a notable exception. But most of these plants carry their foliage quite far back on the stem—you can prune quite heavily and get regrowth.

Though you can shear many of the random-branching conifers, pruning selectively is often a better choice. For example, you can selectively cut back the vase-shaped shrubby junipers and yews *(Taxus)*. Selective pruning often enhances the natural shape of the plant; shearing usually ruins it.

Limit the upward growth of many upright large shrubs by cutting out the leader. To begin, remove 1 or 2 year's growth. Soon new growth from the side branches will fill in the top. When the plant becomes taller than you want, cut back the new growth at the top until only about an inch of it remains. Small branches will grow to cover the bare spot. In later years, to prevent the shrub from growing taller, repeatedly cut back new growth.

If a single-trunked tree loses its central leader, tie a splint to the top—the splint should extend above the break. Tie the branch closest to the old leader to the splint. This branch will become the new central leader. Remove the splint once the new leader is growing upright.

Snip conifers carefully to avoid marring their shapes.

Whorl-branching

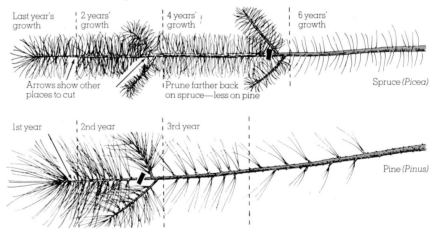

Last year's growth · 2 years' growth · 4 years' growth · 6 years' growth · Spruce *(Picea)*

Arrows show other places to cut · Prune farther back on spruce—less on pine

1st year · 2nd year · 3rd year · Pine *(Pinus)*

Whorl-branching. Cut back to whorl to force branching, compactness.

Random-branching

Make cuts almost anywhere · Juniper *(Juniperus)*

Random-branching. Cut back stems anywhere along leafy portion.

stems to develop. Otherwise, head them back carefully—indiscriminate cutting mars the graceful arch of the stems. Cut stems back to strong side branches that arch outward.

To renew a neglected shrub you have two choices. You can cut back heavily; vigorous growth will sprout readily from old wood. Or you can convert a large, overgrown shrub into a multitrunked shrub-tree by removing all branches below shoulder height and thinning out weak stems.

If plants suffer winter damage, remove dead stems. You can delay pruning until you determine the extent of the damage after buds break and new growth begins.

Cotoneasters are susceptible to fireblight, an infection that shows as blackened leaves and stems beginning at branch tips. Cut out all blighted wood a foot below the infection. Disinfect shears after each cut.

Cotoneaster. For graceful shrub, cut back to stems that arch outward.

COTTONWOOD.
See Populus.

COYOTE BRUSH.
See Baccharis.

CRABAPPLE.
See Malus.

CRANBERRY.
See Vaccinium.

CRAPE MYRTLE.
See Lagerstroemia.

CRATAEGUS. Hawthorn. Deciduous trees. Prune in late winter, early spring, before growth starts.

Though most hawthorns are naturally dense and twiggy, they need little pruning. Grow them as single-trunked specimens (see page 14 for training of young trees) or let them develop several trunks. To grow a single-trunk tree, cut back all but 3 to 5 branches on a young tree. This will prevent overcrowding later.

Thin out weaker and overcrowding branches occasionally to open up tree's crown and let storm winds pass through easily. Remove suckers from the tree's base and along the trunk.

You can grow hawthorn for hedges. Start with young, unbranched trees and plant them 3 feet apart. Stop their upward growth at the desired height by topping the main stem. After that, prune only to maintain the height and width you want. You can shear plants for a formal shape or selectively cut back branches for a looser outline.

In some areas, fireblight infects hawthorns; leaves and stems turn black and die, starting at stem tips. Cankers may also develop on large branches; they can eventually girdle and kill these branches. Cut out blighted and cankered branches well below the diseased parts. Disinfect pruning shears after each cut.

CREAM BUSH.
See Holodiscus.

CREEPING FIG.
See Ficus.

CRINODENDRON patagua (C. dependens, Tricuspidaria dependens). Lily-of-the-valley tree. Evergreen tree. Prune any time.

Plants are normally shrubby, with branches to the ground. For a single-trunked tree, give the early training described on page 14. Once tree is established, remove new growth from along the trunk and periodically thin out brushy growth in the tree's center. Basically, this tree grows upright, but some branches will grow downward; you can cut these out.

CROSS VINE.
See Bignonia.

CROTON.
See Codiaeum.

CROWN OF GOLD TREE.
See Cassia.

CRYPTOMERIA japonica. Japanese cryptomeria. Evergreen coniferous tree. Prune any time.

Because growth is symmetrical and even, you need do little pruning; occasionally you may have to cut back a branch that breaks the regular outline. Prune out all dead wood.

Variety 'Elegans' grows as a dense, broad pyramid to 25 feet, with foliage to the ground. You can prune it for an oriental effect by taking out selected branches so that remaining ones are arranged in tiers.

To create an informal topiary (see page 106), cut out all interior branches and foliage, leaving only clusters of foliage at branch tips for a pompon effect. Dwarf varieties, used for rock garden planting, need no pruning.

CUNNINGHAMIA lanceolata. China fir. Evergreen coniferous tree. Prune in early spring.

Give normal training and guidance to young trees (see page 14). Remove occasional dead branches; otherwise, little pruning is needed. Cut back any awkward limbs to side branches. Remove suckers that come up from base of trunk.

CUPANIOPSIS anacardioides (Cupania anacardioides). Carrot wood, tuckeroo. Evergreen tree. Prune any time.

Grow this broadleaf plant as a single or multitrunked tree, following guidelines on page 14. Prune only to enhance the structure of the tree as it develops its permanent framework; remove weak, excess branches from tree's center. Don't stub back branches; make all cuts to laterals or to the trunk.

CUP-OF-GOLD VINE.
See Solandra.

CUPRESSOCYPARIS leylandii. Evergreen coniferous tree. Prune any time.

Growth is exceedingly fast, narrow, and upright, making this a good plant for a hedge or high screen. Plants will tolerate shearing for formal hedges, but usually are quite even and neat without shearing. Prune mainly to limit height and to maintain an even top on the hedge or screen (you may have to trim down the tops more than once a year). Individual plants become broader and looser with age.

CUPRESSUS. Cypress. Evergreen coniferous trees. Prune any time.

Cypresses range from large, often picturesque trees to tall, pencil-thin accent plants. They can be planted as individual trees or in rows for tall screens or windbreaks. They need little pruning; in general, just remove dead wood.

Two kinds—Tecate cypress (*C. forbesii*) and Arizona cypress (*C. glabra*)—often grow too fast for root systems to support them in storm winds. To slow growth rate, give plants infrequent watering. If you live where winds are strong, selectively thin out branches to let wind pass through.

Some pyramidal and columnar cypresses will take shearing as formal hedges. The best-known columnar kinds are varieties of Italian cypress (*C. sempervirens*). At times, their branches may pull away from the narrow column, spoiling their impeccable vertical form. Don't tie a straying branch back into place: instead, cut it off just inside the point where it grows away from the column. This will force side growth to fill in and restore symmetry.

CURRANT, GOOSEBERRY. Deciduous shrubs. Prune in late winter.

Currants bear their fruits at the base of 1-year-old wood on short branches (spurs) of 2 and 3-year-old wood. To stimulate new growth, prune each year to remove wood that is heading into its fourth year and to reduce the length of remaining stems.

When you plant a currant, cut back stems, leaving only 3 to 4 buds per stem, with the top bud facing outward. The next winter, shorten 5 to 8 main stems to one-third their lengths, cutting back to outward-facing buds. In the following winter, remove all but 8 or 9 of the strongest, best-placed stems; cut each stem back by half its length to an outward-facing bud.

In subsequent winters, remove all stems more than 3 years old, along with any twiggy, dead, or broken stems and any that grow downward. On these mature bushes, shorten side branches but don't cut back main stems.

If plants suffer winter damage, delay pruning until buds swell so that you can determine how much dead wood to remove.

Currant. Each winter, cut off 3-year-old stems, shorten side branches. Cut off downward-growing stems.

CURRANT (ornamental).
See Ribes.

CYPRESS.
See Cupressus.

CYPRUS CEDAR.
See Cedrus.

CYTISUS, GENISTA, SPARTIUM. Broom. Evergreen and deciduous shrubs. Prune after flowering.

Brooms range from rock-garden shrublets to shrub-tree plants such as Mt. Etna broom (*Genista aethnensis*). In a garden, small sorts need little pruning; remove spent flower spikes (to prevent seed formation) and cut off weak and dead twigs.

To offset legginess of large types, prune back stems that have flowered to half their length, cutting to a side branch or to growth that is just beginning. Thin out weak and crowded wood and any dead twigs.

Two of the leafy *Cytisus* species (*C. canariensis* and *C. racemosus*) make good hedges that can be clipped to a fairly formal, even surface. Shear as often as needed during the growing season to maintain the hedge's shape.

You can't rejuvenate an old, overgrown, leggy broom by cutting it back severely. At that stage, either cut out excess branches and twigs to accentuate the plant's picturesque irregularity, or remove it and start anew.

DABOECIA. Evergreen shrubs. Prune in early spring, before growth starts.

These low shrubs are heath and heather relatives. Bloom season ranges from early spring to early autumn. During bloom, cut off spent flower spikes below lowest flower. In early spring, cut or shear back plant to two-thirds its size.

DAHOON.
See Ilex.

DAPHNE. Evergreen and deciduous shrubs. Prune during bloom.

Though daphnes will respond to heavy pruning, they rarely need anything more than an occasional snip to correct the shape of the plant. Cut branches back to laterals or to spots just above obvious growth buds. Cutting to outward-facing buds promotes spreading; cutting to inside buds directs growth upward. You can cut stems of the deciduous species for bouquets while in bud; brought indoors, the buds will open.

DATE PALM.
See Palm.

DATURA.
See Brugmansia.

DAUBENTONIA.
See Sesbania.

DAVIDIA involucrata. Dove tree. Deciduous tree. Prune after flowering.

When young, dove trees need routine training (see page 14). Grow them either as single-trunked or multistemmed plants (especially where plants can suffer winter damage).

Remove dead and broken branches and any crossing or crowded limbs. Make all cuts to a side branch or to the trunk. (Cuts more than ½ inch wide can allow disease to enter because wounds heal slowly.) Pay close attention to early training so that you won't have to remove major branches later.

DELONIX regia. Royal poinciana, flamboyant. Deciduous tree. Prune any time.

Give young plants routine early training (see page 14). Once tree shape is established, the royal poinciana will develop into a stout-trunked

(Continued on page 51)

ESPALIERS

Espaliers are trees and shrubs trained to grow in predominantly flat patterns against a wall, fence, or trellis, or on parallel wires. Plants can be espaliered either for fruit production or for decoration.

Espaliering began in Europe where, to save space, gardeners trained various fruit trees in *cordons* (the word "cordon" means rope). These trained plants gave a large yield of good fruit for the small amount of space each plant required. But espaliered fruit trees require much work.

Espaliering is also a way to train plants in decorative patterns. Today, plants are espaliered more for decoration than for fruit bearing.

To espalier a plant, you just direct its growth, pruning frequently during the growing season and during the dormant period to guide it into the shape you want. It may take several seasons of training before the plant conforms entirely to the shape you want it to take. Even after a new growth pattern has been established, you'll need to prune regularly to maintain its shape.

Maintain espalier shape by frequent selective snipping.

Formal espalier of fruit tree

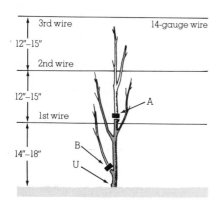

Planting time. Newly planted tree stands next to wires. Bud union (U) is 1 to 2 inches above ground. (A) Cut off top, leaving three well-placed branches or buds (here, one bud at top of stem and two branches). (B) Remove all other branches and buds from trunk.

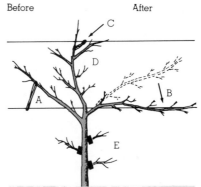

First growing season. (A) Let two branches for first tier grow out at 45° angle. (B) Later, tie down full-grown branches to wire. Don't pinch off tips. (C) Tie stem to wire. (D) Choose two branches for next tier; pinch off tips of all others. (E) Remove side growth.

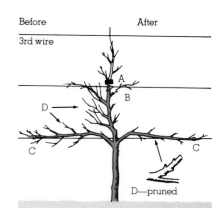

First dormant season. (A) When leaves drop, cut off tip at wire and retie. (B) Leave top two branches for second tier; cut back others to stubs with two or three spurs. (C) Tie tips to wires; prune tips only for balance. (D) shows laterals before/after pruning.

You can train a plant either formally, directing it into a specific geometric shape, or informally, letting it display a more natural shape.

Formal. Formal espaliers need close attention. The illustrations (at right) show some of the most common patterns for formal espaliers. The training directions (below) are for fruit trees—apple or pear, for example. You can apply the directions to ornamental plants as well, though with these you won't have to be concerned with the development of fruiting buds or spurs.

Informal. Informal espaliers are trees or shrubs trained against a flat surface without being shaped into a definite pattern. Often you prune them to expose their trunks or limbs or to encourage an interesting shape. Generally you follow the natural shape of the plant and give free rein to your sense of artistry when you prune. You'll still need to regularly cut off or prune back stems and shoots that don't enhance the shape you want.

Kinds of espaliers

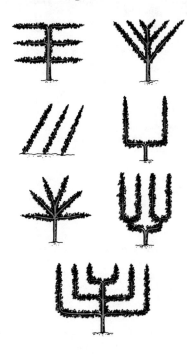

Espaliers can be trained into many shapes. These are some popular ones.

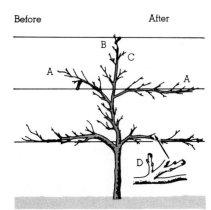

Second growing season. (A) Train second-tier branches to wire. (B) Tie top stem to wire. (C) Pinch off tips of laterals. (D) Cut back shoots on all first-tier laterals to three buds; buds will become fruiting spurs.

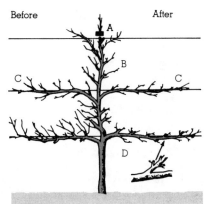

Second dormant season. Train third-tier branches: (A) cut off tip and retie; (B) leave top two branches, cut back others to two or three spurs. (C) Tie tips to wires, prune same way as first-tier branches a year ago. (D) Cut back side shoots to three buds.

plant with a wide-spreading, domed crown. Normally, just remove any dead or broken branches. Make all cuts back to side branches or major limbs.

DENDROMECON. Bush poppy. Evergreen shrubs. <u>Prune after flowering.</u>

Two species are sold: island bush poppy (*D. harfordii*), a spreading shrub or small tree, and *D. rigida*, a shrub that grows to 8 feet. You can severely cut back both species to renew untidy, overgrown plants, but don't cut back into branches that are more than 1 inch thick.

To prune island bush poppy, cut out dead wood and old branches that aren't producing strong new growth; head back overlong shoots. To keep *D. rigida* compact, cut back stems to about 2 feet, thinning out any that are dead and weak.

DEODAR CEDAR.
See Cedrus.

DESERT HONEYSUCKLE.
See Anisacanthus.

DESERT WILLOW.
See Chilopsis.

DEUTZIA. Deciduous shrubs. <u>Prune after flowering.</u>

Because flowers appear on stems that grew after last year's bloom, you prune to encourage renewal wood after blossoms fade. It's a good idea to prune before the flowers are completely finished—new growth starts before flowers fade.

Ordinarily, prune the tall kinds heavily (*D. lemoinei* and *D. scabra*, for example). Cut back all wood that has flowered to a point well below the blooms. For low-growing sorts (such as *D. gracilis* and *D. rosea*), cut oldest stems to the ground every other year.

Where stems are killed by winter cold or broken by snow and ice, cut out dead and damaged wood as soon as possible in early spring.

DIOSMA.
See Coleonema and Diosma.

DIPLACUS.
See Mimulus.

DIPLOPAPPUS.
See Felicia.

DISTICTIS. Evergreen vines. <u>Prune in late autumn to early spring.</u>

Three twining vines range in order from restrained to rampant growers: vanilla trumpet vine (*D. laxiflora*), blood-red trumpet vine (*D. buccinatoria*, also still known by its former names, *Bignonia cherere* or *Phaedranthus buccinatorius*), and royal trumpet vine (*D.* 'Rivers').

Go over vines every year to untangle stems, to cut out excess growth, and to restrain as much as necessary. During the growing season, cut out all new growth that is heading out of bounds. (This will save on autumn pruning work.)

DIZYGOTHECA elegantissima (*Aralia elegantissima*). Threadleaf false aralia. Evergreen shrub. <u>Prune in spring.</u>

This is a character shrub with stems rising from the ground, each topped by a crown of large 7-fingered leaves. With 3 or more stems, the plant makes a handsome, graceful accent shrub, growing about 12 feet tall.

To encourage foliage at various heights, cut back tallest stem to base; a new stem will quickly sprout from base of cut. To maintain the overall foliage height and balance you prefer, do this for several years in a row, or as often as you like.

In time, lacy juvenile foliage gives way to much broader, coarser, mature leaves—a faster process on unpruned plants.

DODONAEA viscosa. Hop bush, hopseed bush. Evergreen shrub. <u>Prune any time.</u>

Fast-growing and dense, this shrub has many upright stems. Left unpruned, it will become a somewhat billowy mass. Plant several, 6 to 8 feet apart, and you'll have a leafy wall. For these informal uses, occasionally cut back wayward growth.

You can also shear hop bush as a formal hedge or train it as an informal espalier (see page 50). To grow it as a tree, cut out all but a single stem and follow guidelines on page 14. Remove all new growth that comes from the ground or sprouts along the trunk. You can also use a large, thinned-out shrub as a multitrunked tree.

Lower limbs

Dodonaea. Remove lower limbs to reveal trunk, convert large, bulky shrub into small tree.

DOGWOOD.
See Cornus.

DOMBEYA. Evergreen shrubs (one can be a tree). <u>Prune in early spring or (in tropical areas) in summer.</u>

You can grow both *D. cayeuxii* and *D. wallichii* as big, bulky shrubs, train them as espaliers, or grow them on arbors. (Espaliers and arbors help to show off the drooping, hydrangea-like flower clusters.) *D. wallichii* will become a spreading 30-foot-tall tree with early training (see page 14).

To prune, each year remove frost-damaged wood, thin out crowding or crossing stems, and head back any awkward, too-long branches. Cut off spent flowers to make plants more attractive.

DOUGLAS FIR.
See Pseudotsuga.

DOVE TREE.
See Davidia.

DOXANTHA.
See Macfadyena.

DRACAENA. Evergreen shrubby and treelike perennials. <u>Prune in spring through midautumn.</u>

Dracaenas resemble their close relatives *Cordyline* (some of which are sold as "dracaenas"). Dracaenas such as *D. deremensis*, *D. fragrans*, *D. marginata*, and *D. sanderana* grow as clumps of stems carrying sword-shaped leaves; they need little pruning. Cut off old leaves as they turn yellow and die. Cut each leaf at

the narrow point close to the stem. If a stem gets too tall, you can experiment and cut it back part way (new growth may sprout from below the cut).

Dragon tree (*D. draco*) grows at least 20 feet tall and wide, each branch ending in a cluster of sword-shaped leaves. Don't prune unless a branch is in your way; in that case, cut it off flush with the branch from which it grows. For neatness, trim off flower stems at ends of branches after flowers have dropped.

DRAGON TREE.
See Dracaena.

DRIMYS winteri. Winter's bark. Evergreen tree. <u>Prune any time.</u>

You can train winter's bark to a single trunk (see page 14), but naturally it grows several trunks—upright and slender to about 25 feet, with somewhat drooping branches.

Prune only to enhance or maintain the tree's natural beauty, removing branches that droop too low and heading back any awkward-looking limbs. Cut out dead or broken branches and any that are rubbing or crowded.

DURANTA. Evergreen shrubs. <u>Prune any time.</u>

These fast-growing shrubs bloom in summer, then bear bunches of small yellow fruits. Sky flower—also called golden dewdrop or pigeon berry—(*D. repens*, also sold as *D. erecta* or *D. plumieri*) is tall (10 to 25 feet) forming multistemmed clumps of arching or drooping branches. Brazilian sky flower (*D. stenostachya*) is more compact, growing 6 to 15 feet tall.

For best appearance, frequently thin and prune back both shrubs. Cut back all branches that have produced berries and any branches that are out of hand. Prune them back to the ground or to unflowered laterals. Don't cut back stem tips; this causes bushy growth just below the cut.

You can train both species as small, open multitrunked trees with arching branches.

DUTCHMAN'S PIPE.
See Aristolochia.

DWARF POINCIANA.
See Caesalpinia.

EASTER LILY VINE.
See Beaumontia.

ECHIUM fastuosum. Pride of Madeira. Evergreen shrubby perennial. Prune after flowering.

In time this plant becomes a tree-like shrub with thick branches, and tufts of foliage at branch tips. To encourage bushiness, lightly cut back stems, but don't cut back into bare wood or new growth may not form. After flowers fade, cut off flower spikes a few inches down in foliage. (If plants are growing where they are difficult to reach, let flower spikes stay until they fall off.)

ELEAGNUS. Deciduous and evergreen shrubs and one deciduous tree. Prune in late spring, early summer.

Whether deciduous or evergreen, the shrubs easily grow into dense masses that usually need little pruning. Best uses are for screens and hedges (clipped or informal). To prune, just cut back any too-long branches.

You can also thin branches selectively to develop small spreading trees with strong arching branches. When old plants have become sparse and lost vigor, remove oldest stems and heavily cut back remaining branches. Plants normally send out vigorous new growth from cut branches and from the ground.

Though Russian olive (*E. angustifolia*) is a tree, you can use it as a large shrub, a small multitrunked

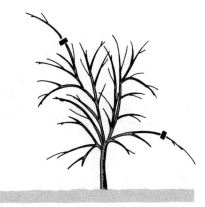

Eleagnus. Cut back branches that grow too long and spoil the balance of the crown.

tree, or a hedge. For training as a single-trunked tree, see page 14. To grow as a multitrunked tree, let several stems grow from the ground, and gradually remove lower branches as the plant gains height. Thereafter, remove dead and broken limbs; if you wish, cut out weak and excess branches that obscure the basic framework.

If any branches suddenly wilt and shrivel during summer, cut them out just below the affected part. Disinfect pruning shears after each cut.

ELDERBERRY.
See Sambucus.

ELM.
See Ulmus.

EMPRESS TREE.
See Paulownia.

ENGLISH LAUREL.
See Prunus.

ENKIANTHUS. Deciduous shrubs. Prune in early spring, before leaf-out.

Upright trunks with tiers of nearly horizontal branches characterize these slow-growing shrubs (*E. campanulatus* may become a 30-foot tree after many years). Growth is so orderly and attractive that there's little need to prune—just cut out dead and broken branches whenever they occur.

EPAULETTE TREE.
See Pterostyrax.

ERANTHEMUM pulchellum (*E. nervosum*). Evergreen shrub. Prune in spring.

Plant naturally grows as sprawling shrub. To promote bushiness and flowering, pinch back stem tips 2 or 3 times early in growing season.

To rejuvenate a leggy, overgrown plant, cut it to the ground. New stems will quickly sprout.

ERICA. Heath. Evergreen shrubs. Prune after flowering.

Various kinds of heath range from less-than-foot-high ground cover and rock garden candidates to 18-foot-tall specimen shrubs. To prune the low-growing types—*E. carnea, E. ciliaris, E. darleyensis, E. doliiformis, E.*

tetralix, E. vagans, and various hybrids—cut or shear off stems that have flowered, removing about half of each stem. When plants get old and die back in center, dig them out and replace them with new plants.

On the taller kinds—*E. arborea, E. australis, E. canaliculata, E. hyemalis, E. lusitanica, E. mammosa, E. mediterranea, E. persoluta, E. regia, E. speciosa, E. ventricosa*—cut off spent blooms just below flower spikes. You can control the shape of larger kinds by cutting back wayward branches to laterals or to a leaf. Don't cut back into leafless wood or new growth may not emerge.

ERIOBOTRYA. Loquat. Evergreen shrub and tree. Prune in early spring, before new growth starts.

Naturally a large shrub, bronze loquat (*E. deflexa*) can be trained as a small tree (see page 14) or as an informal espalier (see page 50) on a trellis or against a wall that does not reflect much heat. As a shrub, it needs little pruning; just remove dead, broken, or weak branches.

Fruit-bearing *E. japonica* grows as a single or multitrunked tree. It needs little pruning except for early training as a tree or espalier. Large leaves form dense canopy; for better fruit production, thin out the crown, admitting some light to tree's center. If tree forms a heavy fruit crop, thin the fruit to improve its quality and to reduce weight on limbs.

Fireblight is sometimes a problem: leaves and stems turn black and die, beginning at the branch ends and working downward. Cut out blighted stems, making cuts 12 inches back into healthy wood. Disinfect shears after each cut.

ERIOGONUM. Wild buckwheat. Evergreen shrubs. Prune in late winter, early spring.

The most widely grown wild buckwheat shrubs—*E. arborescens, E. fasciculatum, E. giganteum*—eventually become picturesque, revealing most of their branches, with foliage clustered at branch ends. Starting when plants are young, you can make them bushier by pinching tips of stems to encourage branching. If older plants become too leggy and open, replace them with young ones.

ERYTHEA.
See Palm.

ERYTHRINA. Coral tree. Mostly deciduous (some nearly evergreen) trees and shrubs. Pruning time varies: generally prune when plants are most dormant or right after flowering.

Erythrina bidwillii and cockspur coral tree (*E. crista-galli*) grow as shrubs or small trees. They bear flowers on new wood and can be pruned severely. In some areas, gardeners grow them as perennials—each winter, cold kills the tops, but each spring a new flowering shrub grows from the roots. Generally you cut off old flower stems and dead branch ends after each wave of bloom. To develop large plants, prune only to shape and to eliminate any badly placed branches.

You can cut *E. bidwillii* to the ground each year to renew the growth of soft-wooded stems that will bear flowers. Do this before new growth begins in spring. Caution: *E. bidwillii* is very thorny. Use long-handled shears and wear gloves when you prune.

For *E. crista-galli*, plants grow soft-wooded stems that bear flowers. These stems usually die back to the point where branches have become woody. A week or more after flowering, cut the flowering stems back to the point where the limbs are woody. New flowering stems will develop for the blooming season. Eventually, as the plant develops more woody limbs, it can become a well-shaped tree.

Trees. The other familiar kinds of coral tree are recognizable as trees. Most must form some woody branch structure before they will flower. Typically, trees have wide-spreading umbrella shapes with several stout branches growing low on the trunk or from the ground. (*E. falcata*, however, is upright.)

Prune only to shape, removing branches that are too low; thin out dead, twiggy, and broken branches. Don't indiscriminately shorten limbs; instead, make all cuts back to another branch. Balance thinning by root-pruning shallow roots. Do this when trees are most dormant in midwinter.

Many coral trees show a rugged, picturesque, angular branch-

(Continued on page 56)

FLOWERING TREES

The familiar members of the cherry (*Prunus*) family produce fruit or nuts: apricot, cherry, peach, plum, and almond. They also have cousins—deciduous trees and shrubs—that gardeners grow strictly for their spring flower display. Since your purpose in growing the purely ornamental plants is to enjoy flowers rather than fruits, you prune them differently from the crop-producing trees. *Prune these trees and shrubs right after flowering.* (For directions on pruning evergreen kinds of cherries, see the entry "Prunus" elsewhere in the encyclopedia.)

Some plants—flowering almond, peach, nectarine, and *Prunus mume*—offer you a choice of pruning methods. Prune heavily to get the most new growth and to increase flower production. Or prune lightly to let plants develop naturally; plants pruned this way will produce a showy but usually smaller display of flowers.

Flowering almond

Prunus triloba is the larger of the two most common flowering almonds. A slow-growing tree, it reaches a height of about 15 feet. You can grow it as a tree (see page 14) or as a large multitrunked shrub. Either way, the plant needs little pruning. Cut off any flowering stems you want for indoor display. You can shape the plant at the same time. Remove twiggy, crowding stems and dead wood, and thin stems to open the plant's center.

Dwarf flowering almond (*P. glandulosa*) is strictly shrubby, with many long stems studded with flowers. Flowers come on year-old growth, so prune heavily after flowering each year to achieve new growth for next year's display. Thin out all crowding stems in plant's center, and cut back remaining stems to about 6 inches. Without heavy pruning, plant becomes twiggy and bears fewer flowers.

Flowering cherry

Flowering cherries are a large, varied group of trees. Some bear flowers only, others (such as chokecherries and bird cherries) bear tiny fruits. Give young trees the early training outlined on page 14.

After basic form is established, prune as little as possible. (Cherries that are headed back usually send out sprouts profusely, making the tree look ugly.) Remove lower limbs, as needed, to raise the canopy high enough to walk under. Remove awkward and crossing branches. Pinch back or cut back any too-vigorous shoots to keep the plant in balance and to promote branching. Remove any dead or diseased stems whenever they occur. A good time to do any necessary pruning is when the tree is flowering—you can use cut-off branches for indoor arrangements.

Shrubby flowering cherries include *P. besseyi*, *P. fruticosa*, *P. tomentosa* (all also producers of good fruit), and sometimes *P. cistena* (see Flowering Plums). These shrubby cherries need only enough pruning to maintain their shape. Thin out crowded stems in the plant's center, eliminating weak, twiggy, crowding, and dead stems. Cut back any long, awkward shoots.

Flowering peach. Flowers appear on year-old stems. After blooming, cut back all stems that flowered.

(PRUNUS)

Flowering peach and nectarine

These trees flower on wood produced the previous year. They give the best flower display where most of the crown is year-old stems.

In early years, train the tree to a central leader (as outlined on page 15) or train according to guidelines on page 87 for fruiting peaches and nectarines. When basic tree framework is established and the tree is about the size you want it to remain, begin heavy annual pruning.

During or just after flowering, cut back stems that flowered to 6-inch stubs. Thin out crowding stems so that new growth from the stubs won't create a tangle of crossing stems. Also thin out old, unproductive wood and dead wood. This pruning plan will give you an almost overwhelming number of flowers, but it will create a lollipop-shaped crown. For a moderate approach leading to a more attractive tree, follow the annual pruning recommendations for fruiting peaches and nectarines on page 87.

Flowering plum

The many kinds of flowering plum range from medium-size trees to tree-shrubs to 3-foot-tall shrubs. For trees, train young plants according to guidelines on page 14. Establish a crown you can walk under. As the crown develops, cut out crossing and inward-growing branches and extra-vigorous vertical branches. Because trees branch densely, thin their centers frequently. However, avoid heading back branches to limit the size of trees; this usually causes trees to sprout profusely. The easiest times to prune are winter, when plants are leafless, or spring, when plants are in bloom. You may also need to thin trees occasionally during summer, as stems become heavy and droopy from the weight of growing foliage.

Trim flowering cherry lightly, mostly for flower arrangements.

Dwarf red-leaf plum (*P. cistena*), also known as purple-leaf sand cherry, forms a multistemmed shrub. Occasionally thin weak stems and dead wood. Prune any branches that grow too long, cutting them back to laterals. With some patience, you can train this plant into a graceful, single-trunked small tree.

Prunus mume

Commonly known as Japanese flowering apricot and Japanese flowering plum, *Prunus mume* is a slow-growing small tree with a distinctive appearance. Like flowering almonds, it produces blossoms on year-old stems. Give young plants early training to develop a good tree form (see page 14).

When the tree is well established, begin annual pruning for flower production. Cut back all long, whiplike stems to 6-inch stubs right after flowering. During the next spring, cut back half of the stems produced from these cuts to 6-inch stubs and leave the rest. The following year, cut back the previously uncut stems, and continue this process of cutting back half the growth each year in succeeding years. When pruning, also remove old, twiggy, and unproductive stems and branches that crowd the tree's center.

ing pattern when out of leaf. Naked coral tree (*E. coralloides*, sometimes sold as *E. poianthes*) usually produces so many interlacing twisted limbs that occasionally you have to do some heavy thinning to enhance its unusual beauty.

Prune the deciduous tree species when they are leafless. These include Kaffirboom coral tree (*E. caffra*), naked coral tree (*E. coralloides*), and *E. lysistemon* (*E. princeps*).

Depending on climate, Natal coral tree (*E. humeana*) may be deciduous or nearly evergreen. It needs little pruning because it blooms from previously formed flower buds. If you must, cut back dry, old flower stems for neatness, but otherwise let tree alone during flowering season from June into November. Do any necessary pruning in midwinter.

E. falcata is nearly evergreen everywhere. Prune it in midwinter when it's most dormant.

ESCALLONIA. Evergreen shrubs. Prune after flowering.

Escallonias range from 3-foot shrubs to 15 to 25-foot shrubs or shrub-trees. Without pruning, they become woody and rangy. You can prune them heavily in winter or early spring—thin out old wood and head back also. To keep them compact, pinch tips of new growth and cut off any spent flower clusters.

To keep the tallest kinds shrubby, prune about one-third of the old stems to the ground each year after flowering. Cut back leggy stems and remove spent blossoms. Alternatively, thin out old stems and cut back laterals on some old, tall stems.

To train taller kinds into trees, let them grow tall and wide. Gradually thin out lower branches to reveal multiple trunks.

You can shear all escallonias as hedges, but this will sacrifice some bloom.

EUCALYPTUS. Evergreen trees and shrubs. Prune in spring and summer.

Though eucalyptus can take heavy pruning—they'll spring back vigorously even from a bare stump—most need little or no pruning. The most common reasons for pruning are to control the size of a too-large plant and to correct broken limbs. If the tree's flowers are important, wait to prune until blooming is finished.

Young trees. Many kinds of eucalyptus grow very rapidly, so early training is particularly important (see page 14).

If a young tree is tall and top-heavy, you can train it to develop a strong new tree. Bend the top down to the ground so that the trunk forms an arch. Hold the trunk in this arched position by wiring the top to a heavy rock or short stake. Before long, new shoots will grow from the base of the trunk. After a year, cut off the old, arched trunk at the ground and remove the weakest new shoots, leaving one or several sturdy new trunks.

Mature trees. When you prune eucalyptus, you usually cut limbs back to another branch or to an obvious growth bud or new shoot. If necessary, however, you can cut right into a smooth trunk. On an established plant, new growth will sprout beneath the cut—often very profusely. When these sprouts are growing vigorously, remove the excess sprouts, keeping only well-placed ones.

Different types. Over 100 eucalyptus species grow in the western and southwestern United States. They can be divided into 3 general categories: *mallees*, shrubby types with multiple trunks; *intermediate trees* with multiple or single trunks; *forest trees* with tall single trunks. Each type has its own pruning requirements.

Mallees. Normally, these form dense clumps without any help (pruning usually detracts from their appearance). To improve the looks of a rangy, leggy mallee, cut it to the ground; this will stimulate the growth of many new shoots from the base. As these develop, select 3 to 5 of the strongest shoots to become the new shrub framework; then cut out the remaining stems.

Intermediate trees. Most of these are attractive with either single or multiple trunks. To develop a single-trunked tree, follow the guidelines on page 14. Leave side shoots on the tree for a while to help it get established; then cut them off the main trunk later.

For a multitrunked tree, cut the main trunk to within 2 feet of the ground if there is new growth sprouting from the base; this will divert the energy into several potential trunks. As these grow, choose the best trunks, remove the rest, and then cut the original trunk to the ground.

If no sprouts are coming from the base, bend the trunk over to the ground as described at left in "Young trees." Select the best trunks from among the new shoots that sprout; then cut off the original trunk.

Forest trees. After the recommended early guidance, these stately skyline trees seldom need pruning. However, if limbs break off from storms or from their own weight, have the stub cut back to the nearest branch or to the trunk. Usually this is a job for a professional tree pruner.

Forest trees that have grown too tall for your garden can be cut back to stumps; they respond quickly by producing many new shoots. As these grow, thin out the weakest and those that are poorly placed. Remaining shoots will form the framework for an entirely "new" tree.

EUONYMUS. Deciduous or evergreen shrubs, evergreen vine. Pruning times vary.

How and when you prune depends on the kind of euonymus you are growing and how you use it in your garden.

Deciduous species. Popular kinds include winged euonymus (*E. alata*), European spindle tree (*E. europaea*), and their varieties.

Winged euonymus forms a large, dense, twiggy shrub. Its variety 'Compacta' generally reaches only 4 to 6 feet. You can use them as unclipped hedges or screens as well as for specimen shrubs.

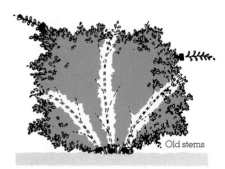

Escallonia. Each year cut off ⅓ of oldest stems at ground, head back wayward ones.

European spindle tree is a large shrub that can be trained into a single-trunked, broad-topped small tree (see page 14).

For shrubs and hedges, prune in late winter or early spring while plants are leafless. Each year cut out about one third of the oldest stems and cut back to laterals any branches that mar the plant's symmetry.

Prune tree forms of European spindle tree after leaf drop in autumn until early spring—just remove dead, broken, crossing, and crowding branches. Head back any lopsided stems to laterals and eliminate any stems that sprout from the ground.

Evergreen shrubs. Large shrubs include varieties of *E. japonica* and *E. kiautschovica (E. patens)*. Primarily, they're used as hedges and screens—either formally clipped or left with a more natural outline.

To prune, cut out dead branches and weak, twiggy stems in the plant's center. During the growing season, clip formal hedges every few weeks. In cold-winter regions, don't shear after midsummer; new growth that starts late in the season may be nipped by frost. Do any major reshaping in early spring, before new growth begins.

To convert older plants of *E. japonica* into multitrunked trees, remove lower limbs on main stems.

Shrubby varieties of *E. fortunei*, such as *E.f.* 'Erecta', 'Sarcoxie', 'Greenlane', and 'Vegeta', make good hedges. They have the same pruning requirements as the other two evergreen species. Used as individual shrubs, most kinds will form mounding plants that are likely to take root when branch tips touch moist soil.

Most shrubby varieties may also be trained as vines (see below).

Variegated kinds of *E. japonica* and *E. fortunei* often develop reverted shoots with normal green foliage. Cut these off at or below the point where they have turned green.

Evergreen vine. Evergreen *E. fortunei* (formerly *E. radicans acuta*) has many named varieties that differ in leaf color and size. More important, they differ in form: vinelike or shrubby. Vinelike varieties behave like ivy (*Hedera*). They will grow as a ground cover on flat land or, with any vertical surface to climb, they will head

upward to form a tightly clinging mat of foliage. Give vinelike kinds the same treatment recommended for ivy (see "Hedera," page 65).

Evergreen ground cover. Purpleleaf wintercreeper (*E. fortunei* 'Colorata') and less common running euonymus (*E. obovata*) are vigorous ground covers that need to be kept in bounds by cutting back runaway shoots. Runaway shoots can be horizontal or vertical (they will climb into other shrubs). For a low, dense mat, set lawnmower blade 3 inches above ground and mow the planting, preferably in spring or early summer.

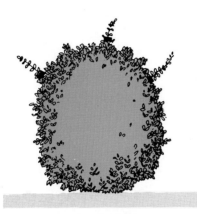

Euonymus. Prune evergreen shrubs to maintain regular outline—cut back any long, awkward stems.

EUPHORBIA pulcherimma. Poinsettia. Evergreen or deciduous shrub. Prune in spring, after bloom is finished.

Prune poinsettias so they will produce strong new growth for the following winter's display. If they're growing among other shrubs, prune the poinsettia back lightly to moderately. Usually, you prune poinsettia in April or May, but in some areas, such as southern Florida, you can prune plants until early September.

You can prune back isolated plants severely. Cut all stems back to 2 or 3 buds or leaf scars, keeping the stump as compact as possible. If growth is crowded, remove some large older stems entirely. As new shoots grow, cut out any stems that are weak or crowding. At this point you have three pruning choices.

You can allow the stems to grow unchecked. This will result in spectacularly large, colorful bracts at the

ends of very tall stems that are bare of leaves for about half their height.

For bushier plants, cut back stems about halfway at 2-month intervals during summer. This produces a shorter branching plant and bracts are smaller than on unpruned stems.

Periodically, you can pinch the tips of new growth through late spring and summer as each stem reaches 1 to 2 feet in length. Pinching requires close attention, but it will give you a bushy plant and smaller bracts without the sacrifice of so much new growth.

EUROPEAN MOUNTAIN ASH.
See Sorbus.

EURYA emarginata. Evergreen shrub. Prune any time; in cold-winter areas, prune in spring and summer.

Slow-growing *Eurya* needs little pruning. Occasionally, it may need some thinning or you may want to train it. When pruning, cut back to a lateral or to an obvious growth bud. You can train this plant to almost any shape, including espaliers. You can even train old ones into small evergreen trees that are especially good for Japanese gardens because they are slow-growing.

EURYA OCHNACEA.
See Cleyera.

EURYOPS. Evergreen shrubby perennials. Prune in summer, after main flowering season.

During growing season, pinch tips of new growth to promote bushiness and to keep plants compact. Cut back leggy or topheavy plants to a semiwoody framework. Try not to cut back into bare stems—look for young shoots or growth buds and prune just above them.

EVERGREEN GRAPE.
See Cissus.

EVERGREEN PEAR.
See Pyrus.

EXOCHORDA. Pearl bush. Deciduous shrubs. Prune after flowering.

Pearl bush grows upright with arching lateral branches. For a

(Continued on page 59)

FORSYTHIA

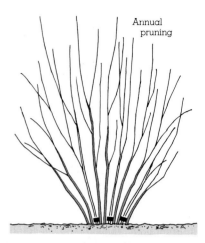

Selectively remove oldest stems on mature forsythia so replacement stems will grow without crowding.

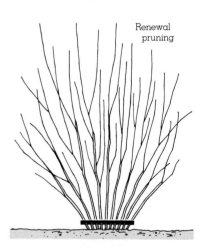

Overgrown forsythia is a thicket of crowded stems. Renew shrub by cutting plant almost to ground.

Cut back forsythia each year to renew flowering stems.

In early spring, forsythias break forth in fountains of color. These yellow-flowered deciduous shrubs bear their blossoms on leafless stems. *Prune when flowering is finished.*

Don't prune forsythias for several years after planting. Once they reach the size you want, prune each year to promote fresh growth. After flowering, cut to the ground one-third of the oldest stems and remove weak, crowded, and dead branches. (You can also cut off stems during bloom for indoor decoration.) Pinch out the tips of new shoots when they are 1 to 2 feet long to stimulate branching and to increase the next year's flower display.

Weeping forsythia *(Forsythia suspensa)* and the hybrid 'Arnold Dwarf' will grow as ground covers. Their branch tips will root when they touch moist soil, extending the area the plants cover. Cut back any stems that stick up awkwardly. Periodically cut out old, weak stems.

To renew an old, neglected plant that's overcrowded with stems, in early spring cut back the entire shrub to within 6 to 12 inches of the ground. Cut to the ground all old, particularly woody stems. As new growth sprouts, remove all weaker and crowding shoots. This procedure sacrifices a season's bloom, but restores a plant to new vigor in 2 years.

...Exochorda (cont'd.)

bushier shrub, head back main stems to promote lateral branching or pinch tips of new growth. Remove spent flower spikes and cut out all weak wood in plant's center.

Every few years, thin out the oldest wood by cutting some stems to the ground; let new shoots replace old ones. To restrict height and spread, cut branches back to strong laterals.

Common pearl bush (*E. racemosa*) will grow 15 feet tall. You can trim it up to a multitrunked small tree by removing the lower branches.

FAGUS. Beech. Deciduous trees. Prune in late winter.

Typically, an unpruned beech will become a tall, broadly pyramidal tree with low branches that sweep the ground. Train young beeches according to the guidelines on page 14. Be careful to remove weak V-shaped crotches. Because beech wood is brittle, narrow crotches are likely to split in storms or just from the weight of foliage.

As a tree grows taller, remove lower limbs if you want to see the trunk or sit or walk under the tree. (It's best to avoid too much traffic under beech trees, since they grow best in uncompacted soil.) In later years, just remove weak, crowding, dead, and broken branches. The only pruning the narrow columnar varieties need is to remove irregular branches that stick out too far.

You can train beeches as a high hedge; you can keep them about 15 feet tall, but as narrow as 18 inches. Shear in normal pruning season, and again in summer when new growth has matured.

FALLUGIA paradoxa. Apache plume. Partly evergreen shrub. Prune in autumn.

Normally, Apache plume needs no pruning—any irregular branching adds to its beauty. If you want to control size or shape, wait until the showy, feathery seed heads have finished their display. Cut back that year's growth to a leaf or growth bud or cut off entire branches, if necessary.

FALSE CYPRESS.
See Chamaecyparis.

FALSE SPIRAEA.
See Sorbaria.

FATSHEDERA lizei. Evergreen vine, shrub, ground cover. Prune any time.

This hybrid of Japanese aralia (*Fatsia japonica*) and English ivy (*Hedera helix*) is about midway between them in appearance—neither shrub nor vine, but a sprawling, snaky plant that can be trained several ways.

For a shrubby mass, pinch growing tips frequently to promote branching. Train *Fatshedera* as a vine to climb a wall or trellis, or use it as an espalier (train stems before they become mature and brittle). If an established plant becomes unmanageable, cut it to the ground. New growth will start quickly, and you can work at training these young stems.

To use it as a ground cover, lay stems flat, and pinch tips to induce branching. Regularly prune back upright stems to maintain desired height.

Note: you can graft any variety of ivy to the top of fatshedera to form an interesting plant you can shape like topiary.

FATSIA japonica (*Aralia sieboldii, A. japonica*). Japanese aralia. Evergreen shrub. Prune in early spring or (in tropical areas) in summer.

Japanese aralia has multiple stems that grow from the ground with tropically bold, fan-shaped leaves at branch tips. Plants need no regular pruning, but respond well to it. If some stems get too tall, cut them back to branches, to the ground, or to any point in between.

Established plants may produce many new stems from ground level—thin out any you don't want. Rejuvenate old, spindly plants by cutting back hard to 6-inch stubs. New growth will start easily; later, thin out crowded shoots.

FEATHER BUSH.
See Lysiloma.

FEIJOA sellowiana. Pineapple guava. Evergreen shrub or small tree. Prune in late spring before flowering, or (in tropical areas) in summer after fruiting.

Pineapple guava naturally grows as a dense shrub with many stems, but it's amenable to any amount of pruning and training. You can train it as an espalier, as a small tree with one or several trunks, or as a hedge or screen.

For shrubs, periodically thin out weak, twiggy, and dead stems in the plant's center. To control height, spread, or any wayward branches, cut back to lateral growth or remove branches entirely.

To train as a tree, select a single-trunked specimen at a nursery. As it grows, remove any other stems that come up from the base and follow directions for training young trees on page 14.

To develop a multistemmed tree, let your plant grow naturally as a many-stemmed shrub for several years. When the plant is growing vigorously and is at least 3 feet tall, select the stems you want for trunks and cut all others to the ground. Thereafter, each year remove new sprouts from the base. Gradually raise the tree's canopy by cutting back the lowest branches flush with the trunks. Remove crossing branches and any weak and dead stems in the canopy.

General directions for hedge training and maintenance are on page 70. For espalier training, see page 50.

Feijoa. To keep shrub symmetrical, cut back shoots that grow too long, cut off any awkward stems.

FELICIA amelloides (*F. aethiopica, Agathea coelestis*). Blue marguerite. Shrubby perennial. Prune in late summer.

This densely branched, leafy plant spreads 4 to 5 feet wide, if not pruned, and becomes untidy-looking in time. Though this plant is likely to be flowering at its best pruning time, as flowers fade shear it back 6 to 8 inches into new growth. Avoid cutting back into old, woody stems. At the same time, thin out weak, straggly stems. New flower-bearing growth will come along quickly. Remove spent flowers to prolong bloom.

FERN PINE.
See Podocarpus.

FETTERBUSH.
See Leucothoe.

FICUS. Ornamental figs. Evergreen or deciduous trees and shrubs, evergreen vine. <u>Prune in spring, summer</u>. Prune any time in frost-free regions.

Ornamental figs range from massive, park-size trees like the Indian laurel fig (*F. microcarpa*) to shrubby mistletoe fig (*F. deltoidea*) to the aggressive vine, creeping fig (*F. pumila*). You can prune all of these as much as you like—back to bare stems, if necessary—but it's best to select a fig suited to the space available so that you will need to prune only to shape rather than to restrain. Make all pruning cuts to well-placed laterals or to leaves.

Below you'll find the popular ornamental fig species grouped according to how they grow. In addition to tree, shrub, and vine, you will notice two special use categories—espalier and hedge. Some species appear in both tree and shrub lists; these are figs that, in time or with training, will become trees.

Trees. *Ficus auriculata (F. roxburghii), F. benjamina, F. macrophylla, F. microcarpa, F.m. nitida (F. retusa), F. nekbudu (F. utilis), F. religiosa, F. rubiginosa*, fiddleleaf fig (*F. lyrata*, formerly *F. pandurata*), rubber plant (*F. elastica*). All of these species will grow as single-trunk or multitrunk trees. Prune them only to shape or repair. Cut back wayward branches; remove lower limbs, if you like, to show trunks; cut out broken, weak, and crowding branches.

Shrubs. *Ficus auriculata (F. roxburghii)*, fiddleleaf fig (*F. lyrata*, formerly *F. pandurata*), mistletoe fig (*F. deltoidea*, formerly *F. diversifolia*), rubber plant (*F. elastica*). Prune all simply to shape or restrain size. Young rubber plants and fiddleleaf figs often produce straight, unbranched stems. To increase branching, pinch back these stems in early summer.

Vine. Creeping fig (*F. pumila*, formerly *F. repens*). It grows as a vine until it reaches the highest point on a wall. Then it develops stems that bear larger and thicker mature leaves and fruit. Soon after planting, cut the plant back almost to the ground. This will encourage several new stems to develop. Spread stems horizontally to get good coverage. They will seek the nearest surface to cling to. Unless restrained, vine can grow to cover a huge area.

To control size, cut the plant to the ground every 3 to 4 years or, if it's growing on a wall, shear it back whenever necessary. You can also allow the plant to develop mature stems at the top of a wall and prune it by thinning stems or trimming back as a hedge. Tolerates any amount of cutting or shearing and, in time, will need regular pruning.

Espaliers. You can espalier two kinds of *Ficus: F. auriculata (F. roxburghii)* and *F. benjamina*. See page 50 for directions.

Hedges, screens. *Ficus benjamina* and *F. microcarpa nitida*. Both grow naturally to be moderate-size trees. But, because they branch freely and have handsome glossy leaves, they make good hedge and screen plants. (See page 70 for hedge instructions.) You can train them formally (shear plants) or informally (cut back any out-of-place branches).

FIG, edible. Deciduous tree. <u>Prune in winter.</u>

The fig is a very accommodating tree. It can take quite a bit of pruning and still bear an ample crop; it also will bear with no pruning at all. In some colder areas, figs will freeze back to the ground but will send up fresh shoots in spring.

Most figs produce two crops a year. In early summer, the first crop comes on wood formed the previous year. The second crop, in late summer, is borne on new growth which is forming while the first crop of figs is maturing. On an unpruned tree, most fruit forms progressively farther from the tree's center, though some fruits can appear anywhere on new laterals.

Ornamental uses. For beauty and shade, let the tree grow naturally. Only remove unattractive or poorly placed limbs and weak, dead, and crossing branches. Cut back any branches that grow beyond the shape you want to maintain. Grown this way, the tree will become spreading, round-topped, and as high as 30 feet.

To control the size, thin out all but the most attractively placed limbs. Cut back branches as needed to limit spread or height. Do major pruning in winter, but cut back new growth in summer whenever necessary.

You can also espalier figs (see page 50). Because you'll need to prune espaliered plants frequently, you can't expect a large crop of fruit.

Fruit production. To increase your fig crop, start by training the young tree to an open center shape (see page 15). Keep the main scaffold limbs close to the ground. As trees grow, control height to keep fruit within easy picking reach.

After a main framework has formed, prune to encourage trees to produce new wood. Thin out weak and unnecessary growth in the tree's canopy to let light into the center. As needed, cut back branches to limit spread or height.

Occasionally, you may have to prune lightly in summer to keep a tree in bounds. Between the two crops, avoid heavy cutting back—this can seriously reduce the volume of the second crop and remove growth that will carry the first crop of the next year.

Edible fig. Annually, thin out crossing branches and watersprouts to make open, well-balanced crown.

FIG (ornamental).
See Ficus.

FILBERT.
See Corylus.

FIR.
See Abies.

FIRETHORN.
See Pyracantha.

FIREWHEEL TREE.
See Stenocarpus.

FLAMBOYANT.
See Delonix.

FLAME BUSH.
See Calliandra.

FLAME-OF-THE-FOREST.
See Spathodea.

FLAME-OF-THE-WOODS.
See Ixora.

FLAME PEA.
See Chorizema.

FLAME TREE.
See Brachychiton.

FLANNEL BUSH.
See Fremontodendron.

FLOWERING ALMOND.
See Flowering Trees, page 54.

FLOWERING CHERRY.
See Flowering Trees, page 54.

FLOWERING CRABAPPLE.
See Malus.

FLOWERING MAPLE.
See Abutilon.

FLOWERING NECTARINE.
See Flowering Trees, page 54.

FLOWERING PEACH.
See Flowering Trees, page 54.

FLOWERING PLUM.
See Flowering Trees, page 54.

FLOWERING QUINCE.
See Chaenomeles.

FLOWERING RASPBERRY.
See Rubus.

FLOWERY SENNA.
See Cassia.

FORSYTHIA.
See page 58.

FOTHERGILLA. Deciduous shrubs. Prune in late winter to midspring.

These graceful shrubs need no routine pruning. Every few years you may want to thin out the oldest twiggy wood to open up the plant a bit. Cut oldest stems to the ground and re-move weak, straggly, and dead branches. Prune during winter when plants are dormant, or in spring, just after flowering, before new leaves open.

FRAGRANT SNOWBALL.
See Viburnum.

FRANGIPANI.
See Plumeria.

FRANKLINIA alatamaha *(Gordonia alatamaha)*. **Deciduous tree or shrub. Prune in early spring.**

In milder regions of the South and West, Franklinia will become a 20 to 30-foot tree. Where winters are cold, growth is slower and the plant makes a medium to large shrub.

You can grow *Franklinia* as a single-trunked tree (see page 14) or as a multitrunked tree. Other than early training, it needs little pruning. If a vigorous branch grows too long, cut it back to a strong lateral. Where limbs have been damaged by winter freezes, cut back to healthy wood in spring.

FRAXINUS. Ash. Deciduous trees *(F. uhdei* is nearly evergreen). **Prune in winter to early spring.**

Ashes are fast-growing trees with rather brittle wood. They tend to form weak V-shaped crotches where scaffold limbs join the trunks. Therefore, give careful early training (see guidelines on page 14) to minimize the chance of major limbs' breaking in later years. In order to stimulate branching, you may need to cut back long, vigorous branches that grow from the young tree's trunk. This pruning will help to develop a stronger scaffold of major limbs.

On several kinds of ash—nota-bly *F. udhei, F. velutina,* and their varieties—1-year-old stems form 2 pairs of buds at each node. This growth characteristic lets you easily stop limbs from forming weak V-shaped crotches. The upper, pri-mary bud normally will produce the next branch and form a V-shaped crotch. The lower, secondary bud will produce a limb that grows at a much wider and stronger angle from the trunk, but normally it won't grow un-less the primary bud is removed.

You can force the secondary bud to grow by rubbing or snipping off the upper bud before it starts grow-ing. (Secondary buds remain alive for a few years; if a branch has al-ready developed from a primary bud, you can still cut it off after one or two seasons and stimulate the secondary buds to grow.)

As the tree develops, prune out any branches that grow vertically within the canopy and cut back any too-long branches that spoil the crown's symmetry. Once the tree's shape is well established, you'll only need to remove occasional dead branches or broken limbs.

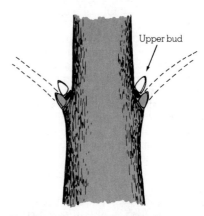

Fraxinus. Each node has 2 buds. To stimulate strong, wide-angled branches, remove upper buds.

FREMONTODENDRON *(Fremontia)*. **Evergreen shrubs or small trees. Prune after flowering.**

These fast-growing plants range from 6 to 20 feet tall, usually forming several trunks or branching close to the ground. Basically, they are big, bulky shrubs, but you can remove the lower branches of established plants to shape them into small trees, or you can train them to grow more or less flat against a wall or building.

Prune plants to control size or to correct irregular shape. Pinch the tips of new growth to promote branching and cut back too-long branches to good laterals. Wear gloves and long sleeves when pruning; seed cap-sules are covered with hairs that irri-tate skin.

FRINGE TREE.
See Chionanthus.

FUCHSIA.
See page 62.

GALPHIMIA glauca (*Thryallis glauca*). Evergreen shrub. Prune in spring through autumn.

Without pruning, plants become leggy, forming long, spindly stems that can break from the weight of leaves and flowers. Pinch or cut back new growth as often as needed to encourage branching and bushiness. *Galphimia* is useful as a clipped or informal hedge (see page 70 for general hedge information).

GAMOLEPIS chrysanthemoides. Evergreen shrub. Prune any time.

Fast-growing gamolepis can become 4 to 6 feet tall, and can spread even wider. Left alone, it may become leggy and untidy. To keep plant compact and neat, start pinching tips of new growth when plants are young. Continue pinching regularly throughout spring, summer, and autumn, or clip plants back after a crop of flowers. If you need to control size, you can cut back plants at any time. They'll respond by putting out new growth quickly.

For leggy, overgrown plants, heavily cut back in late winter. Gamolepis will do well in a mass planting. Also, you can use it as a clipped hedge, but this will sacrifice some of the flowers. If plants become too untidy and don't respond well to pruning after several years, dig them out and replace them.

GARDENIA. Evergreen shrubs. Prune during bloom and in early spring.

Most gardenias need little pruning to maintain a neat appearance. During bloom, thin out any weak stems that are producing no flowers and that have few or small leaves. At the same time, on leggy plants, (especially *G. radicans* 'Mystery'), lightly cut back stems to encourage branching.

To renew an old, rangy plant, start in early spring before warm weather and before new growth begins (this pruning will sacrifice a year's bloom). Thin out twiggy stems and old, unproductive branches. Cut back oldest, weakest stems to 6 to 8-inch stubs; this will stimulate new growth from the plant's base. A year later, remove more old, weak wood. Continue this process annually until all stems are young and vigorous.

GARRYA. Silktassel. Evergreen shrubs. Prune after flowering.

Silktassels need little pruning. To shape shrubs, cut back awkward limbs to strong laterals or to a pair of leaves. Coast silktassel (*G. elliptica*) may grow 20 or more feet tall. You can trim it up to become a small tree by following the directions on page 14. Any of the species are useful for screens or informal hedges.

GAULTHERIA. Evergreen shrubs. Prune in spring.

Most common *Gaultherias* are low shrublets or spreading ground covers. Prune them only to remove dead or broken stems or awkward branches.

Salal (*G. shallon*) is an exception. A variable shrub, it grows 2 to 10 feet tall (depending on conditions) and needs only occasional pruning. Remove dead, weak, or straggly branches. Don't shear plant; cut off branches where they join other stems. (You can remove branches at any time.) Cut branches make long-lasting arrangements.

In the Pacific Northwest, to renew an old planting, cut plants to the ground and cover the ground with fir bark mulch. In a year plants will fill in the area again.

GEIJERA parviflora. Australian willow, Wilga. Evergreen tree. Prune any time.

Give young trees routine training as outlined on page 14. After that, trees need little pruning. Cut out dead and broken branches and head back any wayward lateral branch to a well-placed one. To encourage the weeping shape this plant produces so well, cut back lateral branches to hanging side stems.

GELSEMIUM sempervirens. Carolina jessamine. Evergreen vine. Prune after flowering.

Carolina jessamine sends out long twining stems that will wind around supports or around each other. Train it up a trellis or fence, grow it along house eaves where branches will cascade gracefully, or use it as a ground cover.

Periodically thin out vines and cut them back to control spread and clean up tangled growth. Plant re-

(Continued on page 64)

FUCHSIA

Most popular fuchsias are hybrids. These showy-flowered evergreen or deciduous shrubs vary in form from vinelike to upright and bushy. Vinelike plants are often called "hanging basket fuchsias." They look best if you grow them in containers from which their stems and flowers can drape attractively. Shrubby, upright fuchsias make good container plants as well as good garden shrubs. Large but less common shrubby fuchsias such as *Fuchsia magellanica* and *F. arborescens* will grow more than 10 feet tall.

Despite differences among fuchsias, you can use a basic set of pruning guidelines in caring for all species. *Prune plants in winter and pinch them back in spring.*

Basic pruning

Fuchsias bloom only on new growth. Prune to develop a good framework from which strong new growth will come.

Container plants. Prune fuchsias in containers severely. Your goal is to keep the plant growing in proper proportion to its container. Pruning encourages new growth that will hide the framework of woody stems.

To prune hanging basket fuchsias, start by cutting back all stems to the container's edge. Cut off upward-growing branches and remove as many crossing branches as possible. Ideally, the framework of stems will point outward like the spokes of a wagon wheel. Cut back each stem of last year's growth to 1 or 2 pairs of buds. Then remove the plant from the container, shake some soil from the roots, and cut back the root mass to half its size. Replant in the container, in fresh soil mix.

Prune upright fuchsias in containers in much the same way. Remove crossing stems and weak stems, leaving a well-balanced framework of woody stems. Cut these remaining branches back to 1 or 2

pairs of nodes, and then prune roots and repot as described above.

For all container plants let about 3 pairs of leaves develop, then pinch off stem tips to stimulate branching. Continue pinching throughout the growing season to make plants bushier and to promote flowering.

In regions where winters are too cold for plants to survive outdoors, store them during cold-weather months in a cool garage, shed, or porch. Take plants indoors when first frost threatens. Let leaves fall off plants, but save most pruning until you move plants out-of-doors again in spring after all danger of frost is past. In some regions of the United States, fuchsias are grown as greenhouse or house plants and moved outdoors in summer. Prune these plants in late winter.

Plants in the garden. You can prune fuchsias growing as shrubs in your garden as little or as much as you want. Prune severely to keep plants small; prune moderately to allow plants to grow larger.

In general, prune to remove crossing and crowding branches and dead, broken, and weak stems. To make plants bushy, pinch tips of stems often during the growing season.

Where winters are occasionally cold enough to injure fuchsias, cut out all frost-damaged stems. Delay pruning in spring until all danger of frost is past.

Special training

You can also train fuchsias as espaliers and as standards (often called "tree" fuchsias).

You can espalier trailing and upright fuchsias and train them either formally or informally. Once you have established the framework, prune heavily each year as you would container plants. Directions for training espaliers are on page 50.

Early pinching leads to abundant blooms.

You can buy fuchsias already trained as standards, or you can develop your own (be patient; this may take 2 to 3 years).

To grow a fuchsia standard, choose a vigorous variety (either upright or trailing). Cut off all stems but the strongest one and tie it vertically to a stake. Allow it to grow up the stake. Pinch off the tip at the point where you want the branches to begin.

Pinch the branch tips frequently to stimulate branching. Pinch off side branches below the top cluster of branches.

Once the tree form is established, each year cut back the stems the way you would cut back those of a hanging basket plant. The pruned plant should have a circle of short stems atop the main trunk.

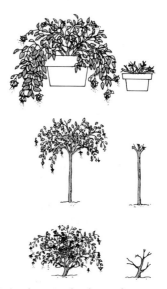

Prune hanging basket and tree fuchsias heavily, leaving compact framework of stems. Prune upright plants in ground to skeleton of short stems.

sponds well to any amount of pruning. To maintain it as a ground cover, just cut back any too-tall stems.

GENISTA.
See Cytisus, Genista, Spartium.

GEOMETRY TREE.
See Bucida.

GERALDTON WAX FLOWER.
See Chamaelaucium.

GERMANDER.
See Teucrium.

GINKGO biloba. Maidenhair tree. Deciduous tree. Prune in winter.

Young trees need routine training as described on page 14. Also, cut off any vertical shoots that grow parallel to the central leader. Young trees may grow asymmetrically; if this occurs, cut back awkward branches to well-placed laterals. Older trees need little pruning; just remove dead, weak, or broken branches.

GLEDITSIA triacanthos. Honey locust. Deciduous tree. Prune in winter.

Most honey locusts are varieties of the thornless form, *G. t. inermis*. Give young trees the training described on page 14. If your newly planted tree has branches along the trunk, cut each branch back to 2 buds. This will promote strong branching close to the tree's center.

As honey locusts grow, they occasionally send out unruly branches; cut these back to strong laterals. Some varieties form V-shaped crotches be-

Gleditsia. On established tree, remove crossing limbs and any limbs that form narrow angle to trunk.

tween major limbs and the trunk. In selecting permanent scaffold branches, choose branches that make an angle greater than 45° with the trunk.

As a tree matures, prune out dead, broken, and crowded limbs as needed. To keep trees open, thin out excess branches, but keep the main parallel branches that are spaced 10 to 12 feet apart.

GLORYBOWER.
See Clerodendrum.

GOATNUT.
See Simmondsia.

GOLD MEDALLION TREE.
See Cassia.

GOLDENCHAIN TREE.
See Laburnum.

GOLDEN LARCH.
See Pseudolarix.

GOLDENRAIN TREE.
See Koelreuteria.

GOLDEN TRUMPET TREE.
See Tabebuia.

GOOSEBERRY.
See Currant, Gooseberry; also see Ribes.

GRAPE.
See page 66.

GRAPE IVY.
See Cissus.

GRAPEFRUIT.
See Citrus, page 38.

GREVILLEA. Evergreen tree, shrubs. Prune after flowering.

Silk oak (*G. robusta*) is the common tree species. Fast-growing and brittle-wooded, it needs careful early training to establish a strong framework (see page 14). After planting, cut back the leader to about 2½ feet and shorten any branches to within 2 buds of the trunk.

As the tree grows, cut back to strong laterals any branches that grow too long. Try to avoid heavy pruning that leaves large cut surfaces—these are slow to heal. Thin mature trees occasionally to allow wind to pass through more easily and reduce the chance for broken limbs.

The several shrubby grevilleas grow to various sizes. Most have arching branches—use as shrubs, unclipped hedges, and screens. You can plant low-growing ones as

shrubby ground covers. They need little pruning; cut out dead, broken, and awkward branches. Prune back to laterals or to another branch. Rosemary grevillea (*G. rosmarinifolia*) can be clipped as a hedge.

GREWIA occidentalis (*G. caffra*). Lavender starflower. Evergreen shrub. Prune in summer and in autumn, after flowering.

This fast-growing, sprawling shrub can be used in various ways. For a 6 to 10-foot-high and wide shrub, let branches grow out long and arch down. To make plant bushier, pinch off tips of stems. Because its branching pattern is flat, this plant is easy to espalier (see page 50). To make a clipped hedge (see page 70), set out plants 4 to 6 feet apart. For a ground cover, let plant sprawl and cut off upright stems.

To cover an arbor or trellis, encourage upward growth. Also, you can train plants on wires as cordons. Or, with early training to a single leader, you can develop a small tree (see page 14).

Heavy bloom comes in late spring. To encourage additional flowers, cut back lightly to force new flowering stems. Do any major thinning or heading back in autumn after flowering stops.

GRISELINIA. Evergreen shrubs. Prune in spring, before growth begins.

Griselinias are neat, compact shrubs. Prune to encourage more branching each spring before growth starts. Cut back any overlong stems to a lateral, leaf, or growth bud.

You can train both *G. littoralis* and *G. lucida* as espaliers. *G. littoralis* will make a fine tall screen or windbreak, or a bushy, sprawling ground cover shrub in a seaside garden.

GUATEMALAN HOLLY.
See Olmediella.

GUAVA.
See Feijoa, Psidium.

GUINEA GOLD VINE.
See Hibbertia.

GUM.
See Eucalyptus.

GUM MYRTLE.
See Angophora.

GYMNOCLADUS dioica. Kentucky coffee tree. Deciduous tree. Prune during winter.

Narrow young trees become broader as they age. Branches are relatively few but picturesquely angled, forming an open foliage canopy. Give young trees routine training, following the guidelines on page 14. Older trees need little attention—remove weak, dead, and broken limbs. You can also thin out any crowding branches that obscure the attractive branching pattern.

HACKBERRY.
See Celtis.

HAKEA. Evergreen shrubs or trees. Prune in early spring.

Hakeas are dense, compact plants. Plant them singly as specimen shrubs or mass them together as windbreaks, informal hedges, or screens. You can train *H. laurina* as a tree (see guidelines on page 14). You can also convert them from large shrubs to small trees as they age. You can clip prickly-leafed *H. suaveolens* into a hedge or let it grow informally to cover a steep, dry slope.

Pinch back tips on young plants to promote bushiness. Mature plants seldom need pruning. Occasionally, you may need to cut back a wayward branch to a sturdy lateral.

HALESIA. Deciduous trees. Prune after flowering.

Give the various kinds of *Halesia* training as single-trunked trees (see page 14). Otherwise, some will grow as large multistemmed shrubs. Established trees need little pruning—just remove crowding, weak, dead, or broken branches.

HAMAMELIS. Witch hazel. Deciduous trees or large shrubs. Prune after flowering.

Witch hazels are multistemmed plants that grow at a slow to moderate rate. In time, Chinese witch hazel (*H. mollis*) and common witch hazel (*H. virginiana*) may reach tree size. To train them as trees, follow directions on page 14. Some plants are grafted. Be sure to cut off all suckers from them.

Witch hazels need little pruning. If branches become crowded, thin out enough old stems to open up the interior. Cut out weak, twiggy, dead, and broken branches. To keep plants small, cut back stems that grow too long to side branches.

You can thin *H. intermedia* and *H. mollis* while bare branches are decorated with flowers; the prunings make attractive arrangements.

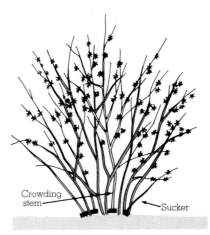

Crowding stem

Sucker

Hamamelis. Each year remove suckers. When needed, remove crowded, weak, dead, or broken branches.

HARDENBERGIA. Evergreen shrubby vines. Prune after flowering.

Against vertical surfaces, these twining vines will form a delicate tracery of branches and leaves. They can decorate the tops of low walls, fences, screens, and arches. They're especially useful as climbers in shade or part shade. Prune to prevent tangling and thin out old, weak stems to keep plants from becoming leggy. To control shape, pinch back tips of new growth during spring and summer.

HARDY ORANGE.
See Poncirus.

HARPEPHYLLUM caffrum. Kaffir plum. Evergreen tree. Prune in spring.

Kaffir plum grows as a single-trunked tree. Start with a young tree and follow training directions on page 14. You can also grow this evergreen with several trunks (plants usually grow this way after severe frost damage). Take care in guiding irregular growth of young trees. Cut back branches to a desirable framework.

After frost danger is past, prune out dead, frost-damaged, and broken branches, cutting back to sound laterals.

This tree is naturally round-headed and dense. You can reveal more of the branch structure by periodically thinning out excess and crowding limbs.

HAWTHORN.
See Crataegus.

HAZELNUT.
See Corylus.

HEATH.
See Erica, Daboecia.

HEATHER.
See Calluna.

HEAVENLY BAMBOO.
See Nandina.

HEBE. Evergreen shrubs. Prune after flowering.

These fast-growing shrubs take well to heavy pruning, and sprout easily from old, leafless wood. To keep plants bushy and compact, cut back stems that have flowered by about half their length. To rejuvenate older, ragged plants, cut oldest and least vigorous stems to the ground; then severely cut back remaining stems.

HEDERA. Ivy. Evergreen vines. Prune from early spring through summer.

Ivy will climb and cling with its aerial roots to almost all vertical surfaces it encounters—fences, tree trunks, walls—and it will make a dense ground and bank cover.

In most situations, ivy needs "haircutting" 2 to 3 times a year. Trim off stems protruding from vertical surfaces and from ground covers, edge ground covers next to lawn or pavement, and edge around windows in ivy-covered walls. Use hedge and pruning shears to keep plantings flat and maintain window margins. For lawn or pavement edging, use a sharp spade or edging tool.

Over several years, ground cover plantings build up a thick mat of stems and need periodic scalping. Use hedge shears or a heavy-duty rotary power mower to cut the twiggy mass back to the ground. Do this in spring when new growth will quickly cover the ground again.

Old plants growing vertically will

(Continued on page 68)

GRAPES

Prune vines annually for bountiful crop.

Grape vines produce delicious fruit and, on an arbor, pleasant shade. Once established, the vines grow rampantly. If all you want from a grape vine is leafy cover for an arbor or patio, you only need to train a strong vine up and over its support and thin out entangling growth each year. But most people plant grapes for fruit, even if they want shade as well. For good fruit production, you'll need to follow more careful pruning procedures. *Prune these deciduous vines in winter or in early spring before buds swell.*

Grapes are produced on stems that will develop from the year-old wood—stems that formed the previous season. Year-old stems have smooth bark; older stems have rough, shaggy bark. The purpose of pruning is to limit the amount of potential fruiting wood to ensure that the plant doesn't produce too much fruit, and to see that it does bear grapes of good quality.

There are several pruning methods for grapes. The two most widely used are *spur pruning* and *cane pruning*.

You can prune all of the common grape varieties by using one of these two methods. Both can be used to train grapes on arbors. In general, you use spur pruning for European table grape and wine varieties (exceptions are 'Olivette Blanche', 'Rish Baba', and 'Thompson Seedless'). Use cane pruning for American varieties, American-European varieties (also known as French-American hybrids), muscadine grapes, and the three exceptions mentioned above.

The following illustrations show each method as it is carried out over time, from the planting of a bare-root grape through the fourth year after planting.

Planting to 2nd spring

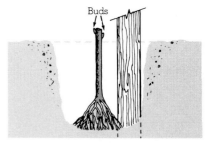

Plant bare-root grape during dormant season. Set plant deep with 1 or 2 buds above soil level. (Post in hole is part of trellis to support growing vine.)

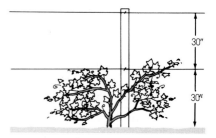

During first year, let vine grow unchecked (don't try to train growth). The more leaves, the better the root development.

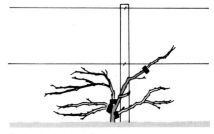

In first winter, select longest, strongest stem for future trunk. Cut off all other growth, tie the single cane upright.

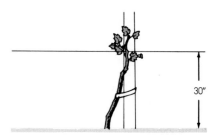

During second spring, new shoots will grow from buds. Select strongest shoot for upper trunk, leave 2 lower shoots to form arms.

Spur pruning

In second summer, when upright shoot tops upper wire, pinch off its tip. Let 2 shoots grow just below tip to train along top wire.

In second winter, dormant vine has 2 pairs of parallel arms. Cut off all side shoots from these arms and remove any others from main trunk.

In third winter, prune off weak side shoots from arms. Leave strong stems (spurs) spaced 6 to 10 inches apart and cut each back to two buds.

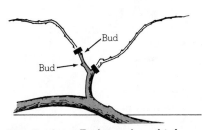

Fourth winter. Each spur from third-winter pruning formed 2 stems and bore fruit. Cut off upper stem. Cut back lower stem to 2 buds.

Cane pruning

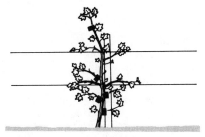

In second summer, pinch off tip of main stem when it grows a foot above top wire. Cut off side shoots on lower half of trunk.

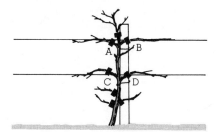

During second winter, cut off main stem just above top wire. Leave 4 side shoots (A,B,C,D) for permanent canes; cut them back to 2 buds.

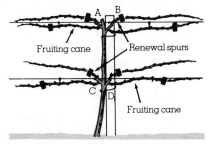

Third winter. Stubs A,B,C,D grew 2 canes each. Cut back upper canes to 2 buds for renewal spurs; cut back lower (fruiting) canes to 12 buds.

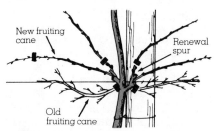

Fourth winter. Cut off each cane that bore fruit. On renewal spurs, cut upper stems back to 2 buds, cut back lower canes (new fruiting canes) to 12 buds.

Training on an arbor

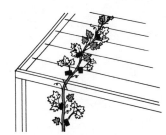

Second summer. When vine reaches top of arbor, bend it over and tie it to wires as it grows across top. Remove side shoots to encourage tip to grow.

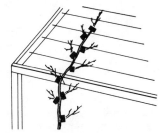

Second winter. Cut back main stem to point just beyond where you want the last set of branches. Cut off all side shoots. In spring, thin new shoots to 1 foot apart.

Third winter, spur pruning. Cut back each selected shoot (from previous summer's growth) to 2 buds. Thereafter, follow basic spur guidelines.

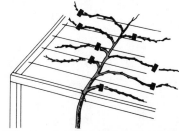

Third winter, cane pruning. Cut back alternately to long canes (12 buds) and spurs (2 buds). Thereafter, each year follow basic cane pruning steps.

produce mature shrubby growth toward the top of the planting. These stiff stems bear unlobed leaves that are shaped differently from juvenile leaves, and clusters of insignificant green flowers that develop into black berries. Growth from these stems will always be shrubby, not vining. Leave this growth unpruned if you like decorative berries. Or you can thin stems or clip them as hedges.

HEMLOCK.
See Tsuga.

HERALD'S TRUMPET.
See Beaumontia.

HETEROMELES arbutifolia. Toyon, Christmas berry, California holly. Evergreen shrub or small tree. <u>Prune in late winter, early spring,</u> when growth begins.

In nature, toyon grows as a shrub or small multitrunked tree. In the garden, you can keep it as a shrub, let it develop into a small tree with several trunks, or train it into a single-trunked tree (see page 14). Toyon also makes a good informal hedge. It will spread out over a bank, if you keep removing upright shoots.

As a shrub or tree it will take any amount of pruning (but see information on fireblight below). Remove twiggy and weak stems to reveal branch structure. Pinch out new growth at branch tips to encourage bushiness and increase flower and berry production. To control size or shape, prune branches to laterals, cutting back young leafy stems to a leaf. For drastic rejuvenation, cut back plant to a leafless skeleton of major limbs or even to the ground.

At the time of new growth in spring, plants are susceptible to fireblight. If a stem dies back from the tip with a blackened, burned appearance, cut it off a foot below the diseased part. Disinfect pruning shears after each cut.

HIBBERTIA. Evergreen shrubs, vines. <u>Pruning time varies.</u>
Shrubby *H. cuneiformis (Candollea cuneiformis)* flowers in spring on new growth. Do any pruning after bloom period. If necessary, cut back stems to limit size and thin out dead and weak stems.

Guinea gold vine *(H. scandens)*

blooms from spring into autumn. Prune in early spring before flowers appear, cutting out any frost-damaged stems. Untangle stems that are intertwined and remove excess stems in the process. On a topheavy vine, cut back the oldest stems to stimulate new growth low on the plant.

HIBISCUS. Deciduous and evergreen shrubs. <u>Prune in winter, early spring</u> (deciduous); <u>prune in spring</u> (evergreen).

Deciduous shrubs. The two most common deciduous shrubs are Confederate rose *(H. mutabilis)* and rose-of-Sharon *(H. syriacus)*. In warmer regions, both can become small trees if they're not heavily pruned.

To prune, annually thin out any crowded stems. Remove dead, broken, and weak stems and old, unproductive branches. To keep plant from getting too large, cut back stems to laterals or growth buds.

Established plants can take almost any amount of cutting back. To encourage largest flowers on *H. syriacus,* you can cut back previous season's growth to 2 buds (this also keeps plant size down). Rose-of-Sharon can also make a hedge plant—cut back stems, rather than shear them, to maintain height and width.

Evergreen shrubs. The flashy Chinese hibiscus *(H. rosa-sinensis)* grows as a tender shrub or small tree in the warmest parts of the West and South. Many named varieties are sold; sizes of mature plants vary considerably.

Young plants seldom need pruning, but pinching back tips of new growth will increase bushiness and the number of flowering branches.

On older plants, you can prune heavily each year to control size, but it is better to select a variety that won't overgrow its allotted space. Flowers come on new growth, so a moderate annual cutting back will encourage blossoming. Cut back about one-third of the last year's growth; remove crossing branches and those that grow toward the plants' center.

To rejuvenate a big, woody, old shrub that produces few flowers, prune heavily in several stages. Start in spring after all frost danger is past, cutting back 1 or 2 old stems each month through August. Plan to cut

back the entire plant at least halfway by the end of the growing season. New growth will quickly sprout after pruning in spring and summer.

You can use Chinese hibiscus as a hedge. To control shape and size of hedge, selectively cut back stems, but don't shear plants.

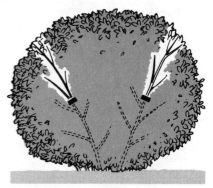

Hibiscus. Renew Chinese hibiscus by selectively heading back stems halfway to well-placed branches.

HIGHBUSH CRANBERRY.
See Vaccinium.

HOLLY.
See Ilex.

HOLLYLEAF CHERRY.
See Prunus (evergreen).

HOLODISCUS. Deciduous shrubs to small trees. <u>Prune after flowering.</u>
Remove clusters of dead blooms in summer, cutting back to laterals. At the same time, prune back any too-long stems to strong laterals. Occasionally, cut out dead, twiggy, old, and unproductive stems.

HONEY BUSH.
See Melianthus.

HONEY LOCUST.
See Gleditsia.

HONEYSUCKLE.
See page 74.

HONG KONG ORCHID TREE.
See Bauhinia.

HOOP PINE.
See Araucaria.

HOP BUSH.
See Dodonaea.

HOP HORNBEAM.
See Ostrya.

HOPSEED BUSH.
See Dodonaea.

HORNBEAM.
See Carpinus.

HORSECHESTNUT.
See Aesculus.

HOWEIA.
See Palm.

HUCKLEBERRY.
See Vaccinium.

HYDRANGEA. Deciduous shrubs, vine. Pruning time varies.

Hydrangeas fall into two groups: those you prune in early spring before new growth begins and those you prune after flowers fade.

Early spring pruning. Hydrangeas that bloom on new spring growth include climbing hydrangea (*H. anomala petiolaris*), *H. paniculata* and varieties, and smooth hydrangea (*H. arborescens*). Prune them in early spring before new growth starts.

Give climbing hydrangea (*H. anomala petiolaris*) little pruning until it is well established and climbing. At that time, cut off any shoots that don't cling to the surface you want the plant to climb. Cut back flowering shoots to 2 buds, if possible.

Smooth hydrangea (*H. arborescens*) and its variety *H. a.* 'Grandiflora' are neater plants with larger flower clusters if you cut them back by at least half. Some gardeners cut back previous year's growth to 2 or 3 buds or cut the entire plant to the ground. This results in the largest flower clusters, but stems can't always hold them up. When you do head back, also cut out dead stems, crowded and weak branches.

Grow peegee hydrangea (*H. paniculata* 'Grandiflora') as a large shrub or train it into a small tree. In either case, the plant develops woody framework that produces new growth.

For a shrub, make sure that some branches grow close to the ground or several stems rise from the ground. If not, cut stems of year-old plant to within 2 buds of the ground to force branching. Each year cut back previous year's stems to 2 to 4 buds, thin out crossing or crowding stems, and remove weak and dead branches. In time you may want to gradually cut out old framework limbs to make way for new growth from low on the plant.

For a tree, select one vigorous stem and let it grow upward. Cut it off at the height you want branching to begin. When branches have formed, cut them back to about 4 buds. In successive years, prune the top as you would a shrub's.

After-bloom pruning. Some hydrangeas bear flowers on stems produced the previous year. These include garden or bigleaf hydrangea (*H. macrophylla*, formerly *H. hortensia*, *H. opuloides*, and *H. otaksa*) and oakleaf hydrangea (*H. quercifolia*). Prune them after flowers fade.

On bigleaf hydrangea, as flowers fade, new growth will begin lower on the stems. Cut back the flowering stems to the strongest pair of new shoots or to a pair of buds that will send out stems where you want them. Make these cuts leaving 2 to 4 pairs of buds on stems that grow from the ground or 2 pairs of buds on side branches. As plant matures, begin to thin out oldest woody stems. Remove crowded crossing, broken, or dead branches.

Oakleaf hydrangea has foliage that some gardeners like even better than its flowers. To grow the plant solely for its foliage, cut the plant to the ground each year in early spring. Because stems freeze to the ground each winter, northern gardeners must grow it this way. To grow the plant for blossoms, cut back halfway stems that have flowered. The plant grows many stems from the ground, and spreads into a clump. Thin out old, weak, and crowding stems.

Hydrangea. After blooming, cut back each stem that bloomed to 2 to 4 pairs of buds.

HYMENOSPORUM flavum. Sweetshade. Evergreen small tree or large shrub. Prune any time.

This slender, graceful, sparsely branched tree is attractive by itself or in a grove planting. Pruning is different for each use.

Give single trees early training as outlined on page 14. Limbs are widely spaced, usually branching in whorls of 3 from the trunk and tending to grow long and weak. To strengthen limbs and encourage more branching, frequently pinch tips of new growth. Cut back to a good lateral any branch that gets too long and floppy.

Sturdy trees that are planted in groves need no staking, pinching, or pruning. But do stake tall, spindly trees until they are well established.

HYPERICUM. St. Johnswort. Evergreen or semievergreen shrubs. Prune in winter, early spring, before new growth starts.

Without attention, these shrubs become twiggy and straggly after several years. Every 2 to 3 years, thin out crowded stems, cutting out the oldest stems and weak, twiggy, or dead stems. Cut back remaining plant one-third to one-half its previous height.

Aaron's beard or creeping St. Johnswort (*H. calycinum*) is a vigorous ground cover that spreads by underground runners. Mow or cut it to the ground every 2 to 3 years. In areas such as the Pacific Northwest, where frost damages leaves, trim plants to the ground each year in spring to remove damaged leaves.

ILEX. Holly. Evergreen and deciduous shrubs and trees. Prune in winter, early spring.

Hollies grow in an almost bewildering variety. They vary both in foliage pattern and in size—from foot-high cushion plants to 40-foot trees. The smallest types serve as useful specimen plants or border hedges. Medium-size kinds make good specimens, hedges, and screens. The largest ones develop into handsome, symmetrical trees.

Hollies usually grow to be dense and symmetrical. Prune mostly to shape plants: cut back wayward branches on shrubs and trees; trim back hedges (see page 70). The December holiday season is a good time to prune—clipped-off branches can be used for indoor decorations. When pruning, cut out all dead and broken branches. Make all cuts back to leaves or to joints with other branches. Don't cut back to a bare stem.

Hollies that are destined to become trees generally start as dense, upright shrubs. To train as a single-leader tree, remove any upright stems that compete with the central leader. If you want a bare trunk topped by foliage, gradually remove lower branches.

ILLICIUM. Anise tree. Evergreen shrubs to small trees. Prune in spring, summer.

Both Japanese anise tree (*I. anisatum*) and Florida anise tree (*I. floridanum*) are dense, compact shrubs that carry foliage to the ground. In time, they can become trees. To convert them into single-trunked or multitrunked trees, remove lower branches.

These plants seldom need pruning. Cut back any wayward branch to a good lateral. Anise trees are good choices for informal hedges (see page 70), screens, or barriers.

INCENSE CEDAR.
See Calocedrus.

INDIA HAWTHORN.
See Raphiolepis.

INDIAN BEAN.
See Catalpa.

INDIAN CURRANT.
See Symphoricarpos.

INDIGO BUSH.
See Amorpha.

INKBERRY.
See Ilex.

IRISH HEATH.
See Daboecia.

ITALIAN BUCKTHORN.
See Rhamnus.

ITEA virginica. Virginia sweetspire, Virginia willow, tassel-white. Deciduous shrub. Prune in early spring.

Growth is open, graceful, and restrained, so plant needs little pruning. Cut out any dead and broken branches and any crowding stems. Occasionally thin out oldest stems that are not growing vigorously.

IVY.
See Hedera.

HEDGES

A hedge is a living fence or barrier made up of many plants, usually just of one species. If planted close enough together, in several years the individual plants will appear to be one unit. Developing a hedge takes considerable planning and care in the first several years. After that time, you can concentrate chiefly on routine maintenance.

Throughout this encyclopedia you'll find plants that are recommended for hedges. These plants are usually dense, carry their foliage to the ground, grow in orderly shapes, and withstand close shearing when necessary.

Types of hedges

Hedges are usually described as formal or informal, depending on how they are pruned.

Formal. Shear formal hedges so that their sides are perfectly flat and their tops are flat or rounded. They should look rigid and smooth. They serve as walls or fences in a landscape.

Informal. Do not shear informal hedges rigidly. Instead, allow the plants to develop much of their natural shape. Prune by selectively cutting back any branches that stick out too far. The overall appearance of an informal hedge is softer or more feathery than that of a formal hedge.

Planting

When you plant, space hedge plants from 1 to 3 feet apart. The exact spacing will depend on how large the plants will grow and, to some extent, on how quickly you want the hedge to fill in.

Early training

After planting, cut back your hedge plants to a height of 6 to 12 inches. This severe pruning forces the plants to branch out close to the ground. Without the lower branches, you'll have a hedge that grows on an unsightly framework of bare trunks.

During the rest of the first growing season, don't prune plants unless a strong stem grows up much higher than the rest. Snip it back even with the rest of the plants.

Pruning guidelines. Though you can train hedges in many different shapes, it's best when trimming to

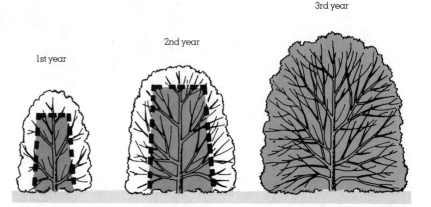

1st year   2nd year   3rd year

Regular pruning makes hedges twiggier, denser each year. Beginning with young plants, prune hedges to the shape you want.

taper the sides so that the bottom is wider than the top. This allows light to reach the entire hedge surface, stimulating growth all over the plant. Lower branches that are shaded will grow more slowly and eventually die, leaving bare spots that won't fill in. As you train a young hedge, be sure to keep the sides tapered.

Second and later years. In the second and succeeding years, continue to pinch, prune, and cut back plants to develop a dense, mature hedge. Cut back any runaway growth (such as leaders) to force branching. Each year cut back new growth by about half to encourage your hedge to branch densely.

You may need to prune extra-vigorous plants more than once a growing season.

Trimming a mature hedge

When a hedge has reached the size you want, give it periodic trimmings to maintain its size. You will need to cut back practically all new growth to near its point of origin, but don't remove new growth entirely. Do this pruning in spring. Prune during the flush of new growth to encourage more branching; prune after the flush of new growth has stopped if you want to prevent the hedge from growing bigger. As you prune, be sure to maintain tapered sides, with the bottom wider than the top.

Some plants need only one shearing per year, but others will send forth new growth after the first trimming. If you live in a cold-winter climate, time your trimming so that new growth will have time to mature before hard frosts come in autumn; this generally means you should plan to do your last trimming in mid to late summer.

Occasionally an old hedge needs to be replaced, if it develops dead areas where no new growth will appear. Dig up plants, replant, and start training hedge again.

Shear or snip hedges as often as needed to maintain their form.

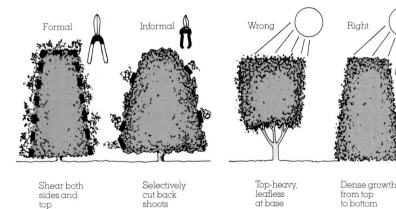

Formal	Informal	Wrong	Right
Shear both sides and top	Selectively cut back shoots	Top-heavy, leafless at base	Dense growth from top to bottom

Formal trimming (left)—use shears to form flat sides, top. Informal trimming —snip back wayward shoots.

Taper hedge sides so that bottom is wider than top (right). Lower leaves, stems die without adequate light.

IXORA coccinea. Jungle geranium, flame-of-the-woods. Evergreen shrub. Prune early spring to mid-autumn.

These brightly flowering shrubs need only occasional pruning. To promote bushiness, pinch tips of new growth when stems are 6 to 8 inches long. Continue pinching with each flush of growth. On old plants, thin out crowded stems in early spring. After that, cut back the remaining stems to about 1 foot if plant is poorly shaped or untidy.

JACARANDA mimosifolia (*J. acutifolia*). Deciduous to semievergreen tree. Prune in spring. In tropical areas, prune in spring to late summer.

Tree forms broad, spreading crown of feathery foliage atop single or multiple trunks. For single-trunked tree, follow directions for early training on page 14. After tree is established, you will have little pruning to do. Cut out any dead or broken limbs. If an awkward limb detracts from tree's beauty, cut it back to a strong lateral. If branches droop from weight of flowers or leaves, you can thin out branches at the ends of main limbs to lighten the load.

To convert a young single-trunked tree to a multitrunked plant, cut off the trunk about 2 feet from the ground. New branches will sprout below the cut. When they do, select 3 or 4 to become main trunks.

A badly frost-damaged young tree may lose most of its trunk, but it should send out several new shoots from the base. To regrow a single-stemmed tree, select the most vigorous shoot as a replacement and remove all others. For multiple trunks, choose several well-placed shoots to retain, and cut off the rest.

JACOBINIA.
See Justicia.

JAPANESE ARALIA.
See Fatsia.

JAPANESE FLOWERING APRICOT.
See Flowering Trees, page 54.

JAPANESE FLOWERING PLUM.
See Flowering Trees, page 54.

JAPANESE PAGODA TREE.
See Sophora.

JAPANESE SNOWDROP TREE.
See Styrax.

JASMINE.
See Jasminum.

JASMINUM. Jasmine. Evergreen and deciduous shrubs and vines. Prune after flowering.

Jasmines range in character from shrubs to shrubby vines (mounding plants with long, flexible stems), to twining vines. All jasmines bloom on year-old wood—that's why you prune after flowering—but blooming time varies among the different kinds.

The pruning method is determined by the plants' purpose—regardless of species, all jasmines used to cover a wall or fence are pruned in the same way; this is true as well for those trained on a trellis and those grown as mounds. Thin out crowded or tangled stems and pinch tips of new growth to encourage branching and compactness. On older plants with overcrowded stems, cut out oldest stems and thin out weak, twiggy, and dead stems. You may even want to cut the plant back to a single character trunk.

To retain a shrub form in plants that grow as shrubby vines, cut back any long stems that stick out of the mound of foliage.

You can train shrubby-vining and vining jasmines to cover banks by cutting out upright stems. Or you can guide them up a wall or over an arch or pergola, and allow flexible stems to cascade.

JERUSALEM SAGE.
See Phlomis.

JERUSALEM THORN.
See Parkinsonia.

JETBEAD.
See Rhodotypos.

JOJOBA.
See Simmondsia.

JUDAS TREE.
See Cercis.

JUGLANS.
See Walnut.

JUJUBE.
See Ziziphus.

JUNGLE GERANIUM.
See Ixora.

JUNIPER.
See Juniperus.

JUNIPER MYRTLE.
See Agonis.

JUNIPERUS. Juniper. Evergreen shrubs and trees. Prune in spring, summer.

Junipers range in size from ground covers to trees and vary in form from symmetrical to twisted or angular. To keep pruning to a minimum, be sure to select the juniper most likely to give you the look you want and one that will fit the space available.

Prune a juniper to correct its shape, to accent its form (usually its irregularity), to limit its size, or to renovate an overgrown plant.

To correct shape. A good time to correct a juniper's shape is before new growth starts in spring, so that new stems will hide pruning scars. But, you won't harm plants if you wait until after new growth stops in summer.

Prune awkward branches that spoil the form you want. With ground cover junipers, cut back a vertical stem to a branch that grows horizontally. Cut it back to the limb from which it originates if this won't leave a gaping bare spot. On angular and upright junipers, cut back irregular stems to another branch that points in the direction you want future growth to go. Don't cut back to a bare stem because it may not grow again.

You can make a scrawny plant more bushy by cutting back new growth about halfway in summer. This will stimulate more branching and denser foliage close to main stems.

To accent irregularity. Pruning to accent irregularity is entirely a matter of personal taste. You can do this in spring or summer. Selectively cut back or remove whole branches to emphasize a twisted or gnarled form, an angular branching pattern, or sprays of foliage held in horizontal planes.

You'll need to look carefully to determine which branches are contributing to the plant's character and which are obscuring it. Remove the obscuring growth. Always cut back to the joint with another branch, limb, or trunk.

To limit size. Prune to limit size only in summer after new growth has stopped. Remove nearly all of the new growth. Cut back each new growth almost to its point of origin, preferably to a small branch that points in the same direction as the

Juniperus. Prune according to shape and use of plants. Cut tall shoots off low-growing kinds, remove wayward shoots on more symmetrical kinds.

branch or shoot you plan to cut out. You can shear junipers that are upright, conical, or regular in form. Selectively cut back all plants with irregular or open growth. Plants that are pruned this way each year will increase in size very slowly.

To renovate. To change an old, overgrown shrub into a multitrunked small tree, remove lower branches and thin out top a bit to reveal the branching and foliage pattern.

JUSTICIA. Evergreen shrubs. Pruning times vary.

Shrimp plant (*J. brandegeana*, formerly *Beloperone guttata*) grows as a 3 to 4-foot mound of flexible stems. Pinch tips of new growth repeatedly to encourage branching. When plant becomes a compact mound, stop pinching and let blooms form at branch tips. When flower bracts turn black, cut back these flowering stems to encourage bushiness.

Brazilian plume flower (*J. carnea*, formerly *Jacobinia carnea*) in some areas will be killed to the ground by hard frost. If roots live, the plant will grow a new top each year. To prune, cut away dead stems in late winter before new growth starts.

Where climate is mild enough for tops to survive, cut back stems heavily (halfway or more) every 2 or 3 years in early spring. Remove old and weak stems. Each year, pinch tips of stems once or twice to increase bushiness and number of flowers.

Gardeners in Southwest desert communities grow 3 drought-tolerant species. Chuparosa (*J. californica*) is an arching shrub with very tiny leaves. Where winter frosts kill

plants to the ground, cut away dead stems before new growth starts. Where plants are not subject to frost damage, occasionally thin out oldest stems as they lose their vigor.

In California, *J. leonardii* is often sold as *Aniscanthus thurberi* (a related plant). In Arizona, Mohintli (*J. spicigera*) often is sold as *Aniscanthus thurberi* or as *J. ghiesbreghtiana*. Pinch the tips of new growth on both *J. leonardii* and *J. spicigera* a few times during the growing season. Also, occasionally thin out oldest stems to make way for strong new growth.

KAFFIR PLUM.
See Harpephyllum.

KALMIA latifolia. Mountain laurel, calico bush. Evergreen shrub. Prune after flowering.

Kalmias seldom need pruning, but they respond well to it when necessary. Cut back to a strong lateral any broken or too-long branch. On an old, leggy plant, you can cut oldest stems—or even the entire plant—to the ground. New growth will rebuild plant in 2 to 3 years.

New growth comes from beneath flower clusters and at tips of stems that have not bloomed. To maintain plant's appearance, break off spent flower clusters carefully so that you won't damage growth buds just beneath. To make a nonflowering shoot form branches, pinch off the new tip growth as it begins.

KANGAROO TREEBINE.
See Cissus.

KATSURA TREE.
See Cerdidiphyllum.

KENTUCKY COFFEE TREE.
See Gymnocladus.

KERRIA japonica. Deciduous shrub. Prune after flowering.

Stems arch gracefully, are covered with golden blossoms. Plant can become a fountain of stems reaching down to the ground.

Blooms appear on stems that grew the previous year. After flowers fade, cut out all stems that have blossomed. Cut most of them to the ground. Cut a few down to the point where new growth is sprouting low on the stem, usually 4 to 5 nodes. Stems that are shortened, rather than cut to the ground, will produce shorter stems that will fill in the lower part of the bush.

KIWI.
See Actinidia.

KOELREUTERIA. Deciduous trees. Prune in winter. In cold-winter areas, prune in late winter. In tropical areas, prune in spring and summer.

Give young trees early training as outlined on page 14. Koelreuterias are also attractive with multiple trunks. Once a tree's growth is established, you'll have little pruning to do.

Cut off any broken or dead branches, thin out any crowded or crossing branches, and remove any sprouts that form along the trunk. Make all cuts back to laterals or to joints on main limbs. Vigorous clumps of new shoots sprout from beneath any cut. Rub off these shoots unless you need to save one for a new branch.

Trees often branch irregularly. To keep tree's shape balanced, cut back any too-vigorous branches.

KOLKWITZIA amabilis. Beauty bush. Prune after flowering or in late winter, before leaves emerge.

Beauty bush is a big shrub with arching branches. With ample room, you need only prune it enough to ensure production of strong new growth each year. Blossoms appear on stems formed in the previous summer; for renewal, cut a few of the oldest stems to the ground just after

(Continued on page 75)

HONEYSUCKLE

To keep in bounds, prune these rambling vines heavily.

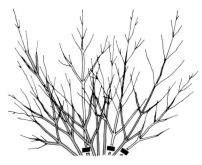

Shrub honeysuckle. Cut back oldest, twiggy stems to the ground every 3 to 4 years.

Honeysuckles *(Lonicera)* are a popular and useful group of plants. They include evergreen and deciduous plants, small to large shrubs, and vines that grow moderately to rampantly. Each type has its own pruning requirements and particular pruning time.

Shrubs. Except for winter honeysuckle (*L. fragrantissima*), these shrubs bloom on new growth. Prune them in winter or early spring before new growth starts. Prune *L. fra-*

grantissima after it flowers.

Limit your annual attention to removing dead and broken limbs. Every 3 to 4 years, cut back some of the oldest stems to the ground to encourage renewal growth.

Most of the small to medium-size shrubs are good for informal hedges or screen plants. You can shear *L. fragrantissima* and *L. nitida* into formal hedges.

Vines. As a rule, prune honeysuckle vines after flowering. Vines generally need more pruning than shrubby honeysuckles; the larger, more vigorous vines require heavy pruning.

Honeysuckle vines climb by twining. Periodically you will need to untangle their stems. Give more training than pruning to the moderate growers: *L. ciliosa, L. heckrottii, L. hildebrandiana,* and *L. sempervirens.* Guide their growth in the direction you want it to go; cut back stems that grow out of bounds; cut out any branches that are headed in the wrong direction or are unwanted. Occasionally thin out older stems to make way for new growth.

Extra-vigorous Japanese honeysuckle *(L. japonica)* and its varieties need considerable care if they are to stay attractive and manageable. Left alone, Japanese honeysuckle becomes a smothering mass that engulfs small plants and invades larger ones, all the time building up a flammable thatch of dead stems beneath the foliage. It's best used as a ground cover or as a mask for chain-link fences.

However you use it, each year prune back this vine heavily—almost to the framework stems—to prevent dead stems from building up, as well as to control its natural aggression. Prune after bloom, or in winter, or both times if necessary. When an old honeysuckle becomes too straggly, you can prune it all the way back to the main stem or even to the ground.

...Kolkwitzia (cont'd.)

flowers fade. Take care not to injure new shoots that should be growing from the ground.

Some gardeners prefer to thin plants in winter when stems are bare. At that time, it is also easy to see and cut out any dead, broken, or weak branches.

KOREAN YEW.
See Cephalotaxus.

LABURNUM. Goldenchain tree. Deciduous trees. Prune after flowering.

Usually trained as a single-trunked tree, *Laburnum* grows into a slender vase shape with main branches forming narrow angles to the trunk. (See page 14 for how to train young trees.) To maintain this shape, pinch back or cut out any secondary branches that grow at wide angles to the main trunk.

Each year after flowering, cut off the developing seed pods. These are poisonous and messy, and they drain the plant's energies. Cut out dead stems and crowding branches in the tree's center. Avoid cutting large limbs, if possible—wounds heal slowly.

You can grow goldenchain trees as large, upright shrubs if you allow stems to grow from ground level and from low on the trunk. To encourage shrubby growth, cut back a young plant's leader so new stems will be forced from the base.

LAGERSTROEMIA indica. Crape myrtle. Deciduous tree, shrub. Prune in winter, early spring.

How large crape myrtles will grow depends both on your climate and on the plant variety. Crape myrtles grow as shrubs or shrubby perennials in cold-winter areas where their roots are hardy. There, branches may freeze back partially or to the ground. Crape myrtles also grow as single-trunked or multitrunked trees in mild-winter areas of the South, Southwest, and West. Nurseries offer some special dwarf shrubby varieties.

Crape myrtles bloom in summer on new branches produced in the spring. To get the best flowers, you will need to prune crape myrtles each year during the dormant season.

Shrubs. In regions where tops are partly damaged by frost, wait until new growth starts, then cut away all dead stems. Where plants freeze to the ground, cut away all dead stems before new growth starts.

For maintenance pruning in the dormant season, cut out weak, twiggy stems and any dead wood. Thin out crossing or crowding branches in plant's center. To promote flowering on dwarf shrub varieties, cut off spent blooms at this time. To promote flowering on large shrubs, cut back last year's new growth by 12 to 18 inches.

Trees. Train young trees according to directions on page 14. Yearly, during your plant's dormant season, remove dead and broken branches and any twiggy, crowding, or crossing stems in center of tree's crown. Cut back any too-long branch to a good lateral. To promote better flowering, cut back last year's new growth by 12 to 18 inches. Remove whole branches if necessary to maintain symmetry.

Lagerstroemia. Each year after flowering, cut 12 to 18 inches off tips of branches that bloomed.

LANTANA. Evergreen shrubs and vining shrub (deciduous in colder climates). Prune in spring.

Lantanas will take almost any amount of pruning and make a vigorous comeback, sprouting from old as well as young wood. Without pruning, the shrubby varieties become ungainly or ratty-looking, while some ground cover ones build up a thatch of dead stems.

After any danger of frost is past, cut back shrubby lantanas as much as you want to control size and shape. Cut back plants in the ground lightly to severely, according to their needs. Cut back plants in containers to a small framework of very short branches (the same procedure as is

recommended for fuchsias in hanging baskets; see page 62). If there are only a few plants to care for, pinch tips of new growth frequently during the growing season to promote branching and compactness. Cut out all broken, dead, weak, and crowding stems.

LAPAGERIA rosea. Chilean bellflower. Evergreen vine. Prune in early spring.

Slender stems climb by twining. Each spring, or whenever necessary, untangle newest stems and tie them where you want them to grow. Plants need little routine pruning. In early spring, cut out any weak, straggly stems and any dead wood.

LARCH.
See Larix.

LARIX. Larch. Deciduous coniferous tree. Prune in winter.

Normally these trees grow tall and straight, with a dominant central leader and branches radiating out regularly from the trunk. They need no routine pruning. Cut out any broken branches and gradually remove lower limbs if you want a tree you can walk under. If a tree forms a secondary leader parallel to the main trunk, cut it off at its point of origin.

LAUREL.
See Laurus.

LAURUS nobilis. Sweet bay, Grecian laurel. Evergreen tree or shrub. Prune in spring, summer.

Dense, compact, and neat—these words sum up the laurel's growth pattern. Without pruning, it grows as a broad-based cone of foliage. Eventually it becomes a tree, usually with multiple trunks. Plants will take heavy pruning and shearing into hedges and geometric shapes, such as globes, cones, or lollipop trees. This is one of the classic topiary plants (see page 106).

For formal uses, shear plants as needed during the growing season. A good rule is to prune whenever new growth reaches about 3 inches long. If you want plants to take their natural form, simply cut back any awkward branches to strong laterals.

LAURUSTINUS.
See Viburnum.

LAVANDULA. Lavender. Evergreen shrubs or subshrubs. Prune after flowering in mild-winter regions; prune in early spring in cold-winter regions.

Unpruned lavenders in time become untidy, floppy, or sparse. Cut back plants each year to keep them compact and attractive.

To ensure that plants are dense and productive, cut off all spent flowering stems and at least an inch of leafy stem below. Cut back the larger lavenders more than the dwarf varieties. You can selectively cut back each stem, or you can shear the plants. English lavender (Lavandula angustifolia) will make a rounded hedge. Old, neglected, overgrown plants can't be restored by severe pruning. Replace them with young plants instead.

LAVENDER.
See Lavandula.

LAVENDER COTTON.
See Santolina.

LAVENDER STARFLOWER.
See Grewia.

LEAD PLANT.
See Amorpha.

LEMON.
See Citrus, page 38.

LEMON VERBENA.
See Aloysia.

LEPTOSPERMUM. Tea tree. Evergreen shrubs or small trees. Prune after flowering.

The most common shrubs are varieties of New Zealand tea tree (Leptospermum scoparium). They grow to various sizes and naturally form attractive plants that seldom need pruning. You can use them as specimen plants or as informal hedges. If needed, cut back an awkward branch to a joint with another branch or to a leaf. Don't cut back into bare wood; new growth is unlikely to sprout. With light shearing you can train these plants as formal hedges.

Australian tea tree (L. laevigatum) becomes a large shrub or small tree. Individual plants often have picturesque, twisting branches with canopies of fine-textured leaves. Prune to accent the individual form. Cut back or remove branches only to guide the plant to grow in the shape you want.

To train as a small tree, select a stem for the main trunk and follow the guidelines on page 14. Set out plants close together to develop a windbreak, thick screen, or clipped hedge. Prune as described for New Zealand tea tree.

If old shrubs get too overgrown and out-of-hand, you can prune them up into graceful trees by cutting out the lower side branches to reveal interesting, irregularly shaped trunks.

Leptospermum. Convert large shrub to small tree by removing smaller lower limbs to reveal trunk.

LEUCOPHYLLUM frutescens (L. texanum). Texas ranger. Evergreen shrub. Prune in winter.

This silvery shrub needs little regular pruning. If necessary, cut back too-long branches to good laterals. Occasionally thin out weak stems. Cut out any dead and broken branches. To renew an old, straggly plant, cut it back to within a few inches of the ground.

Planted close together, these shrubs will serve as a formal or informal hedge.

LEUCOTHOE. Evergreen and deciduous shrubs. Prune in winter.

Plants are clump-forming shrubs with many branching stems. Pinch back new stems to encourage branching and compactness.

Do major pruning in winter (for deciduous leucothoes) or late winter (for deciduous leucothoes) or late winter after danger of heaviest frosts has passed (for evergreen leucothoes). In winter, prune stems that grow too tall or straggly, cutting them back to a good side branch or prominent bud. Occasionally cut out oldest stems to make way for strong new growth. To renew an old, straggly, unattractive plant, cut it to the ground. New stems will spring up.

Prune off old flower heads from Sierra laurel (Leucothoe davisiae); plants may bloom again in autumn.

LIGUSTRUM. Privet. Evergreen and deciduous shrubs and small trees. Prune from late winter through summer.

Privets are classic hedge plants. Their growth is dense and compact, and they can withstand frequent shearing. You can also use privets for unclipped hedges, screens, or barriers, as specimen shrubs, and as trees.

To develop and maintain a privet hedge, refer to the information on page 70. As a general rule, prune privets heavily in winter or early spring. Shear plants as often as needed in summer. To keep informal hedges, screens, or barrier plantings neat, cut back any wayward branches to good side branches.

For specimen shrubs, prune as much or as little as is necessary to maintain the shape you want. Pinch back new stems to encourage bushiness. Cut back or thin out branches that detract from the shape you want to develop, pruning selectively to side branches or to main limbs.

You can train glossy privet (Ligustrum lucidum) as a large shrub or as a single-trunked or multitrunked tree. See page 14 for tree training guidelines.

LILLY-PILLY TREE.
See Acmena.

LILY-OF-THE-VALLEY SHRUB.
See Pieris.

LILY-OF-THE-VALLEY TREE.
See Clethra, Crinodendron.

LIME.
See Citrus, page 38.

LINDEN.
See Tilia.

LINOSPADIX.
See Palm.

LIQUIDAMBAR. Sweet gum. Deciduous trees. <u>Prune in winter or summer.</u>

American sweet gum (*Liquidambar styraciflua*) is in youth a tall, narrow tree. It broadens with age. Chinese sweet gum (*L. formosana*) is more irregular in shape. Oriental sweet gum (*L. orientalis*) is shorter with a broader, rounded crown. All need training when young (see page 14). Give special attention to developing a strong central leader. If a young tree forms a forked leader, cut off weaker or more off-center fork.

To develop a strong central leader, don't cut off any side branches for the first 3 to 4 years of the tree's life. Instead, pinch back (during dormant season) side branches to divert energy to the top of the tree. After the fourth year, cut off as many lower branches as is necessary to make the tree easy to walk under. Note: Trees also look beautiful with branches all the way to the ground.

You may need to thin a young tree's crown to encourage it to develop a well-spaced framework of branches. In dormant season, cut back to major limbs or to trunk.

Prune a mature tree only to remove stubs of broken limbs.

Liquidambar. Leave all side branches on young tree to strengthen trunk. Head them back to direct growth upward.

LIRIODENDRON tulipifera. Tulip tree. Deciduous tree. <u>Prune in early summer.</u>

Tulip trees naturally grow tall and straight. Give young trees early training as outlined on page 14. Remove any upright stems that compete with the central leader. Trees need no routine pruning after this time.

Occasionally, a branch may grow too long. Pinch it back (if it is still soft-wooded) or cut it back to a lateral to prevent the need for later pruning. Cuts heal slowly, so avoid leaving large cut surfaces whenever possible.

Because wood is brittle, you may sometimes need to cut off broken limbs or branches. Make all cuts to a lateral or to a joint with another limb or trunk.

LITCHI chinensis. Litchi, litchi nut. Evergreen tree. <u>Prune in summer; in tropical areas, prune in summer to mid-autumn.</u>

Tree is rounded and fairly slow-growing, and it spreads as wide as tall. Grow it as a single-trunked tree (see guidelines on page 14) or with several trunks.

Growth is dense. You may want to thin out weak, crossing, and crowded branches in tree's center to open up the canopy. Make all cuts back to laterals or joints with other limbs. Fruit is carried at ends of new growth. Traditionally, you prune this tree as you gather its fruit by cutting off 10 to 12-inch branch tips with fruit attached.

LITHOCARPUS densiflorus. Tanbark oak. Evergreen tree. <u>Prune in spring.</u>

Tanbark oak naturally grows multiple trunks. You can train young trees to grow a single trunk by following guidelines on page 14. Either let branches grow all the way to the ground or remove lower limbs so you can walk under the tree.

Occasionally, with a mature tree you may need to cut out a dead or broken branch or cut back an awkwardly placed limb. Otherwise, tree needs no routine pruning.

LIVISTONA.
See Palm.

LOCUST.
See Robinia.

LOQUAT.
See Eriobotrya.

LOROPETALUM chinense. Evergreen shrub. <u>Prune after spring bloom.</u>

This shrub naturally grows in a neat and orderly fashion with tiered,

arching, or drooping branches. Train a young plant in a pot, drape it over a wall, or grow it against a wall or fence. Prune a mature plant only to remove dead and broken limbs.

LYONOTHAMNUS floribundus. Catalina ironwood. Evergreen tree. <u>Prune in winter.</u>

To establish a good trunk, give young trees the training outlined on page 14. Mature trees need only occasional pruning to control shape. Cut back any excessively long branches to good laterals. Remove sprouts from the base if they occur. Spent flower clusters at branch ends are unsightly—cut them off for best appearance.

LYSILOMA thornberi. Feather bush. Evergreen to deciduous shrub or small tree. <u>Prune in spring.</u>

Feather bush is a multistemmed shrub with filmy foliage. You can train it to a single trunk by following the guidelines on page 14. Prune to remove frost-damaged, dead, and broken branches. To accentuate plant's filminess, thin crowded and weak branches in its center. You can completely remove some branches to further enhance the see-through quality.

MACADAMIA. Macadamia nut, Queensland nut. Evergreen tree. <u>Prune in spring, summer.</u>

Train young trees to develop a central leader (see guidelines on page 14). Prune so that permanent scaffold branches are spaced about 6 inches apart and with adjacent branches not above each other. After a basic shape is established, trees need little routine pruning. Cut back any wayward limbs to good laterals within the crown. Cut back broken branches to laterals, and remove any dead wood.

MACFADYENA unguis-cati (*Doxantha unguis-cati, Bignonia tweediana*). Cat's claw, yellow trumpet vine. Partly to completely deciduous vine. <u>Prune after flowering.</u>

This rampant-growing vine climbs by hooked, clawlike tendrils. It tends to produce leaves and flowers at ends of stems and to have sparse foliage at the base. After bloom, cut out weak and oldest stems. Cut back some stems nearly to the ground to stimulate leafy growth low on the plant. Cut back or remove straggly and wayward stems. During the growing season, pinch new shoots to control length and promote branching.

MACLURA pomifera. Osage orange. Deciduous tree. Prune in winter.

Left alone, osage orange is a fast-growing, spreading, open tree that can reach 60 feet tall. Branches are formidably thorny. You can grow it as a single-trunked shade tree, following guidelines on page 14.

The tree is also popular as a large hedge, screen, or barrier plant. For these uses, leave all lower branches uncut and let plants grow together. If you start with single-stemmed plants, cut them back nearly to the ground to encourage low branching. Cut back branches as much as necessary (cut to laterals) to maintain the desired height and spread. You can keep it as low as 6 to 10 feet or let it grow higher.

MADRONA, MADRONE.
See Arbutus.

MAGIC FLOWER.
See Cantua.

MAGNOLIA. Deciduous and evergreen trees and shrubs. Prune in summer.

Magnolias usually require little pruning. If training is necessary, you can prune them to conform to a desired shape. But be careful: cuts are slow to heal, and large wounds invite disease. Make all cuts back to laterals or main branches. Never leave stubs. Be sure to remove any dead, diseased, and storm-damaged wood.

The tree magnolias need early training as outlined on page 14. Though Southern magnolia or bull bay (Magnolia grandiflora) is usually grown as a tree, you can train it as an espalier; as such, it will grow in climates where it would not survive if planted in the open.

Prune shrub and shrub-tree magnolias only enough to encourage development of a good branch framework. Remove interfering branches, and thin out crowded and weak branches from the plant's center. Remove sucker growth, especially from below the graft union of a grafted plant. Prune any winter-damaged wood, cutting it back to healthy tissue.

The best pruning for magnolias is preventive. If you see new growth (especially suckers) showing where you don't want it, cut it off before it becomes hardened. Pinch back tips of stems that grow too long.

MAHOBERBERIS. Evergreen shrubs. Prune after flowering.

Growth is upright and usually dense. If a plant looks leggy or unbalanced, cut back straggly branches to good laterals. You can occasionally cut an old stem to the ground if plenty of newer growth is available to replace it.

MAHONIA. Evergreen shrubs. Prune after flowering.

All mahonias are shrubby, but individual species vary considerably. Some make good sculptural accent plants, others become bulky bushes, and still others grow as ground covers. Each type has different pruning requirements.

Accent plants. Mahonia bealei, M. fortunei, M. lomariifolia. These plants consist of vertical stems, unbranched or sparsely branched, with tufts of large leaves at tips of branches. The beauty of these plants is in their sparse, linear shape; it's not good to try to prune them to become low and dense. If an old stem grows too tall for its space, cut it to the ground. New stems will sprout from the base.

You can increase branching a little on M. lomariifolia by cutting back stems at varying heights. New branches will grow from close beneath the cut. On the other hand, don't cut back the leader if you want a tall, dramatic plant.

Shrub types. M. aquifolium, M. fremontii, M. 'Golden Abundance', M. nevinii, M. pinnata. Prune newly planted shrubs to promote the growth of low branches and new shoots from the base. Plants are generally compact and branching, but will occasionally become leggy and sparse. You can cut back any wayward branches severely. New growth will sprout from beneath the cut. Any long, unbranched shoots that protrude beyond the outline you want can be cut back to the ground. To induce more branching, pinch back new growth. When plants become too big and bulky, cut the oldest woody stems to the ground.

Ground covers. M. aquifolium 'Compacta', M. nervosa, M. repens. These mahonias spread by underground stems to form low colonies of upright, somewhat branched stems. Prune only to trim stems that grow above the level of foliage you want to maintain. (A good time to cut back these few tall stems is during winter, when you can use foliage for indoor decorations.)

Mahonia shrub. To renew plant, cut back oldest, woody stems to ground. Pinch new stems for branching.

MAIDENHAIR TREE.
See Ginkgo.

MALUS. Crabapple. Deciduous trees, a few shrubs. Prune in winter or after flowering.

A crabapple's growth is dense and twiggy. Young trees need early training as described on page 14. Be especially careful to remove awkward or crossing branches. Once you've succeeded in establishing the tree's form, annual pruning will consist mostly of thinning. Cut out dead wood and remove weak and crowding branches in the tree's center. Your goal is to open up the crown and emphasize the major limbs.

The time of year you prune will affect the way a crabapple grows. If you prune in winter, it's easy to see what you're doing. But winter pruning is likely to stimulate strong spring

(Continued on page 80)

LILAC

To most gardeners "lilac" means one plant: Common lilac *(Syringa vulgaris)*. In midspring it produces showy clusters of intensely fragrant flowers. But many other lilacs exist as well. Most are deciduous shrubs. *Prune lilacs after flowering.*

The pruning directions that follow are for common lilacs, their hybrids, and other similar shrubby lilacs, such as *S. prestoniae* and *S. swegiflexa.*

Young plants. Young plants need no pruning for several years while they are becoming established. Just pinch any stems that grow too long.

When plants are old enough to bloom, remove their spent flower spikes just above the first leaves beneath the bloom clusters. The growth buds there will provide the next year's blossoms. On young flowering plants, cut back any wayward or crossing stems to laterals or to joints with other branches. To increase the bushiness of young plants, look for shoots that did not flower. You can cut back any shoots that have a single terminal bud to encourage branching. (Shoots with two terminal buds are likely to produce flowers.)

Older plants. As plants grow older, their main stems become thicker and woodier. They produce new growth progressively higher on increasingly bare limbs. You can prune these plants up into small trees. On the other hand, to keep plants full of foliage, prune them for continual rejuvenation. Each year cut back several of the oldest stems to the ground. Lilacs produce enough basal shoots to easily replace old stems you cut out. Thin out excess basal shoots, removing weak and crowding stems.

To rejuvenate an old, overgrown, woody lilac, cut out one-third of the old wood each spring for 3 years. When you do this, the shrub will always produce some spring

Careful annual snipping will keep lilac flowering.

flowers, and after 3 years, you will essentially have a new plant.

Other lilacs. Apply these same general pruning directions to other shrubby lilacs: Chinese lilac *(S. chinensis)*, Hungarian lilac *(S. josikaea)*, Persian lilac *(S. persica)*, *S. laciniata*, *S. villosa.* These lilacs usually need less pruning.

Japanese tree lilac *(S. reticulata,* also known as *S. japonica* or *S. amurensis japonica)* grows differently from other lilacs. If you let it branch from low on the plant and from the ground, it makes a large shrub that's good for windbreak and screen plantings. When you train it as a single-trunked tree (see guidelines on page 14), it can reach 30 feet tall, with handsome, cherrylike bark. For a tree or shrub, annually thin oldest, weak wood and remove dead and broken branches.

Lilac. To keep leafy growth from top to bottom give old plants renewal pruning. Cut oldest stems to the ground: new stems will replace them.

growth that may need pruning out the next year. Summer pruning stimulates less new growth on the tree, but is more difficult for the pruner.

Save yourself pruning work by pinching, breaking, or rubbing out any new growth that appears in unwanted places during the growing season.

You can choose from among many crabapple varieties. Shapes vary from narrow and upright, to broad and spreading, to weeping. Prune according to the variety's natural shape. Don't try to make a narrow-upright tree out of one that is naturally spreading.

Shrubby crabapples, such as *M. sargentii* are also dense and branching. Several main stems rise from the ground or close to it and carry branches and foliage to ground level. Give them the same thinning as described above.

Prune crabapples grown for jelly as you prune apples (see page 22).

Malus. Crabapples are vigorous, densely branched. Each year thin out weak, crowding branches.

MALVAVISCUS arboreus. Turk's cap. Evergreen shrub. <u>Prune in spring, summer, autumn.</u>

Turk's cap is a dense, sprawling shrub. Popular as a clipped hedge (see page 70 for hedge training), it needs heavy trimming to keep growth in check.

Use Turk's cap as an informal hedge or as a specimen shrub. Prune as needed to keep growth orderly. On a congested shrub, thin out weak,

twiggy stems and cut out oldest branches if they stop producing vigorous new growth.

You can also train Turk's cap as an informal espalier (see page 50), an ideal way to show off the plant's attractive blossoms.

MANDEVILLA. Evergreen and deciduous vines. <u>Prune in winter; in tropical areas, also in spring, summer.</u>

Tangling is the chief reason you'll need to prune Chilean jasmine (*Mandevilla laxa*). Thin out tangled stems severely during the plant's leafless period. You can cut a neglected or extremely snarled vine to the ground. New stems will grow in spring and bloom in the same year.

Tangling is less likely with evergreen *M.* 'Alice du Pont'. To increase bushiness, pinch tips of new stems on young plants; pinch tips of new growth on older vines if necessary.

MANGIFERA indica. Mango. Evergreen tree. <u>Prune after fruit is harvested.</u>

With adequate early training (see page 14), mangos become large, attractive shade trees. No routine pruning is necessary. Cut out any dead branches and cut back broken limbs to sturdy laterals.

MANGO.
See Mangifera.

MANZANITA.
See Arctostaphylos.

MANZANOTE.
See Olmediella.

MAPLE.
See Acer.

MAYTEN TREE.
See Maytenus.

MAYTENUS boaria. Mayten tree. Evergreen tree. <u>Prune in spring.</u>

Because young mayten trees often grow many side branches, give them early training if you want a single-trunked tree (see page 14). If you want a multitrunked tree, let a few of the lowest branches grow, being sure to leave any shoots that sprout from ground level.

After tree form is established, you'll have little pruning to do. You can thin out crowded, weak, dead,

or broken branches, as well as any growing toward the tree's center on overly dense crowns. In order to walk or mow the lawn under the tree, you may need to remove low-hanging branches from time to time. Cut them back to sturdy laterals. Cut back any big arching branches to laterals so that they don't look chopped.

MELALEUCA. Bottlebrush. Evergreen trees and shrubs. <u>Prune any time.</u>

Various melaleucas can be grown as single-trunked or multi-trunked trees, large dense or open shrubs, irregular character plants, informal screening plants, and clipped hedges. Except for clipping hedges, do all pruning by cutting back stems to side branches. Never cut back to bare wood; stems may not send out new growth.

Prune or thin melaleucas only to accent the individual plant's shape, or to transform an overgrown shrub into a small tree. You can't rejuvenate these plants by cutting back heavily to stimulate renewal growth.

Dotted melaleuca (*Melaleuca hypericifolia*) is a shrub that can also be used as a hedge (see page 70 for basic hedge training information). It will bloom more heavily if you clip it informally rather than shear it.

The melaleucas that grow as shrubs or small trees include drooping melaleuca (*M. armillaris*), heath melaleuca (*M. ericifolia*), lilac melaleuca (*M. decussata*), and *M. elliptica*. They all make good specimen shrubs. To make plants treelike, thin out heavy growth and trim the plants to show off interesting bark and branching patterns. Drooping melaleuca is useful as a hedge or barrier screen.

The following are trees: cajeput tree (*M. quinquenervia*, usually sold as *M. leucadendron*), flaxleaf paperbark (*M. linariifolia*), *M. styphelioides*, and pink melaleuca (*M. nesophila*). (They are also known as paperbarks because their layered paperlike bark comes off easily.) Give young plants early training as outlined on page 14 for single-trunked trees. *M. styphelioides* looks best when trained to grow several trunks. You can use pink melaleuca as a clipped hedge or a large screen plant. Without tree training, it will form a sprawling character plant.

MELIA azedarach. Chinaberry. Deciduous tree. Prune in late winter.

Young chinaberry trees may need early training (see page 14). Once the tree has reached the height you want, you can shorten branches to encourage branching if necessary.

On mature trees, the only regular pruning you'll need to do is repair work—chinaberry wood is brittle and subject to damage in storms. Cut back all broken branches to sound laterals or to the trunk.

MELIANTHUS major. Honey bush. Evergreen shrub. Prune in early spring.

When left alone, honey bush becomes an irregular, sprawling, unkempt mass of big leaves and snaky stems. Pruning to guide this shrub's random growth will increase its attractiveness.

To develop a spreading plant, prune the bush to branch low. When stems start growing upright, cut some or all of them to within a foot of the ground. When new growth surges forth, pinch tips of stems that threaten to grow too long.

For a tall plant, select several stems that are vigorous and well spaced. Cut excess stems to the ground, then stake remaining stems upright. Pinch growing tips only where you want more branching.

To restore an overgrown, shabby plant, cut it back to within 1 to 2 feet of the ground. When strong new growth appears, train as you prefer.

MESCAL BEAN.
See Sophora.

MESQUITE.
See Prosopis.

METASEQUOIA glyptostroboides. Dawn redwood. Deciduous conifer. Prune in late winter, early spring.

Normally these trees grow tall and straight naturally. Occasionally, a limb may grow too long. Cut it back to a pair of laterals. Trees are handsome with branches all the way to the ground, but if you want a tree to walk under, gradually remove lower limbs as the tree grows taller. On trees that are planted together in groves, lower limbs will eventually be shaded out by higher ones. When lower limbs stop growing vigorously and decline, cut them off.

METROSIDEROS. Evergreen trees or large shrubs. Prune in late spring.

Two common kinds of *Metrosideros* are trees: New Zealand Christmas tree or Pohutukawa (*Metrosideros excelsus*, sometimes sold as *M. tomentosus*), and North Island rata (*M. robustus*). Slow-growing Southern rata (*M. umbellatus*, sometimes sold as *M. lucidus*), takes many years to reach tree size. Treat it as a large shrub. *M. kermadecensis* (*M. villosus*) is a shrub that becomes a tree with a more columnar shape than *M. excelsus*.

The two trees need careful early training (see page 14) to develop well. These plants usually branch heavily from the ground up. Refer to *Feijoa sellowiana* on page 59 for instructions on training as either single-trunked or multi-trunked trees. To keep plants as 6 to 10-foot-high shrubs or windbreak plants, cut back upright growth each year.

On shrubby *M. kermadecensis* and slow-growing *M. umbellatus* you will need to periodically thin out weak, twiggy, and dead branches in the plant's center. To control height, spread, or wayward branches, cut back branches to laterals or remove branches entirely at joints with other limbs.

MEXICAN FAN PALM.
See Palm.

MEXICAN ORANGE.
See Choisya.

MEXICAN PALO VERDE.
See Parkinsonia.

MICHELIA. Evergreen trees or shrubs. Prune in spring.

Banana shrub (*Michelia figo*, sometimes sold as *M. fuscata*) is a slow-growing, big, dense shrub. You can allow it to grow naturally (cut back any wayward growth to laterals), shear it as a large hedge, or train and prune it as an espalier (see page 50 for general espalier instructions).

M. doltsopa is a large shrublike plant that eventually becomes a tree. Its shape varies from bushy to narrow and upright. You can easily train the upright growers into single-trunked trees (see page 14). You can prune shrubbier plants the same way as *M. figo* (above), or train them to become multitrunked trees by allowing several strong stems to form the main framework. As plants grow, gradually remove lower branches to reveal trunks.

MIMOSA.
See Albizia.

MIMULUS (*Diplacus*). Monkey flower. Shrubs and shrubby perennials. Prune in early spring through summer.

Growth varies from upright to sprawling, but all kinds become rangy without pruning. Pinch new growth several times to induce branching. If growth gets out of hand, cut back as much as you like to force new branches to grow from a compact framework. Do any major cutting back before growth starts. To encourage more flowering, cut back again lightly after first flush of bloom is finished.

MIRROR PLANT.
See Coprosma.

MONKEY FLOWER.
See Mimulus.

MONKEY HAND TREE.
See Chiranthodendron.

MONKEY PUZZLE TREE.
See Araucaria.

MORAINE LOCUST.
See Gleditsia.

MORUS. Mulberry. Deciduous trees. Prune in winter, early spring.

The commonly planted mulberries, fruitless forms of *Morus alba*, are exceptionally fast-growing shade trees. Young trees need the early training outlined on page 14. Stake them securely. The crown develops so quickly that it may be snapped from the slender trunk by high winds. During the tree's first few years its branches may grow very long and become drooping. Shorten these limbs by cutting each back into the canopy to an upward-facing branch or bud.

Each year at pruning time, thin out excess growth in the tree's crown: remove weak branches, crowded limbs, and any dead wood. Shorten all overly long branches. Make all cuts back to laterals or joints with other limbs or to the trunk. Be especially careful not to leave stubs; they

(Continued on page 83)

MOCK ORANGE

Cut back old stems to keep orange-fragrant flowers coming.

Mock oranges *(Philadelphus,* often misnamed "syringa") are popular shrubs, valued for their vigorous growth and for their bountiful late spring flower display. Several common species and many named hybrids exist. Most kinds of mock orange are deciduous shrubs (one is evergreen) with fountainlike growth. Their size varies from 3 to 10 feet or more. *Prune them after flowering.*

All mock oranges bloom on stems that developed the previous year. Prune to remove spent flowering wood and to encourage the growth of new stems to bear the next season's flowers.

Plants begin to send out many new shoots after the blooming period. Some stems come from the ground; others sprout from low on stems that have flowered. Young plants and lower-growing varieties usually need to keep most or all of this new growth. Prune stems that have flowered, cutting them back to a pair of vigorous new shoots. Thin out new shoots only if some are growing too close together.

In time, you will have to remove some of the oldest stems to give any new stems room to grow and to keep plants attractive. Do this more often for the extra-vigorous, tall-growing kinds of mock orange than for the smaller kinds. Cut to the ground the oldest canes that are no longer producing strong new shoots. You may not need to prune plants every year, but make an annual check to determine if you need to do any thinning.

Mock oranges look best if they have enough space to develop to full size naturally. Plants that are cut back to fit a limited space look lumpy and graceless.

Evergreen mock orange *(P. mexicanus)* produces such long, supple stems that it does best as a ground or bank cover. With support, it grows as a vine to 20 feet. Cut out flowering stems and the oldest, unproductive canes, just as you would with the deciduous shrubs.

Cut back young, vigorous stems to strong new side shoots during or after flowering.

Renew established plant some each year by cutting oldest, played-out stems to ground.

...Morus (cont'd.)

are likely to die back and rot.

You can also train mulberries as multitrunked trees. Start with a nursery plant that already has several trunks. Or plant a single-trunked small tree, let it grow for a year, and then cut it to the ground in winter. In spring, select several vigorous new shoots to become the future trunks. Then prune and train as you would single-trunked trees.

Several weeping forms of *M. alba* are sold, both fruiting and fruitless. These require staking as young trees but need almost no pruning then or in later years. From time to time, thin out crowding branches.

MOUNTAIN ASH.
See Sorbus.

MOUNTAIN LAUREL.
See Kalmia.

MOUNTAIN MAHOGANY.
See Cercocarpus.

MUEHLENBECKIA. Wire vine. Evergreen vines. Prune whenever needed.

Mattress vine (*Muehlenbeckia complexa*) grows as a tangled mass of wiry stems and tiny leaves. It will climb as high as 30 feet or sprawl on the ground or over rocks, stumps, or debris piles. If it strays out of bounds, shear it or cut it back as much as you like; it will regrow vigorously.

Creeping wire vine (*M. axillaris*, sometimes sold as *M. nana*) is a less aggressive plant than mattress vine. It spreads by underground runners but grows only a few inches high, occasionally forming mounds up to a foot tall. Shear or cut it back as needed for uniformity. Limit spread by digging out unwanted new stems.

MULBERRY.
See Morus.

MURRAYA paniculata (*M. exotica*). Orange jessamine. Evergreen shrub. Prune in early spring; in tropical areas, also in summer.

In its natural state, orange jessamine grows as an open shrub with pendulous branches 6 to 15 feet high and wide. If you choose to allow it to grow naturally, shorten any wayward branches to keep the plant's outline somewhat regular.

You can train orange jessamine into a shrub-tree. Select several

strong, fairly upright limbs for trunks and gradually prune away lower branches. Thin out crowding growth in the plant's center and cut any especially spreading branches back to laterals.

You can also train it as a hedge (see general directions on page 70), though the so-called "dwarf" variety (sold as *Murraya exotica*) might be a better choice. It grows more slowly, is more compact and upright, and reaches a size of only about 6 feet tall and 4 feet wide.

MYOPORUM. Evergreen shrubs and small trees. Prune in spring.

Myoporums range from several-inch-tall ground covers to 30-foot trees. Despite size differences, these plants are all basically shrubby.

Tree-size myoporums—*Myoporum insulare*, *M. laetum*, and *M. l.* 'Carsonii'—carry branches to the ground and grow as dense, billowy clumps. To train plants as valuable seaside windbreaks, encourage branching to the ground. To maintain windbreak plantings, just prune off wayward growth. Cut back too-long branches to good laterals. Because topheavy plants can be blown over, periodically thin out stems to allow some wind to pass through.

You can train tree-size myoporums as attractive multitrunked trees. Select several well-placed upright limbs for trunks, cut any competing stems to the ground, and cut off lower limbs to desired height.

Ground cover shrubs *M. debile*

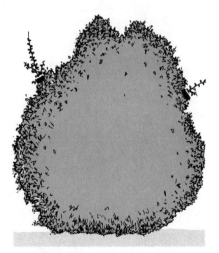

Myoporum. Cut back to sturdy laterals any vigorous stems that spoil plant's outline.

and *M. parvifolium* need no routine pruning. If some stems grow upright, cut them back to joints with horizontal stems.

MYRICA. Evergreen and deciduous shrubs. Prune in late winter, early spring.

The common myricas include bayberry (*Myrica pensylvanica*, sometimes sold as *M. caroliniensis*), a deciduous shrub, and Pacific wax myrtle (*M. californica*) and wax myrtle (*M. cerifera*), two evergreen shrubs that can also be trained as small trees. All grow as multistemmed plants, generally neat and compact. None need routine pruning, but they will look better with occasional attention.

You can let Pacific wax myrtle and wax myrtle grow naturally as big shrubs. To create attractive small trees, thin out the stems at ground level, leaving several for permanent trunks. Cut off lower branches and thin out crowding stems in the crown. You can also use these two wax myrtles as screening plants or as hedges. Prune them either informally or formally (see page 70 for hedge information).

To prune bayberry, thin out excess and old stems from time to time, remove any dead wood, and dig out any unwanted root sprouts (these enlarge the clump's spread). Use bayberry, too, as a formal or informal hedge that's smaller than the other two common myricas.

MYRSINE africana. African boxwood. Evergreen shrub. Prune whenever necessary.

From a rather floppy young plant, *Myrsine* matures into a neat, orderly, very dense shrub. A good specimen shrub for a garden or a container, it also makes a first-rate boxwoodlike hedge (for hedge pruning, see general guidelines on page 70). If you don't want to shear the shrub, pinch or selectively cut back any growth that protrudes beyond its basic shape.

MYRTLE.
See Myrtus.

MYRTUS communis. Myrtle. Evergreen shrubs. Prune whenever necessary.

True myrtle is a rounded, dense, bulky but fine-textured shrub that grows 5 to 15 feet tall with a greater spread. You can grow it as a specimen shrub (needs no pruning), as a character shrub or shrub-tree (thin selectively to reveal basic limb structure), or as an informal hedge or screen. Myrtle also withstands the shearing needed for topiary work (see page 106).

To reveal the plant's branching pattern, cut out unwanted small branches at its base, and remove lower branches on major limbs. To open the foliage on top of the main stems, selectively remove branches at joints with other branches or with the main trunks. Instead of a solid foliage canopy, the plant will exhibit clumps of leaves and open spaces.

Use dwarf varieties as border plants (these require no pruning), or grow them sheared formally or pruned informally as low hedges.

NANDINA domestica. Heavenly bamboo, sacred bamboo. Evergreen and semideciduous shrub. Prune during winter or early spring; in tropical areas, also in summer.

Each plant forms a clump of vertical stems with few or no branches. Foliage lasts for several years. If new stems keep forming at the base, plants remain leafy to the ground. In time, unpruned clumps usually become topheavy and bare at the base. Prune established plants each year to avoid this. Choose one or more of the oldest stems that are mostly bare except for some foliage near the top, and cut them to the ground. This will encourage new stems to grow from the base.

To fill in plant bases with foliage, you can also cut back a few of the oldest stems to 6 to 12 inches from the ground. New stems will sprout from these stubs.

Rejuvenate plants that are too tall and straggly in two stages. First, cut half the stems to 6 to 12 inches above the ground. After these stubs have sent out good new growth, cut back the remaining stems to the same height.

Dwarf nandinas need little pruning. Just cut back unsightly or wayward stems.

NATAL PLUM.
See Carissa.

NECTARINE.
See Peach and Nectarine, page 87.

NEOPANAX arboreus (*Nothopanax arboreum*). **Evergreen tree. Prune in spring.**

Restrict this tree to a single stem and it will grow as a small tree with an open crown of large, tropical-looking leaves. Let it develop several stems from the base and it will become a shorter, multitrunked shrub-tree. No pruning is needed unless a branch grows where you don't want it. If this happens, cut undesirable growth back to a joint with another branch.

NERIUM oleander. Oleander. Evergreen shrub. Prune in early spring, summer.

Oleander grows naturally as a bulky shrub with many stems. You can let it grow unpruned for several years. Eventually you may need to prune it to direct its shape or size or to renew the plant.

To limit size and help rejuvenate plants, cut oldest stems to the ground. If necessary to limit height, cut back remaining stems. To restore basal growth, cut back outer stems hard to stimulate new growth low on the plant. During the growing season, pinch stem tips to encourage branching.

Cut a leggy and unattractive old shrub to within a few inches of the ground. Vigorous new growth should spring up to form a new plant.

Oleanders make handsome trees, either with a single trunk or with multiple trunks. To train as a single-trunked tree, select a young plant with one vertical stem, and follow guidelines on page 14. Because plants sprout freely from the base, you will have to keep these shoots in check. Pull them off while they are succulent—don't cut them off, or you'll leave dormant buds at their bases from which more shoots will emerge. After removing the shoots, you can apply a commercial sprouting inhibitor to prevent their continued regrowth.

To grow a multitrunked tree, begin with a young plant and select several stems to become trunks. Remove all other basal sprouts as they appear. If you want to convert a many-stemmed shrub into a tree, cut weaker and unwanted stems to the ground, leaving just a few well-spaced stems to become trunks.

You can maintain oleanders as

big hedges, but the amount of trimming they require reduces or eliminates flowers.

All parts of the plant are extremely poisonous if they are eaten. Be careful to keep prunings away from children and animals. Never burn prunings: smoke from the wood is severely irritating.

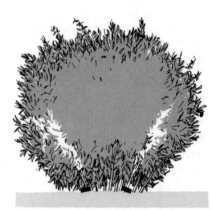

Nerium. Periodically cut out oldest stems to encourage strong, new growth.

NET BUSH.
See Calothamnus.

NEW ZEALAND CHRISTMAS TREE.
See Metrosideros.

NEW ZEALAND LAUREL.
See Corynocarpus.

NEW ZEALAND TEA TREE.
See Leptospermum.

NIGHT JESSAMINE.
See Cestrum.

NINEBARK.
See Physocarpus.

NORFOLK ISLAND PINE.
See Araucaria.

NOTHOPANAX.
See Neopanax.

NYSSA sylvatica. Sour gum, tupelo, pepperidge. Deciduous tree. Prune in winter.

Part of this tree's charm lies in its crooked branches, which will provide your garden with intriguing patterns during the tree's dormant season. You'll need to pay special attention to early training (see page 14). Limit the tree to just one leader and cut out spindly, twiggy stems and crossing branches.

Once you've succeeded in guiding a young tree to develop a good framework, you'll have little pruning to do. Remove dead wood, broken branches, any vertical stems, and any vigorous irregular branches that mar the plant's basic form or that cross other branches.

OAK.
See Quercus.

OCEAN SPRAY.
See Holodiscus.

OCHNA serrulata (O. multiflora).
Bird's-eye bush. Evergreen shrub. Prune in early spring.

Young plants need little pruning but will benefit from pinching to promote branching and bushiness. Any branches that grow too long can be cut back to sturdy laterals.

Older plants need occasional thinning. Cut out weak, twiggy wood in the plant's center, and cut off older branches that have stopped producing vigorous growth.

OCTOPUS TREE.
See Schefflera.

OEMLERIA cerasiformis (Osmaronia cerasiformis). Oso berry, Indian plum. Deciduous shrub. Prune in winter.

This shrub usually grows as a thicket of slender, upright stems. Periodically cut oldest stems to the ground when they stop producing healthy new growth.

You can grow oso berry as a multitrunked tree. Select the stems you want to keep; remove the others. Cut out basal shoots each year. To train shrub as a single-trunked tree, limit it to one vertical stem and pull out all basal shoots.

OLD MAN.
See Artemisia.

OLEA europaea. Olive. Evergreen tree. Prune in early spring (for ornamental use) or summer (in tropical areas); prune after harvest (for fruit production).

Olives are appealing trees that look equally attractive with one or several trunks. Without training, a young olive will grow as a shrub for many years, producing numerous basal sprouts and side branches. To speed up the tree's development, you must direct its early growth.

To grow a single-trunked tree, start with a young tree that has only one trunk, then follow directions on page 14 for early training. Olives sprout profusely from the base and put out many watersprouts from along each trunk. Rub the sprouts off while they're very small. Don't cut off basal sprouts that have already grown long; you will leave many latent buds beneath the cut. Instead, pull off these longer sprouts so that you remove the base of each sprout with a bit of tissue and bark. To prevent regrowth of these shoots, also apply a sprouting inhibitor to the area.

For a multitrunked tree, select a young plant that has several good stems growing from the base. Encourage the upward growth of these stems. Cut back side branches regularly and continue to remove new shoots from the base.

After a tree has become established, do annual thinning to reveal the trunk and branch structure. Cut out weaker branches at their joints with stronger limbs. Remove all lower side branches as the tree gets taller. Olive trees have naturally irregular, interesting shapes. Prune to reveal these branching patterns.

To prevent trees from setting fruit that can stain patios and sidewalks, spray flowers with a plant hormone, naphthaleneacetic acid. Pruning after flowering will also reduce the fruit crop.

Olea. Thin out tree's leafy canopy to reveal handsome branching pattern.

OLEANDER.
See Nerium.

OLIVE.
See Olea.

OLMEDIELLA betschlerana. Guatemalan holly, Costa Rican holly, manzanote. Evergreen large shrub or tree. Prune in early spring.

Dense, orderly growth defines this plant's pattern of development. Mature shrubs or trees need no pruning. Just give young plants early training to guide initial growth. For a single-trunked tree, choose one vertical leader and cut out any competing trunks. If you want a tree you can walk under, gradually remove side branches. If you allow side branches to remain, the plant will grow into a gigantic, pyramid or gumdrop-shaped shrub.

For a multitrunked tree or shrub, start with a plant with several stems growing upright from the base. To increase bushiness, pinch out tips of upward growth.

Plants will exhibit foliage to the ground unless you remove their lower branches. You'll also find that these shrubs make good barrier, screen, and formal or informal hedge plants (see page 70 for basic hedge training).

ORANGE.
See Citrus, page 38.

ORANGE JESSAMINE.
See Murraya.

ORCHID TREE.
See Bauhinia.

ORCHID VINE.
See Stigmaphyllon.

OREGON GRAPE.
See Mahonia.

OREGON MYRTLE.
See Umbellularia.

ORIENTAL ARBORVITAE.
See Platycladus.

OSAGE ORANGE.
See Maclura.

OSMANTHUS. Evergreen shrubs to small trees. Prune in spring and summer.

Three of the four common kinds of *Osmanthus* and their varieties are dense, compact shrubs that can eventually reach tree size: *Osmanthus fortunei*, *O. fragrans*, and hollyleaf osmanthus (O. heterophyllus, sometimes sold as O. aquifolium or O. illicifolius).

To cultivate them as background shrubs, occasionally cut back any wayward branches. Pinch tips of new growth on young plants to encourage bushiness. These shrubs also make fine formal or informal hedges (see page 70 for hedge guidelines). To train plants as trees, remove lower branches and thin out weak, crossing, and crowding limbs.

Delavay osmanthus (O. delavayi, sometimes sold as Siphonosmanthus delavayi) is an arching shrub that grows to 6 feet high and more than 6 feet wide. If the plant has sufficient room to grow in, little pruning will be necessary. Remove dead and weak branches as needed. You can train it as a graceful espalier (see page 50).

OSMARONIA.
See Oemleria.

OSO BERRY.
See Oemleria.

OSTEOSPERMUM. African daisy. Evergreen subshrubs and shrubby perennials. Prune after flowering.

Pinch new growth to decrease the need for pruning. Pinch frequently to promote branching and counteract the plant's tendency to sprawl. Cut back rangy and unattractive older plants to young side branches. Begin pinching once new growth is underway.

OSTRYA. Hop hornbeam. Deciduous trees. Prune in winter.

Grow hop hornbeams as single-trunked trees by following guidelines on page 14, or let them develop with 2 to 4 trunks. Gradually remove lower limbs. Mature trees need little pruning. Remove dead or broken branches whenever they occur. Make cuts back to joints with other branches.

OXERA pulchella. Evergreen vine or vining shrub. Prune after flowering.

With no support or guidance, this plant forms a mounding, shrubby mass about 6 feet high. If you prefer such a shrub to a more vinelike plant, pruning is unnecessary. But you can guide and tie stems on trellises, over arbors, or along low fences where flexible stems will reach about 10 feet long. Thin out dead and broken stems. Cut back or cut off any stems that are unwanted or are obscuring the vine's pattern on its support.

OXYDENDRUM arboreum. Sourwood, sorrel tree. Deciduous tree. Prune in late winter, early spring.

Give young tree early training (see page 14) to develop a single trunk, or allow it to grow several trunks. Mature trees require little pruning. Remove dead, broken, and crossing branches.

PACHISTIMA.
See Paxistima.

PACIFIC WAX MYRTLE.
See Myrica.

PAEONIA suffruticosa hybrids. Tree peony. Deciduous shrubs. Prune in early spring as growth begins.

Prune these magnificent flowering shrubs as little as possible. If winter cold damages stems, cut to nearest growth bud in healthy wood. Cut off any dead or broken stems at the nearest lateral or healthy bud.

Beyond damage maintenance, prune lightly only to shape a plant. Cut back any awkwardly long stem to a sturdy lateral. After flowers fade, cut them off to the nearest leaf beneath bloom.

PALM. Evergreen treelike and shrublike plants. Prune whenever necessary.

Strictly speaking, palms don't require pruning. What they may need, instead, is maintenance grooming. Many palms retain their dead fronds (leaves), which can detract from the plant's beauty. Because the oldest fronds die continually, rather than seasonally, you may want to groom a palm more than once a year. Occasionally you may need to remove fronds that have been damaged by frost, storms, or pests.

Though exceptions exist, palms generally fall into two groups: feather-leafed and fan-leafed. Feather-leafed palms display leaflets arranged on both sides of a long midrib; each leaf resembles a feather. Fan palms display leaflets radiating from one point at the end of a leaf stalk.

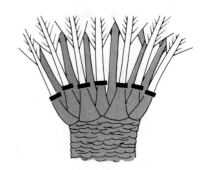

Palm. Cut off oldest fronds (the lowest ones) close to their bases.

One year later, old frond bases will be dead; cut them off flush with trunk.

Feather palms, especially, and many fan palms, will look much neater if you cut off old, brown fronds as close to the trunk as you can, leaving only the leaf bases. Some palms will later shed these old leaf bases naturally. If yours don't, you can remove the leaf bases the following year when you cut off more dead fronds. Use a large, sharp knife to slice off the leaf bases flush with the trunk.

Some fan palms—Washingtonia is an example—wear perennial skirts of dead leaves hanging from their trunks. These dead leaves drop naturally only after many years. Some gardeners prefer this natural appearance and don't remove the skirt of dead leaves, but it's a significant fire hazard. To eliminate it, cut off the dead fronds close to the trunk. The trimmed leaf bases will form an attractive lattice pattern.

Most ornamental palms grow as a single trunk topped by a tuft of leaves. But some grow naturally in clumps and some, like the date palm (Phoenix dactylifera), send up sprouts from the main trunk's base. If a clump-forming palm has too many stems, you can cut the extra ones to the

(Continued on page 88)

PEACH AND NECTARINE

Fast-growing, popular peaches and nectarines need more pruning than any other deciduous fruit trees. They bear their crops on year-old stems. (In contrast, apples, apricots, cherries, pears, and plums bear on fruiting spurs that remain productive for several years.) Without pruning, peaches and nectarines produce their fruits farther and farther away from the tree's center. The weight of the fruit puts a great strain on the branches and may break them, resulting in misshapen trees. *Prune these deciduous trees in winter.*

Train peaches and nectarines to the open-center system illustrated on page 15. When you plant a young tree, cut it back to 2 feet from the ground. Make sure that growth buds exist lower on the stem. From the growth that develops the first year, select three well-placed, strong stems to become the tree's permanent framework. During the first winter after planting, cut out all stems but the three you selected. Cut back those three by one-third, each to an outward-facing bud. New branches will grow from the three cut-back limbs.

The following winter, thin out all upward-growing stems and ones that cross through the center, then shorten any remaining stems by one-third. In the third winter, again thin and cut back the new stems that formed during the year. This should complete the training of the tree's permanent scaffold.

When a tree begins to bear fruit, start to prune for compactness. Each year's new growth of long, willowy shoots will bear fruit during the following summer only. Use one of the following methods to cut out as much as two-thirds of the previous year's growth: remove two of every three branches that grew during the year; cut back each branch to one-third of its length; or, better still, cut out the weak and crowding new stems and cut back the remaining branches to one-third of their length.

Cut back heavily to keep bearing limbs compact.

To obtain a compact tree, cut back the youngest stems to fruiting-bud clusters. You can distinguish dormant vegetative buds from dormant fruiting buds because fruiting buds come in clusters of three (the outer two are flower buds, the central one is vegetative). Don't worry about cutting away some of the fruiting buds; trees usually bear heavily and need some fruit thinning no matter how hard they were pruned previously.

Genetic dwarf peaches and nectarines form shrubs that look like shaggy green mops. Prune them mostly to shape. To encourage ample fruit, you may have to occasionally thin stems in the centers of these plants to allow light to reach the innermost fruiting buds.

Mature peach and nectarine trees need heavy annual pruning. Cut out two-thirds of previous year's growth.

ground. Some of the basically single-trunked palms produce basal sprouts. Cut off the sprouts to make these palms more attractive.

A few of the more popular palms—*Trachycarpus*, for example—bear a heavy overcoat of fiber on their trunks. If you prefer the beauty of smooth trunks, you can strip off the fiber without harming the palm.

PALMETTO.
See Palm.

PALO VERDE.
See Cercidium.

PANDOREA. Evergreen vines. Prune whenever needed.

Vines may be damaged by frost. Cut back damaged portions to healthy stems when new growth begins in spring. At the same time, thin out any tangled or undesirably placed stems. For the vigorous wonga-wonga vine (*Pandorea pandorana*), cut back branch ends heavily after spring bloom is finished.

PAPAYA.
See Carica.

PARKINSONIA aculeata. **Jerusalem thorn, Mexican palo verde. Deciduous tree. Prune as needed.**

A young tree needs early guidance as described on page 14. You can train it to branch either high or low on the trunk. After the tree is established, you'll have little pruning to do. Occasionally, you may need to cut out dead branches from inside the tree's crown.

PARROT BEAK.
See Clianthus.

PARROTIA persica. **Persian parrotia. Deciduous tree or large shrub. Prune in winter and summer.**

Densely leafed branches spread wide, and most grow in horizontal planes. Without guidance, the plant will grow as a large shrub or multi-trunked tree. For a single-trunked tree, follow the early training directions on page 14. You can encourage the plant to grow taller and more treelike by shortening its side branches during summer. Remove these short side branches when the young tree has reached the height where it shows a framework of canopy limbs.

PARTHENOCISSUS (all species formerly included in *Ampelopsis*). Deciduous vines. Prune in winter and during growing season.

All kinds of *Parthenocissus* climb by means of tendrils that have sucker disks at their ends. Some kinds, such as Boston ivy (*Parthenocissus tricuspidata*), depend largely on their disks' adhesive qualities to cover a surface, while others, such as Virginia creeper (*P. quinquefolia*), rely more on the twining of tendrils to climb. Virginia creeper and its close relative *P. inserta* need to cling to wire, a trellis, or some sort of scaffold in order to cover vertical surfaces. Both can be used as scrambling ground covers. Silvervein creeper (*P. henryana*) and Boston ivy cling easily to flat surfaces.

Think carefully about the wall's surface before you plant. Boston ivy, especially, can get under boards and shingles. It can also leave unsightly remains of its suckers on wood or stucco walls when it's removed.

When vines reach their desired size, prune them each winter to restrain their spread. Cut vines away from doors and windows and cut out wayward stems. For Boston ivy and silvervein creeper, cut back any stems that have pulled away from their support to areas where stems are still firmly attached. Detached stems will not reattach.

During the growing season, do any trimming needed to limit or direct growth. Cut off streamers that hang over windows or doors or that

Parthenocissus. Cut off loose stems and unwanted streamers of new growth.

grow out over walkways. Boston ivy often completely covers a wall, but you can train it and other parthenocissus into an openwork tracery. To do this, limit the number of stems that climb a surface. Whenever necessary, cut out any new growth that begins to fill in the open areas.

PASSIFLORA. Passion vine. Evergreen, semievergreen, and deciduous vines. Prune in spring, summer, autumn.

Without care these vigorous vines will become thickly tangled masses of stems and leaves. They climb by wrapping wiry tendrils around anything they come in contact with, including their own stems.

After a vine's second winter, give it at least one pruning annually. Remove some stems to keep the vine open and untangled. During the growing season, cut back excess and wayward growth to other stems or to the ground.

In colder areas, winter freeze damage will mean you'll need to do some repair pruning. Be sure to cut out dead and damaged stems. You'll still need to prune during the growing season in these regions to remove stems that are crowding others or are heading where you don't want them. If a vine gets completely out of hand, cut it to the ground in spring after all danger of frost is past.

PASSION VINE.
See Passiflora.

PAULOWNIA tomentosa (*P. imperialis*). **Empress tree. Deciduous tree. Prune during winter.**

Give young trees routine early training as outlined on page 14. To encourage rapid upward growth, be sure to head back any extra vigorous side branches and remove any sprouts that erupt from the plant's base. After the tree becomes established, prune only to remove dead, frost-damaged, weak, and broken branches, and to eliminate crossing or vertical branches that detract from the branching pattern.

PAXISTIMA (*Pachistima*). Evergreen shrubs. Prune whenever necessary.

These short, dense, tidy shrubs are best used as small-scale ground covers, edging plants, and low formal or informal hedges. For basic hedge directions, see page 70. Unless you treat plants as hedges, you need do little pruning. Cut back wayward stems any time.

PEACH.
See page 87.

PEAR.
See page 90.

PEARL BUSH.
See Exochorda.

PECAN.
See Carya.

PELARGONIUM. Geranium.
Shrubby perennials. Prune from autumn to early spring (see text).

Widely known as geraniums, these common plants are actually pelargoniums. True geraniums are nonshrubby perennials and annuals.

Pinching is the secret to growing well-filled-out pelargoniums. From the time a plant is young, pinch the tips of all stems to promote branching as close to the plant's base as possible. If you have a very small plant, just pinch out the growing tip. On stems that are more than 4 inches long, snap off each stem tip just above a leaf. When new stems are about 4 inches long, pinch their tips. Repeat this several times to develop a well-branched plant that will be full of leaves.

Don't pinch off the tips of plants of the seed-grown strains of *Pelargonium hortorum*, such as the Sprinter and Carefree series. These are self-branching plants.

During the flowering season, pinch back any too-vigorous or unbranched stems.

Dormant pruning. When you prune will depend on your climate's winter temperatures. In frost-free regions you can prune in autumn or in winter. Flowering will resume on new growth fairly early the next year. Where frosty winter weather is expected (but where winters are not cold enough to kill plants), delay pruning until late winter or early spring, after danger of frost is over.

P. domesticum. Cut back the larger-growing, woodier *P. domesticum*—commonly called Martha Washington or Regal geranium, or Lady Washington pelargonium—to half its size. Cut out weak and straggly growth. When new growth resumes, start routine pinching again.

In time, plants can become leggy, showing leaves just at the ends of woody stems. You can try to renew these plants in either of two ways:

1) Cut back plants gradually, starting just after the heavy spring bloom. Cut each stem back to the lowest pair of leaves. When new growth breaks out below these leaves, cut back to the lowest new growth or to stems that are headed in a good direction. Do this with all old stems until the old plant has been reduced to a compact "new" shrub.

2) Cut back plants to within a few inches of the ground in early spring after any danger of frost is past. This method of pruning has two drawbacks: you're likely to lose most or all of the bloom, and old, woody plants may not resprout.

P. hortorum. The common geranium (*P. hortorum*) has softer stems that usually put out new growth easily when you cut them back severely. To prune these geraniums, cut out oldest stems or cut them back to a point where a strong new stem has grown. Then thin out all crowding and weak stems. Cut back the remaining stems fairly hard. Cut above a leaf, above new growth that's just emerging, or above a growth bud. When new growth begins, pinch to cultivate bushiness.

To rejuvenate an old, overgrown plant, follow the first set of directions (preceding) for *P. domesticum*, but do so in early spring after all danger of frost is past.

All geraniums root easily from cuttings. Starting a new plant is often a more successful venture than trying to restore an old, neglected plant.

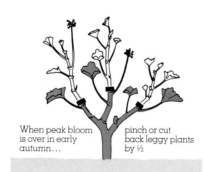

When peak bloom is over in early autumn… pinch or cut back leggy plants by ½

Pelargonium. Prune heavily each year to keep compact framework of stems.

PEPPERIDGE.
See Nyssa.

PEPPERMINT TREE.
See Agonis.

PEPPER TREE.
See Schinus.

PEPPERVINE.
See Ampelopsis.

PEPPERWOOD.
See Umbellularia.

PERNETTYA mucronata. Evergreen shrub. Prune in early spring, autumn.

Pernettya's growth is generally compact, and consists of many slender, twiggy stems. Plants spread into clumps by underground runners. In early spring and whenever needed, cut back any unattractively wayward stems. Autumn pruning will provide you with cuttings bearing colorful berries. Use these sprigs for indoor decoration.

If a plant looks ratty, cut the oldest stems back halfway to encourage branching. Cut out weakest twiggy stems and, if necessary, cut back any of the remaining stems to make plants uniform or compact. To prevent underground stems from invading areas where they're not wanted, sever them from the main clump with a sharp spade.

PEROVSKIA. Deciduous shrub. Prune in late winter, early spring.

Give these soft-wooded shrubs a heavy annual pruning. Cut all stems to within a few inches of the ground. Cut out entirely any weak and crowding ones. Make cuts just above a pair of growth buds. Each succeeding year, prune newest growth to the lowest pair of growth buds and thin out crossing and crowding stems. Occasionally cut back old stumpy stems to allow for new growth from the base.

To grow a taller plant, make your first pruning cut less severe—cut stems 6 to 10 inches from the ground. In years that follow, cut back new growth as described in the preceding paragraph.

PERSEA.
See Avocado.

PERSIAN PARROTIA.
See Parrotia.

PEAR

Modest pruning will keep pear tree fruitful.

Pears produce many upright stems that crowd tree's center. Cut out all but a few needed to give new fruiting spurs.

Pears are large, long-lived trees. They produce fruit on short spurs that remain productive for many years. Pears will naturally grow upright—taller than wide—and develop many branches that are vertical or nearly so. This characteristic influences early pruning.

Training young trees

At planting time, a young pear tree will be 3 to 6 feet tall—either a whip (trunk without branches) or a trunk with some branches. You can select one of several training systems.

Open center system. An open center tree has no central leader. Instead, several major limbs grow outward from the top of a short trunk.

To train an open center tree, cut back the newly planted tree to 24 to 32 inches in height, depending on how low you want the major limbs to form. Strong, well-spaced limbs 6 to 10 inches below the cut will become primary scaffold branches.

If the newly planted tree has some side branches, cut back the leader to 24 to 32 inches. Select well-placed side branches—ones that point out from the trunk in different directions in the 6 to 10-inch space below the cut—to become scaffold branches. Cut back these well-placed branches to 2 to 4-inch stubs and cut off all other side branches. By the end of the first growing season the major scaffold limbs should be formed. See page 15 for full directions on the open center system.

Modified central leader system. This method produces a taller tree than the open center system. You prune to develop 4 to 6 major scaffold limbs along the upper 2 to 3 feet of trunk. It may take two or more seasons to get this many scaffold limbs.

At planting time, cut back a whip (unbranched trunk) to a point where it is 24 to 32 inches from the ground. During the next growing season, allow the uppermost stem to become the leader. At the end of the growing season—the second dormant pruning—select primary scaffold branches at the height you want above the ground. Cut back these primary scaffold branches by a fourth to half their length, and cut off the rest of the weaker or badly placed side branches.

If necessary, continue this process for another pruning season until you have chosen 4 to 6 major scaffold branches. Then let the leader become the top scaffold.

For an already branched trunk, begin as you would for a whip: at planting time, cut back the trunk until it is within 24 to 32 inches from the ground. Select well-placed side branches, if any, to become main scaffold branches. Cut these well-placed branches back to 2 to 4-inch stubs and cut off all poorly placed branches. If there are no well-placed branches, cut off all branches and prune the tree the same as a whip.

Espaliers and cordons. Pears make very good subjects for these carefully controlled kinds of pruning. For directions, see page 50.

Dwarf trees. You can find many standard pear varieties that have been grafted onto dwarfing rootstocks. To train them as small trees, use the central leader system (see page 15). For espaliers and cordons in a small space, dwarf pears are better than full-size trees.

Pruning mature trees

Once the main branch framework is established, annual pruning consists mostly of thinning. Remove weak, broken, and dead branches. A vigorous pear tree will produce many upright shoots. You will need to thin out most of these shoots to let sunlight enter the tree's canopy. To control the tree's height, cut back upper branches to outward-pointing side branches. Avoid cutting back lower branches.

Dwarf trees. Prune dwarf pear trees each year about the same way you do full-size trees. You won't need to do as much pruning because dwarf trees grow less.

When your dwarf pear tree reaches the height you want to maintain, cut back the central leader to a strong side branch. In later years, do this whenever necessary.

Fireblight. Fireblight is a disease that requires pruning as soon as you notice it. If a twig or limb suddenly turns black and burned-looking, cut it off a foot below the affected part. Disinfect pruning shears after each cut to avoid spreading the disease.

PERSIMMON *(Diospyros).* Deciduous trees. Prune in winter.

Young trees need early training as described on page 14 to develop straight leaders and good scaffold branches. Wood is brittle, and a heavy load of fruit can break a weak branch. Be careful to select only limbs that form strong, wide angles to the trunk for scaffold branches. If a tree is spreading too widely, cut back the overreaching limbs to good laterals.

After the tree's main framework is established, each year remove dead wood and watersprouts, and thin out crowded twigs and branches in the crown. Cut back any awkward branches. Make all cuts to laterals or joints with other limbs.

Conspicuous fruits and handsome foliage make persimmons striking informal espaliers. Start with a young tree and follow guidelines on page 50.

PHAEDRANTHUS.
See Distictis.
PHILADELPHUS.
See Mock Orange, page 82.

PHILLYREA decora *(Osmanthus decora).* Evergreen shrub. Prune in early spring.

This neat, dense shrub ordinarily needs no pruning. If a branch grows out too far, cut it back to a pair of branches or to a pair of leaves. You can also pinch back any too-vigorous shoot to prevent it from becoming a wayward branch that will need pruning later.

PHLOMIS fruticosa. Jerusalem sage. Usually evergreen shrubby perennial. Prune in autumn.

Unpruned plants become rangy and unattractive. Cut back the season's growth by one-third and remove weak stems. To promote further flowering, cut back stems by about half after each flush of bloom.

PHOENIX.
See Palm.

PHOTINIA. Evergreen or deciduous shrubs and small trees. Prune in late winter, early spring.

You can train Chinese photinia (*P. serrulata*) and *P. villosa* as trees,

following guidelines on page 14. You also can grow them as shrubs with the same pruning as shrubby *P. fraseri* and Japanese photinia (*P. glabra*).

All photinias are vigorous growers. Pinch new growth to encourage bushiness, particularly to promote branching low on the plant. Pinch a new stem while it is 1 to 2 feet long. Pinch the resulting branches if they become too long.

Whenever stems become crowded, thin out some of the oldest, least vigorous ones and any dead branches in the plant's center. Make all cuts to a lateral, to a joint with another branch, or to the ground.

PHYSOCARPUS. Ninebark. Deciduous shrubs. Prune in late winter.

Ninebarks generally grow into good-looking shrubs with no assistance. For a more dense shrub, pinch young plants frequently. On mature plants, periodically thin out some of the oldest stems and cut out weak, twiggy stems.

To renew an old, straggly, unattractive shrub, cut out all of the old stems over a period of 4 to 5 years. Don't just cut stems back, because many twiggy shoots will sprout from the end of each pruned branch.

PICEA. Spruce. Coniferous evergreen trees and shrubs. Prune in spring.

Spruces are symmetrical plants that need little or no pruning—in fact, indiscriminate pruning can permanently damage their form. Nevertheless, situations arise which do call for some selective attention. If a plant develops a second trunk (double leader), cut out the weaker of the two. Do this as soon as possible so that lopsided branching won't develop.

Occasionally a branch will grow out too far. Cut it back to a lateral within the regular outline. To make a tree denser or limit its growth, you can cut back (not shear) each new shoot by half. Don't make indiscriminate cuts into older branches and don't cut back into bare, needleless wood (refer to Conifers on page 46).

PIERIS. Evergreen shrubs. Prune after flowering.

These graceful, elegant plants need little pruning. Plants grow densely and fairly symmetrically. Some irregularity of shape is attractive. If you need to shape a plant, cut back a stem where it joins another branch.

To promote branching of an unbranched stem, cut it back to a group of leaves at the base of a season's growth. Several dormant buds will sprout. (If you cut back midway on a stem, only one dormant bud is likely to grow.) Try to forestall the need for pruning by pinching out any shoot that will produce an unwanted stem.

PINE.
See Pinus.

PINEAPPLE GUAVA.
See Feijoa.

PINK POWDER PUFF.
See Calliandra.

PINUS. Pine. Evergreen coniferous trees, rarely shrubs. Prune in spring.

You can shape all pines to some extent by pruning, but you must do it carefully, with knowledge of how pines grow. Pines are whorl-branching conifers. You'll find a description of this growth pattern, along with general pruning guidelines for conifers, on pages 46–47.

A pine's new spring shoots take their name from the resemblance they bear to candles. You can prune pines to limit or control growth when the candles have elongated but before they have sent out needles. To keep a branch from growing longer, remove the entire candle. Growth buds at the candle's base will sprout to form several side branches in a whorl. To reduce the length of new growth without stopping growth completely, cut back the candle part way. The shortened candle will develop a new terminal bud to carry on further growth next year. By shortening candles each year, you can effectively slow the growth of a pine without distorting its natural shape.

In time, the lower limbs of most pines will die naturally. When this happens, cut them off. Remove any other dead branches when you notice them. You can cut out any unwanted branches to shape a pine or to accent its branching pattern. Remember that once a branch is removed, a new one won't sprout to take its place. If you leave a gaping hole in the canopy, the best you can hope for is that new growth on nearby branches will cover the blank spot.

To shape a pine in the oriental manner requires some skill but is not difficult. Cut out any branches that interfere with the effect, shorten other branches, and create an upswept look by removing all twigs that grow downward. Cutting the main vertical trunk back to a well-placed side branch will induce side growth. Wiring or weighting branches will produce a cascade effect.

Pinus. Pinch back candle (new shoot) to slow or stop elongation, increase branching.

PISTACIA. Pistache, pistachio. Deciduous or semievergreen trees. Prune in late winter.

Because young trees often grow irregularly, you need to give particular attention to establishing a good branch framework (see page 14 for general guidelines for training young trees). Cut off downward-growing branches and stems, and cut back too-long branches. For permanent framework limbs, select well-spaced branches with wide-angled crotches.

After a tree's form is established, little pruning is needed. Cut out dead and broken wood, remove any unwanted or crowding branches in the tree's center, and cut back any wayward limbs to joints with other branches.

PITTOSPORUM. Evergreen shrubs and trees. Prune any time.

Pittosporums are versatile, good-looking plants. Despite their natural differences in size, nearly all can be grown as shrubs, trees, and hedges.

Tree kinds. Following guidelines on page 14, you can train these as single-trunked or multitrunked trees: P. crassifolium, P. eugenioides, P. phillyraeoides, P. rhombifolium, P. tenuifolium, P. undulatum, and P. viridiflorum. Mature trees seldom need major pruning.

You can grow all but P. phillyraeoides and P. viridiflorum as tall hedges and maintain them at any height over 5 feet almost indefinitely. To force bushiness, shear off a plant's top 2 to 6 inches several times each year between March and November. As plants grow larger, begin to shear sides to limit their spread. Continue trimming 2 or 3 times a year until hedge reaches the size you want. Shear a full-grown hedge's surfaces as needed—typically, once each in spring, summer, and autumn.

For a softer, more natural-looking surface, cut back protruding branches to laterals or growth buds inside the outline of the hedge. Don't cut branches that end approximately at the hedge's surface.

When an older hedge becomes woody at the base or just too large, cut it back heavily in spring to a bare framework. Start training the new growth as though it were a new hedge.

Shrub kinds. You can use bulky P. tobira as a specimen shrub, a formal or informal hedge, or a container plant. It's easy to convert tall, older plants into small trees. Remove lower limbs to reveal the major trunk and limb framework.

Resembling a larger version of P. tobira, P. viridiflorum is suitable for all of the same purposes. You can convert older plants from shrubs to trees.

P. napaulense (P. floribundum) is strictly a specimen shrub that's neither dense enough for hedging nor tall enough to be a shrub-tree.

All unclipped pittosporums need shaping from time to time. Thin out weak and dead branches. Cut back any wayward branches that detract from the plant's form. Make cuts to the base of a shoot or to joints with other branches.

PLATANUS. Plane tree, sycamore. Deciduous trees. Prune in winter.

All plane trees need early training (see page 14) to establish a good, straight leader. Once this basic framework is formed, you'll have no routine pruning to do. Occasionally you may want to thin out smaller branches to reveal more of the plant's rugged branching and patchy bark. Cut out any dead, diseased, or broken wood, making all cuts back to another branch.

Because of their beautiful natural form, American sycamores *(P. occidentalis)* need little pruning. You can thin out smaller branches to reveal their trunk and limbs.

California sycamore *(P. racemosa)* can be trained as an upright tree, but it's also appealing as a tree with multiple trunks or with one or more trunks leaning at interesting angles. Start to develop these characteristics by training when plants are young. On older trees, remove dead twigs and any erratic growth that results from blight disease.

PLATYCLADUS orientalis. *(Thuja orientalis, Biota orientalis).* Oriental arborvitae. Evergreen coniferous shrubs, trees. <u>Prune from late winter to early spring.</u>

Though botanists bestow a distinct identity upon this arborvitae, to most gardeners this species and its many named varieties are simply oriental versions of the American arborvitae. For pruning directions, see *Thuja occidentalis* on page 14.

PLUM.
See page 95.

PLUMBAGO auriculata *(P. capensis).* Cape plumbago. Semievergreen shrub or vine. <u>Prune in late winter after all danger of frost is past.</u>

With no guidance, Cape plumbago becomes a large mound of arching stems. With enough room, this is an attractive way to grow it. Occasionally nip back wayward stems.

To grow it as a more compact, stiff shrub, prune its long, pliable new shoots, cutting them back by about one-third. This will promote branching. After a few years, begin removing oldest stems that are no longer putting out vigorous growth and flowers. Do this each year immediately after flowering stops, to renew the shrub from its base.

To grow Cape plumbago as a vine on a wall or trellis (it will need support and tying), let all new stems grow without restraint. Pinch or head back side branches at first to encourage long stems that will fill the wall or trellis.

Whenever frost damages a plant, cut out all dead and damaged stems below the injured areas. To renew an old, ratty plant, cut it to the ground. Vigorous new stems will soon appear.

Plumbago. Shrub makes irregular mound. Cut back rangy stems for compactness.

PLUME CEDAR.
See Cryptomeria.

PLUMERIA. Plumeria, frangipani. Evergreen and deciduous shrubs or small trees. <u>Prune any time.</u>

Typically, these thick-limbed plants carry large leaves at branch tips, enabling you to see much of the plant's framework. No routine pruning is needed. Should branches grow too vigorously and unbalance the plant's shape, prune to restore a pleasing outline, cutting stems back to laterals or to joints with other branches.

PODOCARPUS. Evergreen coniferous trees and shrubs. <u>Prune in spring, summer.</u>

Unlike most other conifers (but like their close relatives, the yews) the different kinds of *Podocarpus* produce more than one flush of growth in a year. Also, they'll sprout from bare, leafless wood. Because new shoots will grow wherever you cut, this makes them easy to prune. It also makes them good plants for clipped or sheared hedges. For general pruning guidelines, see "Whorl-

branching types" under Conifers on page 47.

Tree types. *Podocarpus falcatus, P. gracilior* (often sold as *P. elongatus*), *P. henkelii, P. macrophyllus, P. nagi, P. totara.* For single-trunked or multitrunked trees, follow early training guidelines on page 14.

Some kinds of podocarpus—notably fern pine *(P. gracilior)*—are slow to develop into trees. Stake them until a strong trunk develops. You can also train fern pines as multistemmed trees by selecting several leaders when plants are young. Depending on your preference, you can allow branches to grow on lower trunks or prune off lower limbs to reveal trunks.

As an alternative, train fern pines as free-form espaliers (see page 50) or even as vines along a fence top or the eaves of a house.

Shrub types. *P. macrophyllus maki, P. nivalis.* The shrubby yew pine *(P. macrophyllus maki)* is a scaled-down version of the more treelike yew pine *(P. macrophyllus).* It makes a good specimen shrub or slow-growing hedge. Alpine totara *(P. nivalis)*, on the other hand, forms a low and widespreading shrub. Aside from specimen use, you can train it as a ground cover by cutting out any upright branches.

POINCIANA.
See Caesalpinia, Delonix.

POINSETTIA.
See Euphorbia.

POLYGALA dalmaisiana. Sweet-pea shrub. Evergreen shrub. <u>Prune throughout the growing season.</u>

Sweet-pea shrub is naturally rangy, with bare-based stems. You can head back, or even shear, stems as often as needed to promote bushiness without sacrificing flowers. If a lighter pruning schedule appeals to you, head back plants moderately after blooming and plant a lower shrub in front of sweet-pea shrub to hide its bare stems.

POLYGONUM. Deciduous vines. <u>Prune in early spring.</u>

These two fast-growing, twining vines—silver lace vine *(P. aubertii)* and Bokhara fleeceflower *(P. bald-*

shuanicum)—require the same pruning treatment.

Where plants freeze to the ground, cut the dead stems to the ground. Though bloom will begin later in summer, new growth will renew the plant.

Where vines don't freeze, in early spring thin out side shoots and cut all main and secondary stems back to the third or fourth growth bud of the last year's growth. During spring and summer, pinch growing tips; cut back and thin out older stems as needed to direct growth and keep the vine in bounds.

To rejuvenate an entangled, neglected plant, cut stems to the ground. New growth will restore the vine.

POMEGRANATE.
See Punica.

POMPON TREE.
See Dais.

PONCIRUS trifoliatus. Hardy orange, trifoliate orange. Deciduous tree. Prune from late winter through early spring.

Though hardy orange grows naturally as a small tree, you can also use it as a formal or informal barrier hedge (see page 70 for hedge information) and as an informal espalier (refer to page 50 for general directions).

As a tree, give it the initial training outlined on page 14. The branching pattern can be attractive, so you may want to periodically thin out the crown to show off its structure better. Remove weak and twiggy stems, then selectively cut out larger branches, if needed, to open up the foliage canopy.

POPLAR.
See Populus.

POPULUS. Includes poplar, cottonwood, balm-of-Gilead, aspen. Deciduous trees. Prune in winter.

The many kinds of *Populus* can be divided into three categories: big spreading trees, columnar trees, and quaking aspen.

The big cottonwoods, poplars, and balm-of-Gileads are not often planted in gardens because of their great size and invasive roots. If you

do plant one, give it routine early training (see page 14) to establish a sturdy, upright trunk. In later years, cut out dead and broken branches.

Columnar accent trees include Lombardy poplar (*P. nigra* 'Italica' and *P. nigra thevestina*) and *P. alba* 'Pyramidalis'. These grow tall and straight with no assistance. Cut out dead branches when they occur and cut out or pull up shoots that grow profusely from the roots.

Quaking aspen (*P. tremuloides*) is the modest member of this group. Though individual trees may become quite tall, they retain a lightweight grace. They're most attractive when planted in groves of several to many trees. You can try to train them into trees as described on page 14, but they usually grow without assistance into handsome curving or angular shapes that training would discourage. Cut off lower limbs to reveal trunks' beauty. Remove dead wood whenever branches die.

PORT ORFORD CEDAR.
See Chamaecyparis.

PORTUGAL LAUREL.
See Prunus.

POTATO VINE.
See Solanum.

POTENTILLA. Cinquefoil. Deciduous shrubs. Prune in late winter or early spring, after flowering.

In winter, remove dead and frost-damaged branches only. Allow the remaining stems to produce a crop of blossoms. After bloom, thin out oldest, least vigorous stems and head back any overlong shoots. You can use the more upright, dense varieties as informal hedges. Clip them lightly to keep plants neat.

PRIDE OF MADEIRA.
See Echium.

PRINCESS FLOWER.
See Tibouchina.

PRIVET.
See Ligustrum.

PROSOPIS glandulosa torreyana. Mesquite. Deciduous tree. Prune in winter.

Think of mesquite as a gigantic shrub. Because plants branch from the base or close to the ground, the

tree is inevitably multitrunked. Prune to remove lower limbs that block access beneath the tree or that detract from the beauty of a particular tree's shape. Cut out dead and broken limbs whenever they occur.

Plant mesquites in a row for a good filmy screen or windbreak.

PRUNUS. Evergreen trees and shrubs. (For deciduous flowering kinds, see Flowering Fruit Trees, page 54.) Prune in early spring.

The growth habits of these evergreen relatives of plums, prunes, and cherries can be summed up in one word: dense. The most common kinds are Carolina laurel cherry (*P. caroliniana*), Catalina cherry (*P. lyonii*), English laurel (*P. laurocerasus*), hollyleaf cherry (*P. ilicifolia*), and Portugal laurel (*P. lusitanica*).

With no pruning they will become increasingly large shrubs until they reach tree size. You can train all of them as trees, following guidelines on page 14. They'll grow either as single-trunked or multitrunked trees.

You also can use them as formal hedge plants (see pages 70–71), keeping them as low as 3 feet if needed. For lower hedges, there are dwarf varieties of Carolina laurel cherry and English laurel. Though you can shear English laurel, the large leaves will look mutilated when they are formally trimmed. For a better appearance, cut overlong stems back to leaves within the foliage.

These evergreen kinds of *Prunus* and their varieties also make handsome privacy screens. To maintain a neat, fairly even appearance,

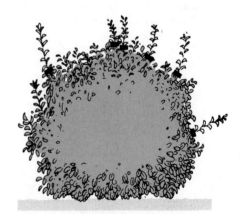

Prunus. Extra-vigorous stems can unbalance plant's shape. Head them back to laterals.

(Continued on page 96)

PLUM AND PRUNE

Plums and prunes bear their tasty fruit in summer. Though different kinds of plums and prunes abound, for pruning purposes you can reduce these to two categories: European plums *(Prunus domestica)* and Japanese plums *(P. salicina)*. All prunes, Damson plum *(P. insititia)*, and various hybrids with American native species are pruned the same as European plums. All kinds bear fruit on lateral spurs. On dormant branches the spurs appear as clusters of buds flush with stems, or they may develop on stubby protrusions from the stems. *Prune all of these deciduous trees in winter.*

Young trees. Train all young plum and prune trees to the open-center systems as illustrated on page 15. Make sure that three or four major limbs are well spaced around the trunk and form wide angles to it.

At the end of the first growing season, select branches from the main trunk to become permanent framework limbs. Cut these limbs back to the point where you want the first branching to occur: cut back to outward-facing buds on strongly upright varieties; cut to inward-facing buds on spreading trees.

In succeeding years, continue selecting strong and well-placed branches for the framework. Shorten them where you want branching to occur. Cut off vertical stems and crowding or crossing stems in the tree's center. When trees are established, prune them according to the two general types.

European plums. European plums are only moderately vigorous. They need relatively little pruning. Remove vertical shoots and cut out crossing and broken branches. Cut back too-long shoots to laterals or to dormant buds, cutting shoots back either to vegetative buds or to fruiting spurs, if necessary. Occasionally strong, young shoots fork to form a Y-shaped crotch; cut out one of the

Prune some varieties heavily, others lightly.

two stems at the fork. Also remove branches that form narrow angles to the trunk or to main limbs.

Japanese plums. Japanese plums are tremendously vigorous, producing many long new shoots each year. Without pruning, a tree will become large and floppy. Limbs may break because of the weight of fruit and foliage on long branches.

After the tree is mature and bearing, annually prune back overlong shoots that formed the previous year. Cut back shoots to laterals, removing them entirely if they are badly placed or crowding. Cut out vertical shoots and thin out crossing or crowding stems.

Many plums produce numerous upright stems. Thin most of them out each year.

head back wayward branches periodically.

An unusual member of this group is Zabel laurel, *P. laurocerasus* 'Zabeliana'. Its branches angle upward and outward from the base, eventually reaching 6 feet high with a greater spread. To keep the shrub low, cut out the vertical branches. To use Zabel laurel as a ground cover, cut back the vertical stems and peg down the spreading limbs. Or you can plant it against a vertical surface and train it as an espalier (see pages 50–51). Cut back any branches that stick out from the flat surface.

PSEUDOLARIX kaempferi *(Chrysolarix kaempferi, C. amabilis)*. Golden larch. Deciduous coniferous tree. Prune in winter.

These slow-growing, spreading trees are whorl-branching conifers. Refer to pages 46–47 for general instructions about pruning conifers.

Young trees need routine early training to develop a straight, single leader (see page 14). After the leader is established, you'll have little pruning to do. In time, if you want a tree to walk under, begin to remove lower limbs. Cut back broken branches to the nearest healthy branch and remove any dead wood when you notice it.

PSEUDOTSUGA menziesii. Douglas fir. Evergreen coniferous tree. Prune in spring.

Douglas firs grow into very large trees. It's wise to plant them only where they will have plenty of room to grow. Attempts to limit their size (other than for hedges, mentioned below) are futile.

Give young trees guidance, as outlined on page 14, to develop a single, straight leader. If the leader is broken, splint up a branch from the closest whorl below to become the new leader. You can cut back a young tree's new side branches halfway to help direct growth upward. Eventually you'll cut off these branches anyway, so annual pruning won't harm the mature tree's appearance.

You can grow a Douglas fir hedge by planting young trees 2 feet apart and then keeping them trimmed and topped. See page 70 for basic hedge information, and pages 46–47 for details on heading back branches of whorl-branching conifers. A Douglas fir hedge is worth cultivating only where the tree is native and plentiful. In regions where it is not, other conifers are more appropriate for hedges.

PSIDIUM. Guava. Evergreen shrubs or small trees. Prune in spring.

Guavas come in several varieties. Mature plants differ in size, but all exhibit open rather than dense growth patterns. In favorable locations they will eventually become small trees if they aren't pruned back. To develop a tree, select three to five main stems you want for future tree trunks while the plant is still young. Then gradually thin out lower branches and weak and crowding branches.

To keep the plant as a shrub, head back the upward growth as needed. Cut stems back to joints with other branches.

To renovate an old, overgrown, rangy plant, cut it back severely. To convert it into a small tree, remove lower branches and selectively cut off excess branches and weak, crossing, and crowding limbs.

PTEROCARYA stenoptera. Chinese wingnut. Deciduous tree. Prune in winter.

Young plants need routine guidance as outlined on page 14. After a sturdy trunk and main limbs are established, you'll have no routine pruning to do. Cut out dead branches whenever they occur, and head back any broken limbs to laterals or joints with other branches.

PTEROSTYRAX hispidus. Epaulette tree. Deciduous tree. Prune in late winter.

For a single-trunked tree, give young plants the early training outlined on page 14. You also can grow epaulette tree as a multitrunked shrub-tree or tree. In either case, you'll have little pruning to do once the trunk or trunks are established. Cut off branches that hang too low or cut them back to a lateral that doesn't droop. Remove dead, frost-damaged, and broken branches whenever they occur.

PTYCHOSPERMA.
See Palm.

PUNICA granatum. Pomegranate. Deciduous tree or shrub. Prune in winter.

Nurseries offer several pomegranate varieties, and these range from 1½-foot shrubs to fruit-bearing small trees.

You can grow the largest kinds as thickets, shrubs, or trees. These plants will naturally become a formless thicket if you let all the new stems grow from the base. For a shapelier shrub, select the stems you want as a permanent framework and remove all others as they grow. For a multi-trunked shrub-tree, cut off the lower branches that grow from the main framework trunks.

If you want a single-trunked tree, select a young plant with one stem that will become the trunk. Or choose a plant with one dominant upright stem and cut away all others when you set out the plant. With any tree, you'll have to continue to remove shoots that grow from the base.

To train pomegranate as an informal espalier (see page 50), select a few strong branches and fasten them in a fan pattern to a vertical support. During the growing season, remove all new shoots from the base and any stems that stick out from the support. In winter, thin out very old and weak stems and any crowding branches.

To maintain the large shrubby varieties, give them the same pruning as recommended above. On the shortest shrubs, such as 3-foot-tall 'Nana' and 1½-foot-tall 'Chico' cut back wayward branches only. Now and then remove the oldest stems from shrubby pomegranates so that stronger, newer branches can replace them.

Punica. Change bushy pomegranate into tree; remove lower branches to show trunks.

PURPLE ANISE TREE.
See Illicium.

PURPLE-LEAF PLUM.
See Flowering plum under
Flowering Trees, page 55.

PURPLE ORCHID TREE.
See Bauhinia.

PURPLE OSIER.
See Salix.

PUSSY WILLOW.
See Salix.

PYRACANTHA. Firethorn. Evergreen shrubs. <u>Prune in winter after
berries drop.</u>

Pyracantha bears spring blossoms and colorful fruits in autumn
and winter. Plants vary in size from
spreading ground covers to low to
tall shrubs. You can train some of the
larger upright kinds as small trees.
Because pyracanthas can take severe pruning, you can grow them as
formal or informal espaliers, hedges,
topiary, and standards. But many
gardeners think pyracanthas look
best when their natural form is main-
tained without severe clipping.

Blossoms and fruits appear on
short, spurlike branches on 2-year-
old-wood. An unpruned shrub's berries will form farther and farther out
on increasingly long branches.
Without attention, a shrub can grow
quite large. Long branches may
droop or break under the weight of a
heavy crop of berries.

There are two ways to control a
shrub's size without clipping it: 1)
Pinch new growth to encourage
branching and compactness; 2) Cut
out branches that have borne berries, and cut back excessively long
branches to laterals growing in desirable directions.

Because they produce dense
growth and thorns, pyracanthas
make fine barrier or hedgerow plants
for your garden. For these uses, prune
back only wayward branches, should
they occur.

Ground cover and low shrub varieties need pruning only to shape.
Cut off vertical stems on ground covers to maintain an even height. On
low shrubs, cut back any wayward
stems that detract from the plant's
appearance.

All but the ground cover and
dwarf varieties are easy to train as
formal or informal espaliers (see page

50). To control growth and tidy berry
clusters on espaliers, cut back flowering stems (except those that form
the main framework) to just above
the first flower cluster. Always make
all cuts back to a lateral or cluster of
leaves. Stubbed branches usually die
back and rot.

Fireblight can be a problem. The
disease causes blackened, burned-
looking stem tips and leaves. If your
plant becomes infected, cut off each
diseased branch about a foot below
the affected area. Disinfect shears
after each cut.

PYROSTEGIA venusta *(P. ignea,
Bignonia venusta).* Flame vine. Evergreen vine. <u>Prune in early spring.</u>

Flame vine is a fast grower,
climbing by means of tendrils. Prune
to control its spread and to prevent
crowding. Before spring growth starts,
untangle any snarled stems. Cut back
stems heading in unwanted directions, thin out excess growth, and remove dead and weak stems.

Because flowers come on new
growth, heavy pruning encourages
flower production. You can severely
prune any side branches growing
from main stems.

PYRUS. Ornamental pear (for edible pear, see page 90). Deciduous
and evergreen trees. <u>Prune in win-
ter</u> (except as noted below).

The deciduous pears include *P.
calleryana, P. ussuriensis,* sand pear
(P. pyrifolia), and willow-leafed pear
(P. salicifolia). To become good single-trunked trees, these plants need
early training as outlined on page 14.

After a tree produces a strong
branch framework, prune only as
needed to thin out the crown. Remove crowding branches (especially
upright limbs that are parallel to the
trunk), weak stems, and dead and
broken branches. Prune any stems
or limbs that are too vigorous, heading them back to well-placed
branches or laterals within the tree's
crown.

Evergreen pear *(P. kawakamii)*
needs considerable early guidance.
You can train it to grow in any one of
several possible ways: as a limber
shrub, as a tree with one or several
trunks, and as a formal or informal
espalier.

Pyrus (deciduous). Thin out crowding
upright stems, head back extra-long
ones.

For a shrub, select a plant with
several stems at its base. Allow the
young plant to grow for a while without pruning. As the shrub develops,
shorten long, wispy branches to encourage the plant to produce additional branches and become bushier. Thin out weak and unwanted
stems as necessary and head back
any wayward stem to a leaf, lateral,
or joint with another limb.

To develop a tree, refer to early
training guidelines on page 14. Stake
it securely until the trunk becomes
thick enough to support the canopy.
Make framework branches stronger
by shortening young ones, cutting
them back to upward-facing buds or
laterals.

Fast growth and limber branches
make this an easy plant for espalier
training. See page 50 for directions
for both formal and informal training. To encourage more bloom on an
espalier, cut off two-thirds of the previous year's growth from each branch
immediately after the plant blossoms.

All pears are more or less susceptible to fireblight, a disease that
results in blackened, scorched-look-
ing leaves and branches. If your tree
shows signs of infection, cut off each
affected branch about a foot below
the infected area. Disinfect shears
after each cut.

QUARTER VINE.
See Bignonia.

QUEENSLAND KAURI.
See Agathis.

QUEENSLAND NUT.
See Macadamia.

QUEENSLAND UMBRELLA TREE.
See Schefflera.

RHODODENDRON AND AZALEA

Prune rhododendron and azalea mainly to shape them.

Technically speaking, all azaleas are rhododendrons, and together they comprise a large group of deciduous and evergreen shrubs. But obvious differences set most azaleas apart from most rhododendrons.

One of these differences is the way in which azaleas and rhododendrons grow. Because they grow differently, you prune them differently. *Prune azaleas and rhododendrons in winter or spring (see text that follows).*

Rhododendrons

A vigorous young rhododendron plant may spend several years becoming established in your garden before it flowers. In order to prune rhododendrons properly, you need to understand how climate affects them and how they grow.

How stems grow. Growth comes in flushes. In areas where the growing season is short, there may be one growth spurt in spring, but two or even three where a mild climate prevails. Each new shoot has a few leaves scattered along its length. When growth ceases, most leaves cluster together to form a rosette at the end of the stem. At the tip of each stem is a terminal bud: growth (vegetative) buds are slender and tapered; flower buds are shorter and rounder. Beneath both kinds of terminal buds lie several growth buds clustered at the bases of the leaves in the rosette.

When to prune. In mild-winter climates, pinch off terminal buds (see "How stems grow" and "Pinching," both on this page) or prune stems in winter or early spring. Where winters are severe, wait to pinch buds or prune stems until spring, after danger of frost is over. (Whatever the climate, you may delay pruning stems until just after flowering, in order to enjoy the most blooms.)

In any climate you can do some shaping while plants are in bloom, using the cut flower clusters for spring bouquets. To prevent seed formation that can reduce next year's bloom, remove spent flower trusses, especially on younger plants. Be careful not to damage the growth buds at the base of each bloom truss.

Pinching. To encourage a bushier plant, remove the terminal growth bud. Do this in spring before the growth bud sprouts or just as it begins to grow. The next flush of growth will stimulate several growth buds in the rosette to sprout. The result will be that several branches will grow, making the plant bushier. (The growth buds of the rosette will be stimulated to sprout naturally after flowering if the terminal bud is a flower bud.)

Pinching off the terminal bud is particularly important on a young plant, where a stem may elongate for several growth flushes without branching unless you remove the terminal bud. By pinching regularly, you can easily guide a young plant's form so that it will need little shaping in its mature years.

Cutting back. For plants that need pruning to correct their shape, cut back a stem to just above a leaf rosette, where dormant growth buds will be waiting to branch out. If you have to cut back into bare wood, look for a band of faint rings on the bark that mark where there once was a rosette of leaves. Make the cut just above the rings. The small bumps under the bark are dormant growth buds. To remove branches entirely, make cuts back to joints with other limbs.

Rejuvenating. You can rejuvenate an old, overgrown, leggy rhododendron over a period of about 4 years. The summer before you do any pruning, fertilize the plant and keep it well watered so that it will be healthy before major surgery.

In the following winter or early spring, cut down one-third of the old limbs to about 8 to 12 inches from the ground. The following year, cut down the second third of the stems, and a year later, cut down the last third of the stems. Try to locate old growth rings on the stems and make cuts above them. If you can't find any growth rings, cut stems back to about 12 inches and hope for regrowth.

Some rhododendron species and hybrids won't take this sort of pruning. Members of the Falconeri series and so-called "tree" rhododendrons in general will not produce new growth from bare wood. Rhododendrons in the Thomsonii series and smooth-barked species and hybrids put out little or no growth from bare stumps. Train these rhododendrons from youth by pinching.

Azaleas

Unlike rhododendrons, azaleas include both *deciduous* and *evergreen* shrubs. For this reason, and because azaleas grow differently from rhododendrons, you will prune them differently.

How stems grow. The new shoots of *deciduous* and *evergreen azaleas* produce leaves that are fairly evenly spaced along the length of the stems. At the base of each leaf is a growth bud. This means that new growth will sprout from almost anywhere you make a cut in an azalea stem, whether it is leafy or bare. Consequently, you don't have to be quite as careful when you prune an azalea as when you prune a rhododendron.

When to prune. Prune *deciduous azaleas* when they are dormant and leafless. In mild-winter climates, do this in winter or in early spring before buds start to grow. In cold-winter climates, prune plants in spring after the danger of severe frost has passed, but before buds begin to sprout.

Prune *evergreen azaleas* at the same time you prune rhododendrons: in mild-winter climates, during winter and spring; in cold-winter climates, during spring, after the danger of severe frost is past. Because of the way they grow (see below), you can pinch or prune *evergreen azaleas* during the growing season. You can postpone this until after flowering.

Pinching. *Evergreen azaleas* grow steadily for a long time each year. (*Deciduous azaleas*, more like rhododendrons, grow with a strong but briefer spurt.) As a result, the stems of *evergreen azaleas* may grow long without branching. You can counteract this by pinching stem tips to promote branching from lateral buds. During the growing season, pinch stems as often as needed to develop the branching you want.

If needed to give balance to a plant, you can pinch the tips of stems of *deciduous azaleas* during the growing season.

Pruning. Shear back new growth on *evergreen azaleas* to keep plants most compact. Do this after flowers fade in the spring. (However, if you don't like the look of sheared plants, prune back long and awkward stems selectively.)

Deciduous azaleas may become woody and unproductive as they grow older. To keep them vigorous, remove old weak stems during winter pruning each year.

Rhododendron. After flowers fall, remove cluster just above top leaf on stem. Don't damage growth bud.

Rhododendron can become leggy. Cut back to whorl of leaves. Stems will grow from buds just beneath cut.

Azalea. Growth buds are all along stem. Pinch or cut back stem tips to develop branching, dense plant.

QUERCUS. Oak. Deciduous and evergreen trees. Prune in winter or summer (deciduous), summer (evergreen).

Young oaks need early training to develop single trunks as described on page 14. They tend to grow so many twigs that none of the branches elongates for many years. To promote rapid vertical growth and thwart the elongation of all growth except the leader's, pinch off tips of unwanted small side branches. Retain as much leaf surface as possible. If a forked leader develops, cut off the weaker fork.

Once a young oak has gained height and has begun to establish a framework of branches, it needs less attention. Thin out twiggy interior branches that are not a part of the main framework. Cut out shoots or stems growing in unwanted directions or in competition with desirable branches. Make all cuts to joints with other branches or the trunk. If you stub back a branch, a brush of new shoots is likely to grow.

Pin oak (*Q. palustris*) is a pyramidal tree when it's young. It forms a rounded top as it matures. During the pyramidal stage, its lower branches are down-sweeping. If you remove the lowest branches to gain walking space beneath the tree, the limbs above will bend into a down-sweeping position. When the tree is mature, the down-sweeping process will stop. You can then cut off lower limbs to create a tree suitable for walking under.

QUILLAJA saponaria. Soapbark tree. Evergreen tree. Prune whenever needed.

Young soapbark trees form dense columns of foliage. Trees carry branches to the ground. For a single-trunked tree, follow early training guidelines on page 14. You can also grow the tree with several trunks. In windy areas, stake the tree securely and thin out twiggy growth in the crown; otherwise, young trees may blow over before their roots are well established.

After tree shape is established, you'll have no routine pruning to do. Thin out twiggy growth and any dead and broken branches whenever needed. Head back any wayward stems.

You can take advantage of soap-

bark tree's dense growth by using it as an informal tall hedge.

QUINCE (*Cydonia*). Fruiting quince. (For flowering quince, see *Chaenomeles*.) Deciduous shrub or small tree. Prune in winter.

To train quince as a single-trunked tree, follow guidelines on page 14. You can also grow quince as a large shrub or shrub-tree, leaving on the lower branches or removing them, as you prefer.

Shaping is the only type of pruning quince requires. Head back to laterals or joints with other limbs any branches that grow too long and unbalance the plant's shape. Thin out branches in the center to keep the canopy open to light and air. Because fruit is borne on new growth, heavy pruning will reduce the fruit crop. The larger the number of short branches that receive good light, the greater the tree's fruit crop will be.

Heavy pruning and/or too much fertilizer results in vigorous soft growth that is susceptible to fireblight. If any branches turn black and burned-looking, cut them out about a foot below the damaged section. Disinfect pruning shears after each cut.

RAPHIOLEPIS. Evergreen shrubs (one a small tree). Prune after flowering.

Neat, dense, and malleable sum up the predominant qualities of *Raphiolepis*. Many kinds exist, ranging from 2-foot-high border shrubs to 6 to 10-foot background and screen plants. One, *R.* 'Majestic Beauty', is robust

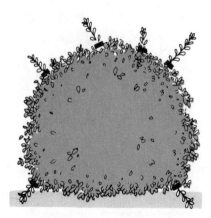

Raphiolepis. After flowering, cut back long stems to keep plant compact.

enough to train as a tree with one or several trunks (see guidelines on page 14).

The various kinds of *Raphiolepis* need little pruning or training. To encourage greater bushiness, pinch back branch tips at least once a year right after flowering. Start when plants are young. For a more open shape, allow plants to grow naturally, and thin out small and crowding branches from the interior. To encourage spreading growth, pinch or head back upright branches. To make plants more upright, pinch or head back horizontal branches.

If distinctively light green, soft leaves appear on stems close to the ground, your plant has been grafted on quince rootstock. Pull these shoots off as they appear.

RASPBERRY.
See Blackberry and Raspberry, page 31.

RATSTRIPPER.
See Paxistima.

REDBERRY.
See Rhamnus.

REDBUD.
See Cercis.

RED CEDAR.
See Juniperus (Eastern), Thuja (Western).

RED CHOKEBERRY.
See Aronia.

REDWOOD.
See Sequoia.

RHAMNUS. Evergreen or deciduous shrubs or trees. Prune in winter (deciduous), spring (evergreen).

Generally, the different kinds of *Rhamnus* need pruning only to direct or control their shape. You can train taller kinds as multitrunked trees or as tall clipped hedges as well as large, handsome shrubs. These include alder buckthorn (*R. frangula*), cascara sagrada (*R. purshiana*), coffeeberry (*R. californica*), common buckthorn (*R. cathartica*), holly-leaf redberry (*R. crocea ilicifolia*), and Italian buckthorn (*R. alaternus*).

Tallhedge buckthorn (*R. frangula* 'Columnaris') is almost exclusively a hedge plant. Very slender in form, it can, without pruning, reach 15 feet tall. The shorter varieties of redberry (*R. crocea*) and *R. califor-*

nica spread as wide as or wider than their height.

With all kinds of *Rhamnus*, head back laterals to any branches that grow too long and unbalance the plant's shape. To keep low growers low, prune upward-growing branches, cutting them out entirely or cutting them back to horizontal side branches. For hedges, clip or shear as needed during the growing season to maintain neatness (see page 70 for general hedge information).

RHAPIDOPHYLLUM.
See Palm.

RHAPIS.
See Palm.

RHODODENDRON.
See page 98.

RHODOTYPOS scandens. Jetbead. Deciduous shrub. Prune in winter.

Jetbead will need no pruning for several years. In time, though, you'll need to cut out oldest stems that are producing only twiggy, weak growth. Replacement shoots will grow from the ground to renew the plant. Pinch some of these to promote branching at the base. To reduce the height of a plant, cut back the longest stem to a pair of laterals or growth buds well down within the plant.

RHOICISSUS capensis (*Cissus capensis*). Evergreen grape. Evergreen vine. Prune during growing season.

Evergreen grape is useful on a vertical surface (with support), on an overhead arbor or trellis, and as a ground cover. On vertical surfaces and overhead structures, pinch tips of new stems to guide growth and keep plant in bounds. If necessary, cut out any unwanted stems that crowd the plant. Ground cover plantings usually need no pruning.

RHOPALOSTYLIS.
See Palm.

RHUS. Sumac. Evergreen or deciduous shrubs or trees. Pruning times vary.

The evergreen sumacs from western America and South Africa differ greatly from the deciduous North American sumacs. Consequently you must prune them differently and at different times.

Deciduous sumacs. *Rhus aromatica, R. copallina, R. glabra, R. trilobata, R. typhina.* Prune in winter, summer.

These sumacs grow in colonies of a few to many stems that spring up from the roots. They're especially numerous if roots have been injured. Because of this characteristic, fragrant sumac (*Rhus aromatica*) and squawbush or skunkbush (*R. trilobata*) make effective bank covers or rough ground covers. Aside from occasionally removing dead stems, you need do no pruning.

The three other sumacs will grow as shrubs or trees. Shining sumac grows 30 feet tall, staghorn sumac (*R. typhina*) reaches to 15 to 30 feet, and smooth sumac (*R. glabra*) grows to 15 feet. These all look quite natural growing in clumps or colonies. To control growth, pull up root sprouts that emerge in unwanted places and cut down or head back stems that grow too tall.

You can also easily train each of these sumacs as a single-trunked tree. A young plant grows a straight, unbranched stem for several feet, then branches out in a "Y" fork. Each year thereafter, each branch usually forks again. Unless a branch gets in your way or becomes permanently bent from the weight of a seed cluster, these trees need no pruning. To remove an unwanted branch, cut it back to a joint with another, but keep an eye on the beauty of the branch structure.

Evergreen sumacs. *Rhus choriophylla, R. integrifolia, R. lancea, R. laurina, R. ovata.* Prune in spring.

African sumac (*R. lancea*) is the only tree in this group. Follow guidelines on page 14 to train it to a single trunk or several trunks. After trunk and branch framework are established, remove only dead and twiggy branches. You can also let this sumac branch from the ground as a tall, filmy-looking shrub. Or use it as a high screen planting, or train and trim it as a hedge (see page 70).

Lemonade berry (*R. integrifolia*), laurel sumac (*R. laurina*), and sugar bush (*R. ovata*) are useful as basic shrubs in and near their native regions. All make fine screen plants, clipped hedges, and espaliers (see page 50). For specimen shrubs, occasionally head back wayward branches to laterals within the plant's outline.

Laurel sumac is more open and rangy than the other two; you may need to pinch it to promote branching. You can convert older plants into small trees by triming off lower branches. *R. choriophylla* is the smallest plant. Occasionally you may need to remove a wayward branch.

Rhus (deciduous). To prune, just remove unattractively placed branches.

RIBES. Ornamental currant, gooseberry. (See Currant for fruiting kinds.) Deciduous and evergreen shrubs. Prune after flowering.

In contrast to the fruit-bearing currants and gooseberries, these ornamental kinds need no special pruning. Alpine currant (*R. alpinum*) is dense and twiggy. You can train it easily as a hedge that's less than 5 feet high (see hedge guidelines on page 70).

Fuchsia-flowering gooseberry (*R. speciosum*), also dense, but spiny, looks better untrimmed. Cut out oldest and dead stems from time to time. Catalina perfume or evergreen currant (*R. viburnifolium*) grows low and sprawling, and makes a good shrubby ground cover.

Golden currant (*R. aureum*), red-flowering currant (*R. sanguineum*), and *R. laurifolium* take similar pruning treatment. Periodically remove old stems that no longer produce vigorous growth or flowers. Don't stub back stems. Make all cuts to laterals, joints with other branches, or the ground.

RICE PAPER PLANT.
See Tetrapanax.

ROBINIA. Locust. Deciduous trees and shrubs. Prune in winter.

Locust trees need early training (described on page 14) to develop strong trunks and branch frameworks. These include *R. ambigua* 'Decaisneana', *R. a.* 'Idahoensis', and black locust (*R. pseudoacacia*) and some of its varieties. After the plant's basic form is established, you'll have little routine pruning to do. Cut out dead and broken limbs as needed, making cuts to joints with other branches. Cut out any branches that you think detract from the tree's overall limb structure.

Two grafted trees need special attention: *R. hispida macrophylla* and *R. pseudoacacia* 'Umbraculifera'. These two usually are grafted onto a trunk of another locust and form dense, rounded crowns of foliage. Stake them securely until roots are well established. Thin out the canopy, removing weak and twiggy stems, so winds can pass through.

Shrubby rose acacia (*R. hispida*) spreads by root shoots to form thorny, thicketlike clumps. Limit the spread of a clump by cutting out the perimeter stems with a sharp spade. Periodically cut the oldest and least vigorous stems to the ground.

ROCKROSE.
See Cistus.

ROCKY MOUNTAIN THIMBLEBERRY.
See Rubus.

RONDELETIA. Evergreen shrubs. Prune after flowering.

In pruning Rondeletia, your main goal is to promote branching and bushiness. Cut back young plants about halfway just after flowering. Pinch tips of new growth. On leggy, older plants, pinch and cut back as needed to restore denseness. Remove spent flower clusters to encourage further bloom.

ROSA.
See Rose, page 102.

ROSE ACACIA.
See Robinia.

ROSE APPLE.
See Syzygium.

ROSEMARY.
See Rosmarinus.

ROSE OF SHARON.
See Hibiscus.

ROSMARINUS officinalis. Rosemary. Evergreen shrub. Prune after flowering.

Rosemary is a dense, rounded shrub that's a bit wider than it is high, with gracefully upsweeping branches. With no pruning, the plant will grow larger and larger, eventually becoming a dense tangle of leafy-tipped woody stems.

Reducing the size of an overgrown plant is a tricky undertaking because bare stems won't sprout new growth. You can only head back into leafy wood. To avoid struggling with an overgrown shrub, plan ahead. Begin to prune a plant when it's still young. Pinch tips of new growth each year or head back new shoots to encourage branching. Cut back any leggy stems to points on the stem where leaves are growing.

Distinctly upright varieties like 'Tuscan Blue' will need more pinching and pruning in their early years to become full, mature plants.

Dwarf or prostrate rosemary (*R. o.* 'Prostratus') grows horizontal stems and branches that may curve upward, then down, then twist or curl. It will form a dense, rather wavy ground cover, cascade down a retaining wall, grow up over a low wall and spread out, or even cover a wire mesh fence. It needs little pruning— just remove wayward stems. To keep it as a flat ground cover, pinch it back or shear it.

ROWAN.
See Sorbus.

ROYAL POINCIANA.
See Delonix.

ROYAL TRUMPET VINE.
See Distictis.

RUBBER PLANT.
See Ficus.

RUBUS deliciosus. Rocky Mountain thimbleberry. Deciduous shrub. Prune in autumn or winter.

Unlike its thorny, sprawling blackberry relatives, this is a graceful, arching shrub with thornless stems. Like blackberries, these stems are biennial. They grow from the ground one year, bear flowers the next year, and die the following win-

(Continued on page 105)

ROSE

Gardeners today have a great selection of roses to choose from. These deciduous shrubs and shrubby vines include modern hybrids, such as hybrid teas, grandifloras, floribundas, various "old-fashioned" types (known as old garden roses), old and new shrub roses, and species roses.

With all roses, the goal of pruning is to remove weak, unproductive, and dead stems and to encourage vigorous new stems to grow. The specifics vary according to the kinds of roses you raise, the way you use them, and the climate.

When to prune. There are two guidelines for when to prune roses.

Prune repeat-flowering roses— roses that bloom several times in the growing season—when they are dormant. In mild-winter climates, prune these in winter or early spring before new growth starts. In cold-winter climates, prune them late enough in spring so that new growth won't be damaged by severe frosts. It's usually safe to begin pruning about 30 days before the date of the last frost.

On the other hand, *prune once-flowering roses—roses that bloom only once a year—in late spring or summer after flowering.*

Light vs. heavy pruning. Most rose growers agree that roses produce the best plants and plenty of good flowers when they are pruned lightly to moderately. Follow this rule for best results.

In cold-winter climates where rose growers usually protect their plants, canes are nevertheless occasionally killed back by winter freezes. When this happens, cut back canes all the way to living wood. Often, this amounts to a heavy pruning—to be avoided unless it's to remove dead wood.

Modern bush roses

These include hybrid teas, grandifloras, and floribundas; polyanthas

and miniatures; and standard (so-called "tree") roses.

Hybrid teas, grandifloras, floribundas. Prune these plants to maintain symmetrical bushes and to encourage plenty of strong new growth. *Prune in winter or spring when plants are still dormant.*

Cut out all dead wood and weak, twiggy branches. Remove old canes that no longer produce vigorous growth by cutting them back to the bud union. Open up the bush by removing all branches that cross through the center. This gives you a vase-shaped plant. Finally, cut back all of the previous year's new growth by as much as one-third of its length. (In the mild-winter areas of the West and South you can develop large specimen shrubs if you avoid cutting into any of the past season's new growth that is thicker than a pencil.)

Unless your rose has especially spreading growth, make all cuts to outward-facing buds.

Look for any canes that have grown from the plant's understock beneath the bud union. Remove all of these stems (suckers) by grasping them firmly, one at a time, with a gloved hand. Pull the suckers away from the plant. This procedure removes latent buds at the sucker's base (buds that remain if you just cut the sucker out).

If you live where winters are severe, remove all dead and damaged wood regardless of how low you must prune your bushes. Even though a cane may be green on the outside, it is damaged if the center is brown. Prune back to wood that is light green to cream white in the center.

Polyanthas and miniatures. These roses are grouped together because they grow in a similar way, though they differ in size. Typically, these roses produce plenty of new growth each year. You can cut them back

Annual pruning brings forth majestic blooms.

severely to limit their size without sacrificing many blooms or the health of the plants. *Prune polyantha and miniature roses in winter or spring when plants are still dormant.*

To prune container plants, thin out stems so that only year-old stems remain. Cut out the weakest of these and cut back the remaining ones to about two buds.

To prune plants that are growing in the ground, thin out all twiggy and unproductive stems, remove crowding stems that cross through the plant's center, and cut back the remaining canes to half their length. Cut the canes to outward-facing buds unless the variety is especially spreading.

Pruned plants should have a

Typical hybrid tea or grandiflora rose—cuts are for moderate pruning.

Rose at left after pruning: old, weak crossing stems, and one-third of each new stem removed.

symmetrical outline. Tip-pinch or cut back any extra-vigorous new growth that unbalances the plant's symmetry.

Standards. Popularly called "tree roses," these plants consist of a bush rose—usually a hybrid tea, grandiflora, floribunda, or polyantha—budded atop a 2 to 3½-foot stem that forms a trunk. Prune them according to the directions for whatever type of rose forms the head. *Prune plants in winter or spring when they are dormant.*

Prune a rose standard a bit more heavily than a regular bush of the same variety to keep the head more compact and in proportion to the trunk. Cut back last year's new growth by one-third to half its length. Prune carefully to keep the head symmetrical.

Climbing roses

The long, somewhat flexible canes of climbing roses need to be tied to some sort of support for most garden uses. Most climbing roses are climbing hybrid teas, grandifloras, floribundas, or modern hybrids that look like these types. Most flower repeatedly during the growing season. Climbers that bloom only in spring receive slightly different treatment (explained below).

Repeat-flowering climbers. It takes several years for plants to become established and produce strong, climbing canes. As strong canes mature, tie them into position. Climbers will give more bloom if you train canes horizontally. For the first 2 to 3 years after planting, prune only to remove dead stems, very weak growth, and spent flowers. *Prune in winter or spring when plants are dormant.*

Long canes will bear flowering laterals and some secondary climbing stems that will produce flowering laterals. On established plants, prune to stimulate the growth of flowering laterals and new canes. These will replace older ones that have lost their vigor.

Each year, remove only the old and obviously unproductive wood, then cut back to two or three buds all laterals that bore flowers during the last year. The best blooms come on laterals growing from 2 to 3-year-old wood. Don't cut back long canes at all unless any grow too long for the available space. During flowering season, remove spent blooms, cutting each back to a strong bud about three leaves up from the shoot's point of origin.

Pillar roses are short climbers whose canes may reach about 10 feet tall and will produce good flower crops when trained upright. Prune these roses the same way as repeat-flowering climbers.

Spring-blooming climbers. These roses are either very woody or have limber canes *(ramblers, see below)*.

Give the woody spring-blooming climbers the same early guidance as repeat-flowering climbers. Because they bloom on growth that formed after last year's flowering, a dormant season pruning destroys potential flowers. *Prune plants immediately after bloom.*

Cut out unproductive old canes and any weak or crossing branches. Train strong new growth as it matures later in the year.

Ramblers produce a great many

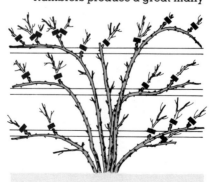

Climbing rose. Leave all vigorous canes, cut back flowering laterals to 2 to 3 buds.

flowering laterals and new canes. These will replace older ones that have lost their vigor.

Typically, canes bear flowers for just 1 year; sometimes they'll bear longer if strong new growth sprouts from a cane that has flowered. *Wait to prune until new shoots are growing after flowering.*

Cut to the ground all canes that have just bloomed and show no signs of producing any strong new growth. Cut back to strong growth any canes that are producing it. As new canes mature, train them into position. These will flower profusely when trained in a variety of ways: as a ground cover; horizontally or vertically; and cascading from atop an arbor, pergola, or wall.

Shrub and old garden roses

This large, general category includes many types and shapes. Most are vigorous and need some annual thinning and shaping, but little cutting back. *Prune the repeat-flowering varieties in winter or early spring, according to your region's climate.* Since most are used as specimen shrubs or as hedges and screens, give them only the amount of shaping the landscape requires. Cut back any awkward shoots. Remove weak wood and old canes that no longer produce flowers or vigorous growth.

Prune once-flowering varieties in spring immediately after the bloom period. Cut out the least-productive old canes. Cut back any extra-long new canes to encourage the growth of laterals that will flower the following spring.

*Some old roses, especially many hybrid perpetuals, produce fairly long, arching canes. Like climbers, they bloom more profusely when canes are trained horizontally, or even arched over with the tips attached to the ground. This encourages flowering laterals to grow from most of the buds along the canes. Prune old roses that are trained this way the same as repeat-flowering climbers.

...Rubus (cont'd.)

ter. Each year, prune all stems that have flowered, cutting them to the ground.

RUSSIAN OLIVE.
See Elaeagnus.

SABAL.
See Palm.

SACRED FLOWER OF THE INCAS.
See Cantua.

SAGE.
See Salvia.

ST. JOHN'S BREAD.
See Ceratonia.

ST. JOHNSWORT.
See Hypericum.

SALAL.
See Gaultheria.

SALIX. Willow. Deciduous trees or shrubs. <u>Prune in winter, spring.</u>

Though the dividing line may appear to blur at times, two groups of willows exist—trees and shrubs. Each has its own set of pruning guidelines.

Trees. <u>Prune willow trees in winter.</u>

These include various weeping willows, such as *S. alba tristis, S. babylonica,* and *S. blanda;* and upright kinds, such as *S. matsudana* and its variety, corkscrew willow (*S.m.* 'Tortuosa'). All of these potentially large trees need routine early training as described on page 14. Pay special attention to establishing a strong, tall leader on weeping kinds so that their permanent branch framework will be high enough to allow their pendulous branches to drape fully down. In later years, thin out dead and weak branches and any vertical watersprouts.

Shrubs. <u>Prune these just before leaf-out in late winter or early spring.</u>

Shrubby willows include rose-gold pussy willow (*S. gracilistyla*), purple osier and dwarf purple osier (*S. purpurea* and *S.p.* 'Gracilis'). Thin out oldest stems and crowded interior branches. If shrubs begin to lose vigor or become too large for their space, cut plants to the ground. Vigorous new stems will renew the plant. You can also use purple osier as a formal hedge (see page 70).

Other shrubs that may grow into small trees are French pussy willow (*S. caprea*) and pussy willow (*S. dis-*

color). To keep them shrubby, cut back upright stems to joints with lower stems or cut them to the ground whenever they grow too large. A simpler alternative is to grow them as shrubs during their early years, gradually allowing them to make the transition into small trees. Once they become trees, periodically thin out dead and twiggy wood, remove dead and broken branches.

Redstem and yellowstem willows are varieties of the tree *S. alba.* Keep them shrubby by hard pruning; they will become thickets of colorful stems in winter. When a young plant reaches 6 to 8 feet high and has several stems growing from the ground, cut out weak stems and head back remaining ones to about 1 foot from the soil. These will send forth brushes of long, vigorous stems that will turn brilliant colors by the next winter. At the end of winter, thin these out and head stems back to about 2 buds. Follow this procedure for several years.

When the plant becomes too large, or the stumps from which its branches grow begin to look too ugly, you can cut the plant to the ground. The following winter, begin to prune again as though your willow were a young plant.

Salix. Remove trunk sprouts, dead branches, and branches that hang too low from weeping willows.

SALTBUSH.
See Atriplex.

SALVIA. Sage. Evergreen and semi-evergreen shrubs. <u>Pruning times vary.</u>

For three of the shrubby sages, pruning is more a matter of personal

taste than necessity. Without pruning, gray-leafed *S. clevelandii* and *S. leucophylla* develop into sprawling but attractive plants that are useful in certain garden situations. To keep them compact, cut back the previous year's growth by as much as half and thin out any weak, crossing, or wayward stems.

You can let densely foliaged *S. greggii* grow at will, but in time the plant may become floppy. For compactness, cut its most recent growth back as much as you wish. You also can grow it as a formal or informal hedge (see general guidelines on page 70).

Mexican bush sage (*S. leucantha*) sends up many stems from the ground and blooms in summer and autumn. As flowers fade, cut older stems to the ground. New bloom-bearing ones will replace them.

SAMBUCUS. Elderberry. Deciduous shrubs and trees. <u>Prune in winter.</u>

Elderberries that grow into trees, such as *S. caerulea,* need early training as described on page 14. You can train them as single-trunked or multitrunked trees. They grow quickly.

After they have become trees, remove dead, weak, and crowding branches. Head back any overlong branches to strong laterals. You also can grow the tree elderberries as mammoth, tropical-looking shrubs by cutting them to the ground each year.

Shrubby elderberries include *S. callicarpa, S. canadensis, S. pubens, S. racemosa,* and their varieties. Let them grow vigorously; plants will form many stems from the ground. Head back stems to shape the plant. Thin out weak, crowding, and dead stems. To make way for strong new growth on established plants, cut out older stems each year. If a plant becomes overgrown, you can cut it to the ground and start over.

SANTOLINA. Evergreen subshrubs. <u>Prune in early spring.</u>

Both gray-leafed lavender cotton (*S. chamaecyparissus*) and its green-leafed counterpart *S. virens* form low, dense, spreading, and mounded clumps of fine foliage. If left unpruned, they will spread extensively, becoming sparse and woody in the center.

(Continued on page 107)

TOPIARY

Snip frequently to develop and maintain geometric or fanciful form.

Simply stated, topiary is plant sculpture. It ranges from the whimsical—plants clipped into animal and bird shapes—to the architectural—plants trained into geometric forms such as pyramids, spheres, and boxes.

Creating a well-shaped topiary requires time, patience, and plenty of attention. Start with plants that are likely to give you good results. The best plants for topiary have many small leaves (or scales or needles for evergreen conifers), as well as dormant buds along their stems. Look for a plant that will make new growth from bare wood.

Your climate will determine your choice of plants, but these are among the best wherever they can be grown: yew *(Taxus)*, boxwood *(Buxus)*, cypress *(Cupressus)*, *Chamaecyparis*, juniper *(Juniperus)*, and myrtle *(Myrtus)*. Some larger-leafed plants are also easy to train—*Cotoneaster*, firethorn *(Pyracantha)*, *Pittosporum*, privet *(Ligustrum)*, *Syzygium*—but close clipping with pruning shears will make the leaves look chopped and ragged.

Select a plant whose natural shape roughly matches the form you intend to create. For example, to sculpt a running dog, you'd want to use a spreading plant. For a living version of a classic Greek column, you'd want a tall, upright plant.

You may need to use more than one plant to create your topiary. For instance, to develop a large topiary elephant, you might need to set out four plants—one to form each leg. Then, as the plants grow, you can prune them together to form the body, head, and trunk.

While you're still developing the topiary, trim it with pruning shears rather than hedge clippers. Make cuts carefully and individually so you can accurately direct new growth toward the shape you want. In general, you can apply the directions for hedge training and maintenance (see page 70) to topiary. Remember that the bottom of your topiary figure needs light to remain leafy. Beyond this, the quality depends as much on artistic talent as horticultural skill.

Topiary. These five examples show various possible shapes—ranging from geometric abstract to whimsical statues in foliage of animal (or even human) figures. What's required are proper plants, imagination, and time.

...*Santolina (cont'd.)*

Each year, head back clumps in early spring to limit their growth. Prune around the edges (as though you were giving the plant a haircut) as much as needed. After blooms fade, shear off spent flowers and some of the plant's stems to maintain neatness.

You can use either kind as a low clipped hedge, shearing as needed to maintain uniformity (see page 70 for general hedge information).

SAPIUM sebiferum. Chinese tallow tree. Deciduous tree. Prune in winter.

You can train Chinese tallow tree to a single trunk by following the guidelines on page 14. Naturally shrubby, it's good for multitrunked training as well. Select the stems you want for trunks, cut out any others from the ground, and pull out any new shoots that arise from the ground or low on the trunks.

Subsequently, you need prune only to shape. Cut out weak, broken, and crowding branches and head back any too-long branches.

Winter cold may kill branch tips. New shoots will quickly cover this damage. There's no need to cut off dead branch tips, because they'll break off later. If new growth comes in too thickly, thin out excess stems.

SAPPHIRE BERRY.
See Symplocos.

SARCOCOCCA. Evergreen shrubs. Prune any time.

These clump-forming shrubs send up many stems from the ground. They can spread into sizable colonies, but they grow so slowly that you don't need to do much pruning. Head back any stems that grow too long. Occasionally, cut old, nonvigorous stems to the ground.

You can cut an old, neglected, ratty plant to the ground in early spring. New stems will grow up to replace the old ones. If you plant *S. ruscifolia* against a vertical surface, it will form a natural espalier.

SASSAFRAS albidum. Sassafras. Deciduous tree. Prune in winter.

Ordinarily, sassafras needs no special training to become a straight, single-trunked tree. Just make sure the young plant has one vertical trunk,

and be sure side branches don't grow at the expense of the leader. If they do, head them back halfway.

As the tree grows, you can cut off lower branches so that eventually you'll be able to walk beneath the canopy. Cut off any broken and dead branches at joints with other limbs or the trunk. Roots often send up sprouts, especially if they've been damaged by digging. Pull up these sprouts whenever they occur.

SAWLEAF ZELKOVA.
See Zelkova.

SCARLET KADSURA.
See Kadsura.

SCARLET WISTERIA TREE.
See Sesbania.

SCHEFFLERA. Evergreen shrub-trees. Prune spring to autumn.

The best-known one is Queensland umbrella tree or octopus tree (*S. actinophylla* or *Brassaia actinophylla*). It grows naturally as a multitrunked, sparsely branched shrub or tree. New Zealand schefflera (*S. digitata)* is similar, both in the way it grows and in how it responds to pruning.

To increase branching and encourage a good leafing pattern, pinch stem tips or cut main trunks down to wherever you want branching to start. It doesn't matter where you cut a stem; new growth will sprout from below the cut. To rejuvenate an overgrown plant, cut it nearly to the ground.

Hawaiian elf schefflera (*S. arboricola* or *Heptapleurum arboricolum)* may grow as tall as the other two kinds, but it has smaller leaves and many more branches. Overall it's much denser and shrubbier. You can pinch or head back stems anywhere to promote branching. If you want to thin out some stems to reveal more of the plant's branches, make cuts to joints with other branches.

SCHINUS. Pepper tree. Evergreen trees. Prune in early spring.

Brazilian pepper tree (*S. terebinthifolius)* and so-called California pepper tree (*S. molle)*—actually a South American native—differ markedly in appearance, uses, and pruning requirements.

California pepper tree develops

a thick, gnarled trunk and heavy limbs that support a canopy of contrastingly delicate, drooping branches and leaves. To grow a tree with a canopy high enough to walk under, give a young tree early training as described on page 14. Early framework training is crucial because this tree is highly susceptible to heart rot, a disease that can start from wounds left by large pruning cuts. If you must remove any branches that are as thick as 3 inches or more, keep cuts well sealed with a pruning compound.

Surprisingly, this tree also makes a fine hedge. Set out plants 2 feet apart, and follow directions on page 70 for training a young hedge. Trim as needed thereafter to keep its informal, billowy shape the size you want.

In contrast to California pepper tree, Brazilian pepper tree forms a broad, dense, umbrella-shaped crown of larger leaves and nonpendulous branches. Use it either as a single-trunked shade tree (see training guidelines on page 14) or grow it with several trunks. Wind, storms, and even the weight of its leaves can break brittle branches. Stake young plants securely, shorten overlong limbs, and thin the canopy in summer to let breezes pass through easily.

SCIADOPITYS verticillata. Umbrella pine. Evergreen coniferous tree. Prune in summer.

A young tree is a narrow, dense cone. Make sure only one leader develops. If a second leader starts to grow, cut it out completely. Otherwise, the plant grows so symmetrically and slowly it needs no routine pruning.

SCIMITAR SHRUB.
See Brachysema.

SEA BUCKTHORN.
See Hippophae.

SENECIO greyi. Evergreen shrub. Prune in early spring.

Each year cut out oldest stems that are no longer producing vigorous branches, or cut them back to healthy laterals. Prune any broken or frost-damaged stems, cutting them back to healthy laterals.

SENNA.
See Cassia.

SEQUOIADENDRON giganteum *(Sequoia gigantea)*. Big tree, giant sequoia. Evergreen coniferous tree. Prune in spring.

Growth is so orderly that pruning is seldom needed. If a second leader develops, cut it out. Tree forms a broad cone that will branch to the ground for many years. Remove lower limbs if the tree spreads too much at ground level, or if you want a tree to walk under.

SEQUOIA sempervirens. Coast redwood. Evergreen coniferous tree. Prune in spring.

Make sure that a young tree develops only one leader (cut out any that try to compete). Because this tree grows so symmetrically, normally it needs no pruning. Occasionally, if a branch grows too long, head it back to a lateral. Trees will keep their branches to the ground for many years. For a tree to walk or sit under, remove lower limbs to create space.

SERVICE BERRY.
See Amelanchier.

SESBANIA tripetii *(Daubentonia tripetii)*. Scarlet wisteria tree. Deciduous shrub or small tree. Prune in early spring.

A fast-growing but short-lived plant, scarlet wisteria tree can be grown as a multistemmed shrub or shrub-tree, or trained as a single-trunked tree (see guidelines on page 14). Each year thin out weak branches. Also cut back year-old side branches on the main framework to stubs with no more than 2 growth buds.

SEVERINIA buxifolia. Chinese box orange. Evergreen shrub or small tree. Prune in spring.

You can train this plant into an attractive, dense, small tree (see instructions on page 14), but its main use is as a barrier hedge—beside each leaf is a pair of spines. Follow the instructions for hedge training on page 70, then shear as needed during the growing season to maintain neatness.

SHADBLOW, SHADBUSH.
See Amelanchier.

SHE-OAK.
See Casuarina.

SHEPHERDIA. Buffalo berry. Deciduous shrubs. Prune in late winter, early spring.

Plants develop into attractive shrubs with no pruning or guidance during their youth. As plants grow older, occasionally remove old, nonvigorous stems. Both *S. argentea* and *S. canadensis* make good hedges (see basic instructions on page 70). Because of its spine-tipped branches, *S. argentea* is useful as a barrier planting, either clipped or natural.

SHRIMP PLANT.
See Justicia.

SHRUB ALTHAEA.
See Hibiscus.

SHRUB ASTER.
See Felicia.

SIBERIAN PEASHRUB.
See Caragana.

SIERRA LAUREL.
See Leucothoe.

SILK OAK.
See Grevillea.

SILKTASSEL.
See Garrya.

SILK TREE.
See Albizia.

SILVER BELL.
See Halesia.

SILVERBERRY.
See Elaeagnus.

SILVER LACE VINE.
See Polygonum.

SIMMONDSIA chinensis. Jojoba, goatnut. Evergreen shrub. Prune in early spring.

Jojoba has dense, boxwoodlike leaves on a compact, rounded mound that grows 4 to 6 feet high. As a specimen shrub, it needs little pruning. Head back to laterals any branches that stick out too far.

Jojoba also makes a good formal hedge plant—a boxwood substitute for low desert gardens. Like boxwood, it can be kept at any height you want by shearing. See page 70 for hedge training information.

SKIMMIA. Evergreen shrubs. Prune in spring, summer.

These slow-growing, compact shrubs need no regular pruning. If an occasional branch grows out too far, head it back to a lateral within the plant's outline.

SKY FLOWER.
See Duranta.

SMOKE TREE.
See Cotinus.

SNOWBALL.
See Viburnum.

SNOWBELL.
See Styrax.

SNOWBERRY.
See Symphoricarpos.

SNOWBUSH.
See Breynia.

SNOWDROP TREE.
See Halesia.

SNOWFLAKE TREE.
See Trevesia.

SOAPBARK TREE.
See Quillaja.

SOLANDRA maxima *(S. guttata)*. Cup-of-gold vine. Evergreen vine. Prune in spring, summer.

Cup-of-gold vine has the woodiness and thick branches of a typical shrub, as well as the vigor and size of a rampant vine. Without pruning, it grows sparsely. For greater branching, denseness, and more flowers, cut back stems and pinch new growth to promote laterals. Prune as much as you want.

You can grow cup-of-gold vine as a rough hedge. Give it plenty of cutting and pinching to keep it under control.

SOLANUM. Evergreen and deciduous shrubs and vines. Prune in late winter, early spring, and whenever necessary.

Most gardeners view these plants as different-sized vines. One of them can be treated as a shrub. Evergreen potato vine (*S. jasminoides*) and deciduous Costa Rican nightshade (*S. wendlandii*) are both vigorous twiners that can cover a lot of space. Cut back potato vine (severely, if necessary) to correct tangling and control its spread. To prevent tangling, first train vine horizontally and low on a wall or fence. Side shoots will grow up to cover area. Cut back and thin out Costa Rican nightshade to untangle stems and limit its growth.

S. rantonnetii, a shrubby vine or

vining shrub, is evergreen or deciduous (depending on winter chill). To keep it as a shrub, head back straggly stems. To use it as a vine, give it support, tying stems to direct their growth. You can let the plant grow naturally to become a sprawling ground cover. It will take any amount of pruning. To train it into a small tree, stake one stem upright. Let it begin branching at whatever height you want, then prune the tree's canopy as though it were a shrub.

SOLLYA heterophylla (*S. fusiformis*). Australian bluebell creeper. Evergreen shrub or vine. <u>Prune in spring.</u>

Without guidance, this sprawling plant's stems will spread out over the ground, twining around each other and any other plants or objects in their path. Use it as a ground cover or trailing vine. For an attractive cascade effect, plant it along the top of a retaining wall.

To grow it as a 2 to 3-foot-high shrub, keep pinching back vinelike shoots that grow out of bounds. To treat it as a vine, give it a support to climb on. Then select and train the strongest shoots, cutting out all others that develop at the plant's base.

SOPHORA. Deciduous or evergreen trees and shrubs. <u>Prune in summer.</u>

Japanese pagoda tree or Chinese scholar tree (*S. japonica*) is the most familiar and largest of this group. You can grow it either as a single-trunked or multitrunked tree by following the guidelines on page 14. Thin out weak, crowding, and unwanted branches from the crown as the young tree develops. After the tree is established, no routine pruning is needed. Cut off any broken and dead branches as they occur.

Two kinds of *Sophora* grow as large shrubs or small trees: mescal bean or Texas mountain laurel (*S. secundiflora*) and Kowhai (*S. tetraptera*). To use these as shrubs, just let them grow naturally. Occasionally thin out weak and crowding branches, and head back any stems that grow irregularly or too tall. To grow them as trees with one or more trunks, follow instructions for *S. japonica* (preceding).

Prune strictly shrubby *S. arizonica* occasionally, thinning or heading back as needed.

SORBARIA. False spiraea. Deciduous shrubs. <u>Prune in late winter, early spring.</u>

These vigorous shrubs form clumps of many stems that can spread to cover a large area. Limit their spread by cutting out perimeter stems with a sharp spade. Flowers come on new wood. Cut back last year's flowering stems to about 2 buds for strong new growth and best flowers.

When a stem has produced flowers for several years, cut it to the ground. Strong new growth will replace it.

SORBUS. Mountain ash. Deciduous trees and shrubs. <u>Prune in winter.</u>

Typical trees include European mountain ash or rowan (*S. aucuparia*). These are handsome either as single-trunked or multitrunked plants. Give young trees early guidance as described on page 14. Cut out any competing leaders. Thin out any vertical or crossing branches in the center of the crown. After the main framework is established, prune to remove any dead or broken branches.

Shrubs, such as *S. tianshanica*, need no routine pruning. If plants produce crowded stems, thin out ones that are nonvigorous or are poorly located. You can train the larger shrubs as shrub-trees by thinning out stems from the ground or limiting their number from the start. Also remove lower branches.

SORREL TREE.
See Oxydendrum.

SOUR GUM.
See Nyssa.

SOURWOOD.
See Oxydendrum.

SOUTHERNWOOD.
See Artemisia.

SPARMANNIA africana. African linden. Evergreen shrub. <u>Prune any time.</u>

When uncontrolled, African linden grows rapidly to 10 to 20 feet as a multistemmed, leggy thicket bearing large, coarse leaves. Prune it heavily to improve its appearance. Either head back longest stems and thin out oldest ones to produce a bulky shrub, or thin out lower branches to make a shrub-tree. Remove old flower heads for a neater appearance.

SPATHODEA campanulata. African tulip tree, flame-of-the-forest. Evergreen tree. <u>Prune in spring or summer.</u>

These large, dense trees grow fairly rapidly. Give them only routine early training (see page 14) to establish a strong trunk and branch structure. Because wood is brittle, you may need to remove broken branches from time to time. Cut them back to joints with sound limbs.

SPARTIUM.
See Cytisus, Genista, Spartium.

SPICE BUSH.
See Calycanthus, Lindera.

SPIRAEA. Deciduous shrubs. <u>Pruning time varies</u> (see below).

Spiraeas fall into two broad categories: those that bloom in spring from wood produced the previous year, and those that bloom in summer on new spring growth. Prune spring-blooming kinds after they flower (or cut stems for indoor decoration). Prune summer-flowering kinds in late winter or early spring, before they leaf out.

Don't head back spiraeas with arching stems—you'll destroy their graceful forms. Instead, cut a few of the oldest stems to the ground each year. Choose stems that show no signs of sending out new laterals that would bear next year's blossoms.

Thin out the oldest stems of upright-growing kinds. You can head back stems to points where strong new growth is coming without damaging the plant's attractiveness.

Prune summer-blooming spiraeas heavily. Thin out old stems and

Spiraea. To preserve plant's arching beauty, periodically cut oldest stems to ground.

head back young stems to as few as 2 buds. This will give you larger flower clusters and a smaller plant. For a larger plant with abundant but smaller flower clusters, head back less, thinning out oldest stems (or just thin out stems).

Prune the low, dense shrublets only to remove old, twiggy stems.

SPRUCE.
See Picea.

STACHYURUS praecox. Deciduous shrub. Prune just after flowering.

Because these shrubs grow slowly and neatly, they need little pruning. Thin out weak and crowding stems if growth is too dense to suit you. If you want to limit height or spread, head back stems to laterals or joints with other stems.

STAR BUSH.
See Turraea.

STAR JASMINE.
See Trachelospermum.

STENOCARPUS sinuatus. Firewheel tree. Evergreen tree. Prune in spring.

Give young trees early training as described on page 14. Once trees are mature, prune only to remove dead and broken branches, or to head back any wayward growth.

STENOLOBIUM.
See Tecoma.

STEWARTIA. Deciduous trees, shrubs. Prune in late winter.

Whether a tree or a shrub, Stewartia needs only a little pruning to guide its shape. You can train trees— S. koreana, S. monadelpha, and S. pseudocamellia—to grow single trunks following guidelines on page 14, or grow them as low-branching or multistemmed shrubs that eventually become trees. For the latter, gradually remove lower branches as the plant grows.

Shrubby S. malacodendron and S. ovata will eventually grow about 15 feet tall. You can allow them to grow naturally as shrubs, or remove their lower branches to convert them into shrub-trees. With any stewartia,

thin out crowding inner branches and cut out any dead and broken branches. Prune any stems that grow too long, cutting back to a leaf or to another branch.

STIGMAPHYLLON. Orchid vine. Evergreen vines. Prune in winter.

To prune orchid vine, thin out unwanted, tangled, and dead stems. During growing season, remove or head back any wayward stems. Rampant S. littorale may need pruning several times a year. You can give smaller S. ciliatum an annual pruning and, during the rest of the year, a bit of pinching.

STRANVAESIA davidiana. Evergreen shrub or small tree. Prune in winter.

Stranvaesia resembles a Cotoneaster but is larger in all its parts. It can become both tall (to 20 feet) and wide-spreading. Like Cotoneaster, it will look best if you plant it where it has room to develop to its natural size rather than in a place where you must curtail full growth.

You can direct shape and control size somewhat, but don't head back stems indiscriminately. Instead, remove a branch back to its joint with another branch. For a multitrunked small tree, cut out lower branches to expose trunk framework. You can prune lower-growing S.d. undulata (S. undulata) the same way. Prune at Christmas time to use berried branches for decorations.

STRAWBERRY GUAVA.
See Psidium.

STRAWBERRY TREE.
See Arbutus.

STREPTOSOLEN jamesonii. Marmalade bush. Evergreen viny shrub. Prune after flowering (in frost-free regions), after danger of frost (in colder areas).

This plant blooms from spring to autumn on new growth. Prune not only to keep plant shapely but to ensure that it continues to produce vigorous new stems. At the proper time for your area, cut back stems that have flowered at least halfway. Thin out weak stems and cut older stems or trunks down to strong newer growth, even if this means cutting the

plant nearly to the ground. To promote branching lower on the bush, head back leggy, wayward stems at any time.

STYRAX. Deciduous trees, shrubs. Prune after flowering.

Japanese snowdrop tree or Japanese snowbell (S. japonicus), and fragrant snowbell (S. obassia), tend to grow as shrubby trees, with several main stems branching from the ground or close to it. You can train them into single-trunked or multi-trunked trees by following the guidelines on page 14.

These two species vary in shape. Japanese snowbell has wide-spreading horizontal branches; fragrant snowbell is much narrower. Both need periodic thinning—remove weak and crowding branches from inside the tree. Prune back to strong laterals any limbs that grow too long for the size of the crown. Cut out any dead or broken branches.

For the large shrubs S. americanus, S. grandifolius, and S. officinalis californicus (S. californica), you'll only need to thin out weak and crowding stems occasionally.

SUGAR BUSH.
See Rhus.

SUMAC.
See Rhus.

SUMMERSWEET.
See Clethra.

SWAN RIVER PEA SHRUB.
See Brachysema.

SWEET BAY.
See Laurus.

SWEET BELLS.
See Leucothoe.

SWEET GUM.
See Liquidambar.

SWEETLEAF.
See Symplocos.

SWEET OLIVE.
See Osmanthus.

SWEET-PEA SHRUB.
See Polygala.

SWEET PEPPERBUSH.
See Clethra.

SWEETSHADE.
See Hymenosporum.

SWEETSPIRE.
See Itea.

WISTERIA

Spectacular spring-blooming wisterias are vigorous deciduous vines. To avoid wrestling with a tangled, overgrown vine, *give wisterias regular winter pruning* and follow-up attention during the growing season.

Training a vine. Train a newly planted vine to produce the branch framework you want. You can choose either one or multiple stems.

For a single-trunked plant, encourage the growth of just one stem by limiting lateral growth. Pinch back all stems except the one you've chosen, so they don't become long streamers. In winter, after the single stem has reached the height you want, cut it back at that height so that horizontal side branches will grow in the following spring.

To develop a multiple-trunked vine, select as many vigorous stems as you want and let them grow. If the plant has just one stem initially, pinch it back to encourage several more to grow. Main stems will in time become substantial trunks and will be very heavy. Give the vine firm support and tie the developing stems where you want them to grow.

Annual pruning. After a wisteria has developed a permanent framework, prune it regularly. Every winter, cut back and thin out unwanted side shoots. Cut back to two or three buds the flower-bearing laterals on these side shoots—you can easily recognize the short, fat-budded spurs that will carry the next spring's flowers. In summer, cut back the long, streamerlike stems before they twine and tangle in the main part of the vine. Save any stems that you want to extend the height or length of the vine and tie them to a support.

Training a shrub. With vigilance, you can train a wisteria as a large shrub or as a multiple-stemmed, small weeping tree. Select well-spaced, vigorous branches to form the framework. Limit growth of all

Yearly trimming encourages best flowering.

other shoots. Pinch or cut back to two or three leaves all potentially long streamers. Continue this until a strong self-supporting framework develops. In years that follow, keep all runaway growth headed back so the plant keeps a shrubby appearance.

Training a tree. You can buy wisterias trained as trees, or you can train your own. Remove all but one main stem and tie it to an upright stake in several places. When the stem has reached the height at which you want the head to form, pinch or cut out the tip to force branching. As branching develops, cut back branches to make them become thicker. Pinch back all potentially long streamers, and rub off all shoots on the trunk.

Wisteria "tree" needs heavy heading back each dormant season to keep top compact.

SYCAMORE.
See Platanus.

SYMPHORICARPOS. Includes snowberry, coral berry, Indian currant. Deciduous shrubs. Prune in early spring.

All of these plants form spreading colonies of stems. Some spread quickly; others are more compact and dense. All bear attractive berrylike fruits from side branches on 2-year-old wood.

To prune, clip twiggy stems that have fruited and aren't producing any vigorous new laterals, cutting them to the ground. Some stems that have fruited will send out vigorous new stems from low on the old stem. Cut these back to strong new growth. Don't just head back these plants. Much of their beauty lies in gracefully arching younger stems. If a plant spreads too far, pull out invasive stems.

SYMPLOCOS paniculata. Sapphire berry, sweetleaf. Deciduous shrub or tree. Prune in early spring.

Sapphire berry is a very large, bulky shrub that needs no routine pruning when planted where it has plenty of room to develop. After a few years, remove a few of the oldest major stems when they stop growing vigorously or become too large and leggy. To encourage more branching low on the plant, head back long, straight shoots from the base or pinch them back before they grow too long.

You can train a young plant as a single-trunked or multitrunked tree, following guidelines on page 14. Remove all additional shoots that spring up from the base or low on the trunk.

SYRINGA.
See Lilac, page 79.

SYZYGIUM. Evergreen shrubs or trees. Prune in spring.

Both of the commonly grown kinds produce dense, polished foliage on compact, upright plants. The smaller of the two is rose apple (S. jambos, or Eugenia jambos). Though it can reach 30 feet, it grows slowly and needs virtually no pruning.

Larger and faster growing is the Australian brush cherry (S. paniculatum, or Eugenia paniculatum). Its most widespread uses are as back-ground, screen, or hedge plant, either formally sheared, or, for a shaggy, informal appearance, lightly clipped. You can train a single plant into a handsome, tall, narrow tree (see guidelines on page 14).

Smaller varieties, such as S.p. 'Compacta' and S.p. 'Globulus', make good choices for areas where you need a lower hedge or shrub. Except for trimming hedge plants, you don't need to routinely prune brush cherry and its varieties. Occasionally, if a branch sticks out too far, head it back to a lateral within the foliage.

TABEBUIA. Briefly deciduous, sometimes evergreen trees. Prune after flowering.

Give young trees early training as outlined on page 14 to become single-trunked specimens. Trees sometimes grow irregularly, so you may need to do some pruning to improve their shape. Head back any lopsided growth to good laterals or joints with other branches until a symmetrical outline is restored.

TAMARISK.
See Tamarix.

TAMARIX. Tamarisk. Deciduous and evergreen-looking shrubs and trees. Pruning time varies.

Tamarisks are often mislabeled in nurseries, but you don't need to know precisely which kind you have in order to know how and when to prune it. If a tamarisk blooms only in early spring, it's flowering on last year's growth; prune it after flowering. If it flowers in spring and summer, or summer, or summer and autumn, prune it in early spring before growth starts.

Tamarisks that bloom only in spring are graceful, airy, arching large shrubs that you can also treat as shrub-trees. Prune out weak and twiggy growth and crossing branches. Try to highlight the shrub's natural outlines. If you have to limit height, cut back upright branches to joints with limbs that grow more horizontally. For a treelike plant, remove lower branches.

The tamarisks that flower in spring and summer, summer, and summer and autumn will become full-fledged trees unless you prune them back. To keep them as shrubs, cut

Tamarix. After spring flowering, thin out crossing and badly placed limbs.

them to the ground in early spring (this sacrifices spring bloom on ones that flower in spring). They will grow to 6 to 12 feet with masses of large flower plumes.

Athel tree (T. aphylla, or T. articulata) blooms in late summer. Potentially the largest of the group, it can easily be trained as a single-trunked or multitrunked tree (see guidelines on page 14). For best use, make it a background tree or windbreak planting. The flowers are not spectacular, and roots are highly competitive. On mature trees, prune only to remove dead or broken branches.

TANBARK OAK.
See Lithocarpus.

TAXODIUM. Deciduous and evergreen coniferous trees. Prune in spring.

Bald cypress (T. distichum) is the characteristic and romantic Spanish-moss-draped tree of southern swamps. Normally, this deciduous tree grows tall, straight, and symmetrically. If a competing leader develops, cut it off. Head back any branches that grow too long to laterals within the crown.

Evergreen in mild climates, Montezuma cypress (T. mucronatum) has a strongly weeping habit. It, too, is a tall grower that you should train to a single leader. In time you may want to remove lower limbs so that you can walk under this tree.

TAXUS. Yew. Evergreen coniferous shrubs and trees. Prune winter through summer.

Yews range from spreading ground covers through shrubs of various shapes to trees that may be needlelike, cone-shaped, or rounded. Commonly, these are selected kinds of English yew *(T. baccata)*, Japanese yew *(T. cuspidata)*, and hybrids of the two species sold as varieties of *T. media.*

Yews are slow-growing, long-lived plants that will tolerate heavy shearing even though they normally need little pruning. They are classic plants for living sculpture such as topiary (see page 106), and make neat knee-high to house-tall hedges.

But you needn't always prune yews formally. Many kinds make handsome garden plants when they're allowed to grow naturally.

Yews are exceptional conifers because they will sprout readily from bare wood. To renovate an old, overgrown plant, you can cut it back to a bare trunk. Shear or head back healthy plants as much as you want.

To cultivate a natural-looking yew, prune only wayward branches that depart from the plant's basic shape. Make cuts within the foliage so cut branch ends won't show.

Shear young yew hedges in midsummer, removing about half the new growth. As the hedge begins to reach its full size, shear 2 or 3 times a year. Do this once in late winter before new growth starts, again when new growth has reached full length, and once more in late summer if plants look ragged.

On older columnar yews *(T. baccata* 'Stricta'), branches often spread outward. To counteract this tendency, head back outward-falling branches to sturdy vertical branches. On very large, old plants you can tie branches together with rope or insulated wire. Join branches on opposite sides of the plant to make them counterbalance one another. This is a better solution than wrapping wire around the plant (a method that is effective but obvious).

TEA TREE.
See Leptospermum.

TECOMA stans *(Stenolobium stans).* Yellow bells, yellow trumpet flower, yellow elder. Evergreen shrub or small tree. <u>Prune in late winter, early spring.</u>

Yellow bells grows as a bushy shrub up to 20 feet. In regions where it gets damaged by frost, prune out all damaged wood and thin out weak and crossing branches.

Where frosts seldom occur, you can train yellow bells as a tree with one or more trunks (see guidelines on page 14). Prune to remove weak and crowding branches, heading back any too-vigorous branches that unbalance the tree's shape. To prolong the bloom period, remove faded flower clusters.

TECOMARIA capensis *(Tecoma capensis).* Cape honeysuckle. Evergreen vine or shrub. <u>Prune after flowering.</u>

With no guidance, cape honeysuckle forms a scrambling mass of stems that will make an effective ground or bank cover. To use it this way, simply cut out stems that grow too high above the foliage.

To grow it as a vine, tie stems to a support—pillar, arbor, fence, trellis, or along eaves. Head the plant back as necessary to fit the space you've alloted it, thinning out crowding stems each year. This will keep the vine from becoming too thick and will also stimulate new flower-bearing growth.

With even more attention to training you can grow cape honeysuckle as an espalier (see page 50). You can also grow it as a 6 to 8-foot shrub. Continually head back any long, sprawling stems.

TERNSTROEMIA gymnanthera *(T. japonica).* Evergreen shrub. <u>Prune in spring.</u>

The slow, orderly growth of *Ternstroemia* means you'll seldom have any pruning to do. Pinch tips of new growth to make plant more compact. Head back any irregular stems to other branches.

TETRAPANAX papyriferus *(Aralia papyrifera).* Rice paper plant. Evergreen shrub-tree. <u>Prune whenever necessary.</u>

Rice paper plant is a character plant with thick stems and enormous tropical-looking foliage. Usually it develops several trunks. Growth proceeds according to a predictable pattern: a stem grows several feet in a season and produces flowers; the next growth flush produces 2 stems from beneath the flower spray. The plant builds up in a succession of these "Y" forks.

You can train it as a single-trunked plant, up to the first fork, or you can allow several main stems to grow from the ground. (The plant may do this naturally; if not, cut the single-stemmed plant to the ground.)

Prune to alter the direction of growth. If you cut in the middle of a stem, 1 to several shoots may emerge from below the cut. If you cut back to a joint with another branch, usually no shoots sprout (and they can be rubbed out if they do). Stems often lean from the weight of foliage, so you'll eventually need to do some pruning. Thin out stems to make an interesting framework.

Rice paper plant often sends up shoots from the roots, especially if roots are disturbed or cut. Pull these shoots to prevent the plant from taking over an area. Cut off flower clusters, after bloom; or, if you don't like their appearance, cut them off as they develop. The extra weight of flowers will pull down branches. One word of caution: the fuzz on new growth is highly irritating to eyes and skin.

TETRASTIGMA voinieranum *(Cissus voinierana).* Evergreen vine. <u>Prune whenever necessary.</u>

With no support, *Tetrastigma* will spread out and become a lush ground cover. But it will climb vigorously if there is anything for its tendrils to wrap around. You can train stems to grow where you want them. Untangle them whenever necessary, cutting back any that grow too long or that head in directions where you don't want them.

TEUCRIUM. Germander. Evergreen shrubs or subshrubs. <u>Prune in late winter, early spring.</u>

You can grow low-growing, spreading *T. chamaedrys* as a foot-high border hedge, a ground cover, or an isolated shrub. For hedges, shear established plants twice in summer. To keep individual plants neat and fairly compact, you can head them back in late winter and again after summer bloom, if necessary.

Bush germander *(T. fruticans)* forms a densely branched, rounded plant that grows about 6 feet high and wide. It stays attractive without routine pruning. Just head back any wayward stems to a pair of leaves. To restrict the plant's size, cut stems back part way and thin out old twiggy stems. You can shear as a hedge, pruning as often as needed to keep it looking neat. To rejuvenate an old, overgrown plant, cut it nearly to the ground, thinning out dead and weak stems.

TEXAS MOUNTAIN LAUREL.
See Sophora.

TEXAS RANGER.
See Leucophyllum.

TEXAS UMBRELLA TREE.
See Melia.

THUJA. Arborvitae. Evergreen coniferous shrubs and trees. Prune in late winter to early summer.

Strictly speaking, *Thuja* includes American arborvitae *(T. occidentalis)* and Western red cedar *(T. plicata)*. But from the standpoint of its garden appearance, uses, and pruning, Oriental arborvitae *(Platycladus orientalis,* see page 93) is covered by the information here on American arborvitae.

American arborvitae. The basic kind, a very large, dense tree, is seldom planted in gardens. Instead, nurseries offer many named varieties that may be pyramidal, columnar, globular, or flat-topped, and that range in height from 2 to 25 feet. These usually exhibit growth that is dense and neat; shaping is rarely necessary. But for a regular geometric shape or a uniform hedge, shear plants as often as you want.

For occasional shaping, prune in late winter. Try to prune within the foliage outline so cuts won't show. Never cut back into a bare branch where there's no indication of green growth; a dormant branch won't sprout new shoots. On all upright and medium to tall varieties, try to maintain a single central leader.

Western red cedar. Western cedar grows naturally as a towering tree, and is rarely found in gardens outside its native territory. Common named varieties usually have a tall, narrow shape that's suitable for high hedges or screens. You can prune these plants the same as American arborvitae, but they're attractive if you let them follow their natural shape rather than shearing them.

TI.
See Cordyline.

THEVETIA. Yellow oleander. Evergreen shrubs, small trees. Prune in early spring.

The common name of one kind— yellow oleander *(T. peruviana)*— points to the resemblance these plants bear to true oleander *(Nerium)*. You can use them as specimen shrubs, screening plants, hedges, or small trees. These have the same pruning needs as *Nerium* (see page 84).

Plants are shallow-rooted and may blow over in windy areas. If you train them as trees, thin branches periodically to let wind pass through easily.

THIMBLEBERRY.
See Rubus.

THREADLEAF FALSE ARALIA.
See Dizygotheca.

TIBOUCHINA urvilleana *(T. semidecandra, Pleroma splendens)*. Princess flower. Evergreen shrub or small tree. Prune in early spring.

Though naturally a rangy, open plant, *Tibouchina* responds favorably to pruning and pinching to control its shape.

For a fairly compact shrub, pinch stem tips on young plants to encourage plenty of branching. Continue this as the plant grows. If the plant

Tibouchina. Occasionally cut back long, lanky stems severely to restore bushiness.

remains too leggy for your taste, lightly head back new growth after each flowering cycle.

Do heavier pruning in early spring after danger of frost is past. Head back plant to restrict size or further encourage bushiness. To rejuvenate an overgrown plant, cut back heavily. New growth will quickly sprout from bare wood.

Because tibouchina is leggy, you can train it as a low-branching or multitrunked small tree. When framework stems are tall enough, begin pinching and lightly heading them back to encourage a more compact crown.

TILIA. Linden. Deciduous trees. Prune in winter.

Young trees need early training (see page 14) to establish a good trunk and leader. Once this is done, you'll have no routine pruning to do. Thin out any crowding branches if they occur. Remove any dead or broken branches.

TIPUANA tipu. Tipu tree. Deciduous or semievergreen tree. Prune in late winter, early spring.

Young, fast-growing saplings need early training as described on page 14. When the trunk is established, you can let the branches grow naturally to form a broad, spreading, umbrella-shaped crown. Thin out any crowding branches in the crown's center to let breezes pass through and to show off the branch structure.

For a more upright, dense tree, encourage young scaffold branches to branch out closer to the trunk by heading them back. Pinch stem tips or lightly head back resulting branches. This will produce compact main scaffold branches that will make the tree narrower.

Branches are brittle. If you live in a windy area, be sure to cut out broken branches when they occur.

TIPU TREE.
See Tipuana.

TOBIRA.
See Pittosporum.

TOTARA.
See Podocarpus.

TOYON.
See Heteromeles.

TRACHELOSPERMUM (*Rhyncospermum*). Star jasmine. Evergreen vines or sprawling shrubs. <u>Prune in spring.</u>

One species, *T. jasminoides*, is much more common in nurseries and gardens than the similar *T. asiaticum*. Both have the same uses and pruning guidelines.

To grow star jasmine as a spreading shrub, pinch tips of branches before they become rangy and vinelike. Continue this as new shoots are produced. To grow the plant as a vine, plant it next to a support—trellis, fence, or post. Let stems grow without pinching, and tie them to the support. Try to select a plant that has not already been pinched to promote bushiness; if possible, purchase one that has been staked upright. For a ground or bank cover, let plants sprawl, cutting or pinching back any upright stems.

Cut back older plants by about one-third each year to keep plants from becoming overgrown and bare-stemmed beneath the foliage. If necessary, you can head a plant back to its main branch framework. New growth and flowers will replace cut branches within a year.

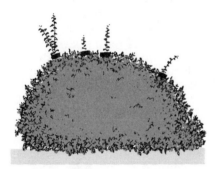

Trachelospermum. To keep plants low, cut back all wispy vertical stems.

TRACHYCARPUS.
See Palm.

TREE-OF-HEAVEN.
See Ailanthus.

TREE PEONY.
See Paeonia.

TRICHOSTEMA lanatum. Woolly blue curls. Evergreen shrub. <u>Prune in spring, summer.</u>

To promote branching and bushiness in young plants, pinch tips of new growth. When plants flower, cut blooming stems for arrangements or cut back stems that have flowered. This will encourage additional flowering and branching.

TRINIDAD FLAME BUSH.
See Calliandra.

TRIPHASIA trifolia. Limeberry. Evergreen shrub. <u>Prune any time.</u>

Plants are dense and orderly with thorny, pendulous branches. Prune off wayward branches and dead stems. Plants' thorniness and naturally neat appearance make them a fine choice for low, informal barrier hedges.

TRISTANIA. Evergreen trees. <u>Prune in spring and summer.</u>

Tristanias are related to eucalyptus. Two kinds are common. Brisbane box (*T. conferta*) grows into a tall tree with a rounded, fairly open crown. Give it early guidance as described on page 14. As main framework branches are forming, head back too-long branches to laterals. Thin out branches to reveal the colorful bark as the tree gets older.

Without pruning, *T. laurina* will grow slowly as a densely branched shrub for many years. To keep it shrubby, pinch some tips or lightly head back wayward branches. Pruned this way, it will grow as a dense dome-shaped column.

For a multitrunked small tree, select several low branches or stems from the ground for trunks. Where you want to develop a shade tree form, encourage plants to develop fewer branches and greater height; trim off lower branches from the trunks and thin out the crown. For a single-trunked tree, follow the guidelines on page 14 to establish a trunk. Only occasional pruning will be necessary thereafter: thin out crowding and weak stems in the tree's center, and head back any wayward branches.

TRUMPET CREEPER.
See Campsis.

TRUMPET FLOWER.
See Bignonia.

TRUMPET VINE.
See Bignonia, Campsis.

TSUGA. Hemlock. Evergreen coniferous trees and shrubs. <u>Prune in early spring.</u>

All the various hemlock species become very large, graceful trees without pruning. With light trimming they make exceptionally handsome background screen plants; with heavy trimming they can be used as large hedges. Canada hemlock (*T. canadensis*) is available in several named varieties that are smaller and have shapes different from those of the species. These make fine specimen and hedge plants.

To train hemlock as a tree, make sure no secondary leader develops. For a hemlock hedge, see guidelines for training a young hedge on page 70. Once your hedge has reached the height you want, give it periodic trimming, primarily in late winter or early spring before growth starts. Shear the hedge again in midsummer if you prefer a flat, formal look to a soft, feathery one.

An exceptional conifer, hemlock will sprout new growth from bare wood. To rejuvenate an old hedge or reduce the size of an overgrown one, you can cut it back heavily—to bare branches if necessary. Do this in late winter or early spring before growth would normally start.

Tsuga. Without pruning, hemlock grows as tall tree (left) but can be trimmed as hedge.

TUCKEROO.
See Cupaniopsis.

TULIP TREE.
See Liriodendron.

TUPELO.
See Nyssa.

TUPIDANTHUS calyptratus. Evergreen shrub or small tree. <u>Prune in spring.</u>

This tropical plant looks like *Schefflera actinophylla* and has the same uses. One difference is that *Tupidanthus* branches from the base more readily and makes a broader shrub.

To convert a single-stemmed plant to a multitrunked one, cut it back to the base. Several stems will start to grow. These will eventually become the trunks of a small tree if you let them grow. Keep upward growth headed back if you prefer a shrubby plant. See *Schefflera* on page 107 for more explicit directions.

TURK'S CAP.
See Malvaviscus.

TURRAEA obtusifolia. Star bush. Evergreen shrub. <u>Prune any time.</u>

Star bush's growth is slow and orderly. It generally remains attractive with little or no pruning. To grow it as a hedge (see page 70), clip or trim whenever necessary to maintain a uniform appearance.

Because lower limbs are nearly prostrate, you can train a young plant as a ground cover by simply removing vertical stems.

UGNI molinae (*Myrtus ugni*). Chilean guava. Evergreen shrub. <u>Prune whenever necessary.</u>

Patience is the key with young plants—they go through a straggly, awkward youth, but with no assistance will fill out into compact, rounded, mature specimens. They make excellent hedges or low screens. Just head back any awkwardly long branches to laterals within the foliage outline.

ULMUS. Elm. Deciduous or partly evergreen trees. <u>Prune in winter.</u>

American elm (*U. americana*) and the large European elms need routine training throughout their early years (see page 14). Prune to encourage the growth of a tall, straight leader. This will promote a main branch framework that begins high on the tree. Once this is accomplished, you'll have little pruning to do. Cut out dead, broken, or diseased wood as it appears. On young

trees, head back any wayward limbs to strong laterals.

Evergreen-to-deciduous Chinese elm (*U. parvifolia*, often sold as *U. p.* 'Sempervirens') and deciduous Siberian elm (*U. pumila*) need more work. Give young trees the routine training described above, taking care to see that branching begins high on the trunk. Branches tend to be brittle and form a dense crown. To lessen wind resistance and reduce the weight of branches, thin out the crown on both young and established trees. Cut out weak, spindly, crowding branches, heading back long, wispy branches to strong laterals to help create a stronger, more compact framework. You'll need to head back Chinese elm's pendulous lower branches to maintain clearance beneath the tree. Cut off all broken limbs whenever they occur. You can grow Siberian elm as a clipped hedge (see page 70), keeping it as low as 3 to 4 feet with repeated shearing.

Ulmus. Chinese elm needs frequent trimming to maintain shape, clearance beneath.

UMBELLULARIA californica. California laurel, California bay, Oregon myrtle, pepperwood. Evergreen tree. <u>Prune in spring, summer.</u>

Though its growth is not rapid, pepperwood will in time become a large, dense tree. Train young plants to one or several trunks, according to guidelines on page 14. After basic tree form is established, prune only to shape. Head back any wayward branches to laterals within the crown, and thin out weak and dead branches inside the crown.

You can also use pepperwood

as a high screen planting or a tall, informal hedge (see page 70 for hedge information). Either way, you will have to head back plants to restrain their size—first in spring and perhaps again in summer.

To reduce an overgrown plant's size or rejuvenate it, cut back heavily to bare wood. Do this in spring, and new growth will soon follow.

UMBRELLA PINE.
See Sciadopitys.

VACCINIUM. Evergreen and deciduous shrubs. <u>Pruning times vary.</u>

The best-known member of this group of plants is blueberry, discussed on page 28. Evergreen huckleberry (*V. ovatum*) is an upright, compact plant that's admired as much for its foliage as for its fruit. Plants need only occasional thinning to remove crowding or old, unvigorous stems. The best time to thin is just after new growth has lost its bronzy tint. You can use cut branches for indoor arrangements.

Cowberry or foxberry (*V. vitis-idaea*) is another evergreen species. It grows slowly to about a foot high and spreads by underground stems. Curtail spreading by cutting perimeter shoots with a sharp spade.

Deciduous red huckleberry (*V. parvifolium*) forms a naturally open and somewhat twiggy plant. Periodically remove some of the oldest, least vigorous wood and crowding branches in the plant's center. Otherwise, let it grow naturally. You can do this in winter, when the plant is leafless, or in spring to use flowering branches for indoor decoration.

VANILLA TRUMPET VINE.
See Distictis.

VIBURNUM. Deciduous and evergreen shrubs and small trees. <u>Prune in winter</u> (summer-flowering kinds), <u>in spring</u> (spring-flowering and evergreen kinds).

Even though there are a great many different kinds of viburnums, directions for pruning them are remarkably uniform.

When you plant a deciduous viburnum, thin out any obviously weak stems and shorten the remaining stems. During the year, thin out any crossing branches and weak shoots. From then on, let the plant develop naturally for several years. Check in winter for dead and broken stems and cut them out. Also cut out weak and twiggy wood in the plant's center. When the oldest main stems stop producing vigorous growth, remove them to encourage strong new stems.

Evergreen viburnums need no initial pruning unless a plant is noticeably lopsided. To correct this problem, cut back overly long stems to laterals to balance the plant's shape. As with deciduous viburnums, thin out dead and weak stems, and any crowding branches in the plant's center. You can head back any wayward stems to laterals, but the rest of the plant may grow and catch up with them.

You can train large viburnums, both deciduous and evergreen, as small multitrunked trees. Select the plant's major stems for trunks and cut out all other stems from the ground. Cut off lower branches up to the point you want the plant to branch out. Keep all basal and trunk sprouts cut off or pulled out.

Viburnum (deciduous). When old stems stop growing vigorously, cut them to the ground.

VICTORIAN BOX.
See Pittosporum.

VIOLET TRUMPET VINE.
See Clytostoma.

VIRGINIA CREEPER.
See Parthenocissus.

VITEX. Chaste tree. Deciduous and evergreen shrubs or trees. <u>Prune in late winter, early spring.</u>

Evergreen New Zealand chaste tree (V. lucens) needs little attention

beyond early training as either a single-trunked or multitrunked tree (see guidelines on page 14). Cut out weak, twiggy, and dead wood in tree's center and cut back any broken branches.

Deciduous V. agnus-castus will grow as a root-hardy perennial in cold-winter regions or as a 25-foot tree where there are no hard freezes. In regions where winter cold damages or kills top growth, cut out all dead and damaged stems in spring. Depending on how much of the branch framework remains, cut back just to sound wood or cut back last year's stems to 2 or 3 pairs of buds. The larger the framework remaining, the larger the shrub will be. Thin out weak and crossing stems in the plant's center and break off new shoots that would create crowding or crossing stems.

In milder climates you can grow V. agnus-castus as a shrub of any size, pruning it heavily, as described for cold climates, or letting most of the growth remain. If you choose the latter, cut out some of the oldest stems each year and thin out weaker, crowding branches in the plant's interior. Head back unbranched, year-old basal stems about halfway.

You also can grow it as a single-trunked or multitrunked tree according to guidelines on page 14, thinning out the crown periodically as though it were a large shrub.

VITIS.
See Grape, page 66.

WALNUT (Juglans). Deciduous trees. <u>Prune in late spring, summer.</u>

All walnuts are handsome ornamental trees. The kinds grown primarily for garden beauty are Southern California black walnut (Juglans californica), butternut (J. cinerea), California black walnut (J. hindsii), Nogal or Arizona walnut (J. major), and black walnut (J. nigra). Give them early training, as described on page 14, to become single-trunked trees.

In selecting branches for a major framework, read the statements listed under English walnut (below) about necked buds. Southern California black walnut almost always grows as a multitrunked tree. California black walnut can also be grown that way.

A mature walnut tree, whether ornamental or nut-producing, needs

little pruning. Cut out extra-vigorous vertical stems within the crown, and any dead branches. Thin out weak, twiggy stems and crossing and crowding limbs. Prune any overly long, drooping branches, heading them back to strong laterals.

English Walnut (Juglans regia). Nut-bearing trees are usually trained to a modified central leader framework. At planting, head back the young tree (usually a single, thick stem) to 4 or 5 buds above the graft union. During the growing season, select a single upright shoot to become the leader—generally one from the topmost bud—and subdue all other shoots by pinching them back. Retain some shoots along the trunk during the tree's developing years to protect the trunk from sunburn. Pinch them back so they'll be leafy but won't really branch out. Remove the lower side branches after the tree's crown has grown enough to shade the trunk.

During its first year, the tree should grow to more than 6 feet tall. In the winter you can head it back at about the 6-foot level, preferably to a bud that faces the prevailing summer wind. If the tree didn't grow tall enough, head back the shoot to good, firm wood (about ½-inch diameter or greater) of the first year's growth. During the next year, train one vertical shoot to reach the desired height.

Having headed back the tree at 6 feet, the following growing season you can begin to select framework branches. These branches can start about 5 feet from the ground. Select

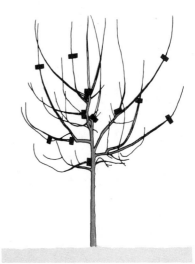

English walnut. Prune young tree to establish strong, well-spaced scaffold limbs.

ones that form a spiral pattern around the trunk with a vertical separation of 6 to 18 inches. If you choose 2 branches to become major limbs each year, you can expect to complete the process in a few years. Each winter during this time, head back the leader to a bud that faces prevailing summer winds.

Continue selecting limbs until your tree reaches its desired height and has enough well-placed limbs (usually from 4 to 6). At this point, stop cutting back the leader. It will bend down a bit during the next season and become the topmost limb.

Branches that grow from year-old wood form at a narrow angle to the old wood. When the resulting branches grow from the trunk, they exhibit narrow crotches that are vulnerable to breakage. On year-old wood, two growth buds exist at each node, one above the other on a very short neck. The uppermost bud will grow first and form a narrow crotch. During the years when your walnut is forming its permanent framework, pinch out or rub out these upper necked buds along the developing trunk before they can grow. All future limbs will grow from the lower buds at a wider angle to the trunk and will be stronger limbs.

WASHINGTONIA.
See Palm.

WASHINGTON THORN.
See Crataegus.

WATTLE.
See Acacia.

WAX MALLOW.
See Malvaviscus.

WAX MYRTLE.
See Myrica.

WEEPING CHINESE BANYAN.
See Ficus.

WEEPING WILLOW.
See Salix.

WEIGELA. Deciduous shrubs. Prune after flowering.
These vigorous, arching shrubs benefit from consistent renewal pruning. After flowers have faded, cut back, to strong new laterals, branches that have flowered. Leave only 1 or 2 pairs of these laterals to each stem. Prune most stems that are more than 2 years old, cutting them

to the ground. Leave only ones that are still producing vigorous new shoots. From new shoots that emerge at the plant's base, retain only the strongest and best-placed ones, cutting or pulling off all others.

You can thin out weak, broken, and dead branches any time. In cold climates, prune in spring after danger of frost is past, cutting out all winter-damaged stems. You can renew an old, ragged plant by cutting it to the ground in late winter or early spring. Many new stems will spring up. Retain only the sturdiest, cutting out the weak and spindly ones.

Weigela. Cut out 2-year-old stems, cut back year-old ones to strong growth.

WESTRINGIA rosmariniformis. Evergreen shrub. Prune in spring, after main bloom flush.
Spreading, somewhat loose growth produces a neat shrub that needs no routine pruning. If you need to guide a plant's shape, head back wayward stems to laterals or joints with other branches.

WHITE FORSYTHIA.
See Abeliophyllum.

WHITE SAPOTE.
See Casimiroa.

WILD BUCKWHEAT.
See Eriogonum.

WILD LILAC.
See Ceanothus.

WILGA.
See Geijera.

WILLOW.
See Salix.

WILLOW-LEAFED JESSAMINE.
See Cestrum.

WINGNUT.
See Pterocarya.

WINTER CREEPER.
See Euonymus.

WINTER HAZEL.
See Corylopsis.

WINTER'S BARK.
See Drimys.

WINTERSWEET.
See Chimonanthus.

WIRE VINE.
See Muehlenbeckia.

WISTERIA.
See page 111.

WITCH HAZEL.
See Hamamelis.

WITHE-ROD.
See Viburnum.

WONGA-WONGA VINE.
See Pandorea.

WOOLLY BLUE CURLS.
See Trichostema.

WORMWOOD.
See Artemisia.

XANTHORHIZA simplicissima. Yellowroot. Deciduous shrub. Prune in winter.
This ground cover plant spreads by underground stems over large areas. Its roots produce stems up to 2 feet tall. Prune any broken and dead stems, cutting them to the ground. Restrict spread by eradicating any stems that come up where you don't want them, digging them out with a sharp spade.

XYLOSMA congestum (X. senticosum). Evergreen or deciduous shrub or small tree. Prune in late winter.
Left unpruned *Xylosma* develops an angular main stem that takes its time zigzagging upward. During this time, side branches grow long and arching or drooping, sometimes reaching to the ground. Eventually the plant becomes a loose, spreading shrub 8 to 10 feet high and about as wide, with long, graceful branches.

Xylosma has a number of garden uses. You can give it little attention and still enjoy a good-looking, arching shrub. You can train it as an informal espalier (see page 50), as a single-trunked or multitrunked tree (see guidelines on page 14), and even as a ground or bank cover (encourage long, flexible growth and cut out upright stems). You can also grow it as a formally clipped or informal hedge; twine long branches into the hedge to fill in gaps faster.

Xylosma responds to heavy pruning by rapidly producing new growth. To revamp an overgrown or unattractive plant, cut back to a skeleton of main framework branches. In about 4 months the bare limbs will be almost completely concealed by vigorous new growth. Thin out superfluous shoots from this new growth, leaving only those that will grow in directions where you want new branches.

With pruning shears and a discerning eye, you can transform an ordinary-looking plant into an interesting piece of plant sculpture. Start by thinning out weak, crowded stems and twiggy growth. Prune to reveal an angular, sculptural branching pattern that will carry clouds of foliage at branch tips. To complete the transformation, head back any overly long leafy branches.

Xylosma. Normally dense shrub (right) can be thinned to reveal branching pattern.

YAUPON.
See Ilex.

YELLOW BELLS.
See Tecoma.

YELLOW ELDER.
See Tecoma.

YELLOW OLEANDER.
See Thevetia.

YELLOWROOT.
See Xanthorhiza.

YELLOW TRUMPET FLOWER.
See Tecoma.

YELLOW TRUMPET VINE.
See Anemopaegma, Macfadyena.

YELLOW WOOD.
See Cladrastis.

YESTERDAY-TODAY-AND-TOMORROW.
See Brunfelsia.

YEW.
See Taxus.

YEW PINE.
See Podocarpus.

YUCCA. Evergreen shrublike and treelike plants. Prune after flowering.

The common *Yucca* plant consists of a hemisphere of swordlike leaves from whose center grows a tall flowering stalk. Some yuccas grow from a single hemisphere. Others form clumps. Still others grow into treelike plants with few to many heavy branches. If you prefer, after flowering remove the flower stalk as far inside the plant as possible.

With clump-forming yuccas you may want to thin out some of the new offshoots from time to time to prevent overcrowding. Cut flush with the bulbous trunk surface. Tree yuccas need no pruning (other than flower stalk removal) unless a branch develops where you don't want it. If this occurs, cut it back to a joint with another branch or to the trunk.

ZANTHORHIZA.
See Xanthorhiza.

ZELKOVA serrata. Sawleaf zelkova. Deciduous tree. Prune in late winter, summer.

You'll need to give young *Zelkova* trees careful training in order to determine their final shape. For a tall, massive tree with a single straight leader, pay special heed to directions on page 14. For several years—more time than with most other trees—you'll need to maintain one dominant leader and cut out all competitors.

In its natural state, zelkova grows as a short, rounded, spreading tree with many major limbs rising from atop a squat trunk. To develop this form, make sure the trunk has reached the height you want before you allow permanent branches to develop. Thin out developing

branches if necessary to relieve crowding. Do all this early pruning in late winter.

After your tree's permanent structure is established, prune only to thin crowding growth and remove dead and broken branches. Do thinning in summer. Remove dead and broken branches any time.

Zelkova. Thin out excess, crowding limbs when tree is in full leaf.

ZENOBIA pulverulenta (*Andromeda speciosa*). Deciduous shrub. Prune in late winter, early spring.

Zenobia grows slowly and openly, with enough branches to carry foliage to the ground. No routine pruning is needed. If a particular branch grows out beyond the rest of the shrub, head it back to a well-placed lateral within the foliage. Occasionally you may want to cut out old stems that are no longer producing vigorous growth.

ZIZYPHUS jujuba. Chinese jujube. Deciduous tree. Prune in winter.

Give young trees careful early training (see page 14) to help them develop a straight leader. Once the plant's basic framework is established, allow the tree to develop according to its natural pattern—zigzag branching with pendulous branches. Then prune to highlight this branching pattern, removing any superfluous branches or ones that droop too low.

INDEX

The entries in this index refer to general pruning information only. Requirements and directions for pruning specific plants are found under the botanical names of the plants in the alphabetical Pruning Encyclopedia, pages 18–119.